DIGITAL MIGRATION

SAGE was founded in 1965 by Sara Miller McCune to support the dissemination of usable knowledge by publishing innovative and high-quality research and teaching content. Today, we publish over 900 journals, including those of more than 400 learned societies, more than 800 new books per year, and a growing range of library products including archives, data, case studies, reports, and video. SAGE remains majority-owned by our founder, and after Sara's lifetime will become owned by a charitable trust that secures our continued independence.

Los Angeles | London | New Delhi | Singapore | Washington DC | Melbourne

DIGITAL MIGRATION

Koen Leurs

SAGE

Los Angeles | London | New Delhi
Singapore | Washington DC | Melbourne

SAGE

Los Angeles | London | New Delhi
Singapore | Washington DC | Melbourne

SAGE Publications Ltd
1 Oliver's Yard
55 City Road
London EC1Y 1SP

SAGE Publications Inc.
2455 Teller Road
Thousand Oaks, California 91320

SAGE Publications India Pvt Ltd
Unit No 323-333, Third Floor, F-Block
International Trade Tower, Nehru Place
New Delhi 110 019

SAGE Publications Asia-Pacific Pte Ltd
3 Church Street
#10-04 Samsung Hub
Singapore 049483

Editor: Michael Ainsley
Assistant Editor: Daniel Price
Production Editor: Neelu Sahu
Copyeditor: Sarah Bury
Proofreader: Rosemary Campbell
Indexer: Gary Kirby
Marketing Manager: Ruslana Khatagova
Cover Design: Francis Kenney
Typeset by KnowledgeWorks Global Ltd

Library of Congress Control Number: 2023930993

British Library Cataloguing in Publication data

A catalogue record for this book is available from the
British Library

ISBN 978-1-5297-0653-6
ISBN 978-1-5297-0652-9 (pbk)

Dedicated to

#NoOneisIllegal
#RefugeesWelcome
#NoBorders
#WeAreHere

All author royalties for this book will be donated to the Alarm Phone. Hotline for boatpeople in distress, https://alarmphone.org/

Contents

About the Author

Koen Leurs is an Associate Professor in Gender, Media and Migration Studies at the Graduate Gender Program of the Department of Media and Culture, Utrecht University, the Netherlands. Leurs is a digital migration studies scholar interested in digital practices of migrants and digital governmentality of migration. He combines mixed methods with creative, participatory and digital approaches. He is Principal Investigator in the project 'Co-Designing a Fair Digital Asylum System' (2022–2023). He was a fellow at the Netherlands Institute of Advanced Studies (NIAS) and the London School of Economics and Political Science (LSE). Previously, he chaired the 'Diaspora, Migration and the Media' section of the *European Communication Research and Education Association* (ECREA, 2016–2021). Recently, Leurs co-edited the *Handbook of media and migration* (Sage, 2020) and special issues on 'Cultures of (im)mobile entanglements' for the *International Journal of Cultural Studies* (2023), 'Digital migration practices and the everyday' for *Communication, Culture & Critique* and 'Inclusive media literacy education for diverse societies' for *Media and Communication* (2022). His previous monograph is *Digital passages: Migrant youth 2.0. Diaspora, gender and youth cultural intersections* (Amsterdam University Press, 2015).

Acknowledgements

This book truly is a passion project. I am indebted to many people who have supported me throughout the years.

First and foremost, I am grateful to all the folks and communities who have let me enter their worlds in the last 15 years of fieldwork. Thank you for sharing your views, experiences, perspectives, critical questions and concerns about migration, technology, mobility, borders, transnationalism, surveillance and identity.

But why this book? Most textbooks suggest that aspiring researchers first read a body of literature and distil a main research question in order to select an appropriate methodology, mode of analysis, way of presenting findings and navigate possible relevant publication outlets. Such books commonly overlook why researchers want to focus on a specific dynamic or process and commit to a particular scholarly debate: research questions, problems and puzzles do not come from writing literature reviews only. Indeed, what is it that drives us? In the words of migration scholar Irene Bloemraad, "the lab coat model" of scholarly researchers is "wrong; most of us build projects from ideas that come from our own lives and our interaction with the society around us" (2012, p. 505). We can take cues from feminist scholarship to embrace and make explicit our drive, passions, frustrations and personal ethics. This is important to realize as it allows for scrutiny of what elements we choose to include in our analysis, and which ones we leave out.

For example, it's often not just a specific 'literature gap' that serves as a motivation to conduct a particular study, but it may be more "a researcher's frustration at the lack of material on a topic" (Harvey, 2020, p. 37). Reflexivity invites us researchers to reflect on our own roles as researchers as a ground to "unpack what knowledge is contingent upon, how the researcher is socially situated, and how the research agenda/process has been constituted" (Ramazanoğlu & Holland, 2002, p. 118). This reflection can include detailing how our positionality, in terms of gender, sexuality, race, nationality, class, age, generation, and/or ability affords or dissafords insights and access to communities, resources and knowledges.

My passion for researching migration and technologies dates back to my youth. I grew up in the small town of Grave, in the south of the Netherlands. Many of my friends lived in a local asylum seekers' centre. In this period, the mid-1990s, residents of the camp had mobile phones and used email to keep in touch with their loved ones abroad. Me and my white non-migrant classmates had not set up email yet, and we were not using mobile phones. After studying media, communication and gender studies a decade later, I realized in hindsight that camp dwellers were early adopters of technologies that would only become mainstream years later. This insight goes against the common stereotype of asylum seekers being backward or unfit to handle advanced technologies. Such stereotypes, for example, featured prominently in the news stories of journalists obsessed with smartphone-carrying and selfie-taking Syrians arriving on European shores during the so-called 'European refugee crisis' in 2015 and 2016. This realization motivated me to tell different stories about migration and technology. In the wake of this so-called crisis, media and migration attracted attention from researchers from a variety of disciplines and fields. It frustrated me to see that these fields were not commonly in conversation outside their own scholarly communities: I noticed discussions were developing in parallel, within the silos of disciplines.

I am grateful to Michael Ainsley, Sage commissioning editor, for believing in the idea of a book outlining the emerging interdisciplinary research area of digital migration studies. Thank you, for challenging me, for supporting me, and for providing generous feedback when I needed it most. The manuscript has been a long time in the making; I first pitched the idea early in 2018. Over time, the cloud document that I used to keep notes kept expanding and expanding. It was reassuring to have your support and guidance, in particular when life got in the way. The Covid-19 health pandemic forced me to slow down during periods of lockdown, quarantine and homeschooling, and completely halted me when the virus got me. Thanks also to Rhoda Ola-Said, for your editorial assistance. Four anonymous reviewers provided important suggestions, challenging me to move beyond discussions of migrants as passive, suffering subjects, problems or victims, and to challenge the dominant Euro-American centredness of media and migration research frameworks.

Thank you JR and your team, for allowing me to include an aerial photograph of your work 'Migrants. Picnic Across the Border' (2017). This work depicts a moment of togetherness of families separated at the United States-Mexican border. For me it illustrates the complexities of migration, movement, securitization and reflects my ethics, drive and motivation. In fall, 2017 the Tunisian-French artist and photographer JR spent a month at Tecate, Mexico, following news about intentions to erect a permanent wall between the U.S. and Mexico. In this period JR had created a meters high installation at the border fence, showing Kikito, a toddler living in Tecate in a house overlooking the border fence. The scaffolding showed Kikito peeking over the fence. JR spent time observing how families were exchanging food, drinks and mobile phones across the actual border. This inspired him to organize a picnic on both sides of the border, on October 8, 2017, the day the scaffolding with Kikito was to be taken down. Food was eaten off the surface of a tarp with a printed photograph, showing the eyes of a 'dreamer', a young undocumented migrant. A band played music on both sides of the fence. JR expected the picnic to be shut down but it was briefly tolerated, and at one point one US border guard shared a cup of tea with the artist. For JR, the artistic intervention shows "another vision" and that there are moments where humanitarian "limits are not where you think they are" (JR, 2017). In this book, similarly I want to draw attention to the messiness and paradoxes of migration in the context of digitization and datafication.

This book builds on discussions with colleagues from various scholarly communities, across geographies. I am grateful for the mentorship of Sandra Ponzanesi and Myria Georgiou. At Utrecht University, I am supported by the Graduate Gender Programme, the Department of Media and Culture Studies, as well as José van Dijck at the 'Governing the Digital Society' focus area and the Digital Migration Special Interest Group. A warm thank you to the 'Co-designing a fair digital asylum system' team: Rianne Dekker, Huub Dijstelbloem, Stefania Milan, Albert Ali Salah, Djamila Schans and Nishant Shah. I have found an academic networked home in the European Communication Research and Education Association Diaspora, Migration and the Media section (ECREA DMM). It was a privilege to serve this community with fellow management board members Kevin Smets and Irati Agirreazkuenaga. Many themes included in this book started from discussions with PhD students, most notably with Melis Mevsimler, Laura Candidatu, Claudia Minchilli of the ERC 'Dream Team', Guanqin He, Marianne Leppik, Fortunat Miarintsoa Andrianimanana, Audris Umel, Olga Usachova and Nerina Boursinou. It was a pleasure to develop projects with inspiring colleauges including Çiğdem Bozdağ, Hemmo Bruinenberg, Sanne Sprenger and Annámaria Neag and to do fieldwork with the brilliant junior researchers Kinan Alajak, Ghadeer Udwan and Jeffrey Patterson.

I benefited from the input from engaged audiences at several in-person and online events.

Thank you for welcoming me to your institution, colleagues and students Saskia Witteborn at the Chinese University of Hong Kong, Dana Diminescu at Télécom Paris, Philipp Seuferling at Södertörn University, Stephan Scheel at Universität Duisburg-Essen. There were also several memorable online events that pushed my thinking, including the 'Cultures of (im)mobile entanglements' workshop organized by Earvin Cabalquinto, the STS 'Mig@Tec Circle', the 'Social Media Use in Migration Research' panel organized by the Canada Excellence Research Chair in Migration and Integration and the 'Migrant Belongings: Digital Practices and the Everyday' conference organized from Utrecht University in April 2021 with Sandra Ponzanesi, Julia de Lange and Frederik Kohler.

In 2020–2021, I was a fellow at the Netherlands Institute of Advanced Studies. I appreciate Jan-Willem Duyvendak's and Fenneke Wekker's leadership, while we were trying to find a way to live and work with the Covid-19 virus. Thanks to all fellows who have shaped my thinking, especially Hein de Haas, Laura Bisailon, Lindsay Braun, Jeff Handmaker, Marika Kelbusek, Iris van Rooij, Maxime Rovère, Myungji Yang and Simon Willmets. From Hein de Haas, I take inspiration to be committed to critically question 'migration myths'. He for example importantly reminds us that international migration has remained stable in the last half-century: around 2.5–3% of the population are international migrants (Haas, 2005). The narrative of growing global migration is fundamentally flawed; a decolonial perspective is helpful, reminding us about the celebration of colonial settler migration or the relative invisibility of forced movement of enslaved populations in accounts of migration. The narrative of migration growth as a security threat only emerged after non-European, non-white people moved to colonial centres in periods of decolonization

Finally, a word of thanks to the dear colleagues who agreed to read chapters and join the Research Dialogues included in this book: Brenda S.A. Yeoh, Huub Dijstelbloem, Dana Diminescu, Amanda Paz Alencar, Radha Hegde, Eugenia Siapera, Saskia Witteborn, Earvin Charles Cabalquinto, Philipp Seuferling and Łukasz Szulc.

Introduction

Digital migration studies is research on migration in relation to digital technologies. As we[1] explore in this book, research addresses the digitization of borders and the datafication of movement for the purposes of surveillance and control, for example, as well as the digital practices of migrants keeping in touch with their loved ones and friends across distances. Methodologically, this emerging interdisciplinary research area covers 'traditional' social science and humanities survey research, qualitative fieldwork and cultural critique as well as digital methods and computational approaches that draw on digital datasets, including social media data or mobile phone call records.

Discussion about and the use of digital technologies have surged in the last decade across various migration contexts, potentially impacting the entire migration cycle. The digital is commonly seen as a 'smart' disruptive tool. Digital solutions are introduced to make migration management and migration control more efficient, while simultaneously promising they will make life easier and safeguard the human rights of migrants. The digital is presented as a key to unlock the transformations required, as we learn from various recent initiatives:

- On January 26, 2022, the World Customs Organization (WCO) celebrated its World Customs Day virtually with the theme of "Scaling up Customs Digital Transformation by Embracing a Data Culture and Building a Data Ecosystem" (WCOOMD, 2022).
- As a response to "global displacement challenges", "digital inclusion" and "data innovation" programmes are high on the agenda of the United Nations High Commissioner for Refugees (UNHCR, 2022a, 2022b).
- In the Association of Southeast Asian Nations region, the International Labour Association embraces "Digitalization to Promote Decent Work for Migrant Workers" (ILO, 2019).
- The slogan "The digital is a game changer for migration" is used by the European Commission (EU EPSC, 2019, p. 12).

The global Covid-19 coronavirus health pandemic (since 2020) has led to a growth in the use of existing and the development of new technologies in migration contexts (McAuliffe, Blower & Beduschi, 2021; Triandafyllidou, 2022). With movement halted under lockdown measures, migrants (ranging from international students, labour migrants, expatriates to refugees) had to rely on digital technologies to keep in touch with loved ones living at a distance (Sseviiri, Alencar & Kisira, 2022). Migration management and border control agencies have embraced technologies such as 'contactless ID controls', remote interviewing and blockchain technologies to facilitate information exchanges between systems as well as artificial intelligence to assist in their decision making (EMN-OECD, 2022). Recruiters and employers of labour migrants have developed new digital products, including apps, web portals and electronic tickets (ILO, 2021). Other experiments with technology include tagging people on immigration bail using electronic monitoring devices in the UK (Global Positioning System-trackers); using automated drones to patrol land and sea borders; testing AI lie detectors across European airports; or using sound canons to deter irregular sea crossings at the Greece–Turkey border (Molnar, 2022). These examples indicate that migration and digital technologies together drive and reflect larger economic, cultural, societal, political and academic developments.

Researchers of digital migration studies are trying to keep pace with these developments. In this book, we develop digital migration studies not as a separate field of study in pursuit of a new academic hype. We are not calling for the establishment of new dedicated journals or new funding streams, taking away scarce resources from established fields. Rather, we acknowledge that the relationship between migration and digital technologies is a thematic area already on the radar of a growing group of scholars from a broad range of disciplines. We will not be able to reverse the specialized character of contemporary academia. However, what we do want to challenge with this book is the lack of dialogue between disciplinary silos. For example, in researching migration, media and technology, scholars commonly do not cite migration studies scholarship and, vice versa, migration scholars are often not aware of developments in media or technology studies. We therefore address digital migration studies here as an interdisciplinary research topic and seek to bring critical scholarship from various fields into the conversation. By doing so, we aim to achieve a more comprehensive and critical understanding of the role of digital technologies in migration contexts, and vice versa.

This book seeks to build on the momentum for such interdisciplinary exchange, as Jordan Hayes notes: "digital migration studies has entered a moment of generative reflection" (Hayes, 2019, p. 661). In the last eight years we have seen a steady growth of publications, conferences, networks and funded research projects addressing digital migration studies. Indicative publications are handbooks such as the *Research handbook on international migration and digital technology* (McAuliffe, 2021), *Handbook of media and migration* (Smets et al., 2020) and *The handbook of diasporas, media, and cultures* (Retis & Tsagarousianou, 2019), monographs like *The digital border* (Chouliaraki & Georgiou, 2022) or *Borders as infrastructure* (Dijstelbloem, 2021) as well as edited volumes like *Research methodologies and ethical challenges in digital migration studies* (Sandberg et al., 2022), *Data science for migration and mobility* (Salah, Korkmaz & Bircan, 2023) and

Information and communications technology in support of migration (Akhgar et al., 2022). Relevant networks are the *Diaspora and media* working group (DIM), established in 2005 as part of the International Association for Media and Communication Research (IAMCR), the *Diaspora, Migration and the Media* section (DMM), established in 2007 as part of the European Communication Research and Education Association (ECREA) and STS Mig-Tec, established in 2019 for scholars working in science and technology studies (STS), migration, security and border studies. Illustrative funded projects include 'AFAR: *Algorithmic Fairness for Asylum-Seekers and Refugees*' (2021–2025), funded by the Volkswagen Foundation, or '*ITFLOWS: IT Tools and Methods for Managing Migration Flows*' (2020–2023), a so-called Horizon 2020 project funded by the European Commission. Finally, there is also the '*Digital Migration Podcast: Migração & Transformação Digital*', hosted by the NOVA School of Law in Portugal (Nova Refugee Clinic, 2022). This book seeks to builds connections between fields by developing a multi-perspectival approach to digital migration studies.

Comprehensive understanding

Despite the growth of scholarship across fields, the work is not done. To date, we lack a comprehensive understanding of how migration and digital technologies are interrelated. In their scoping review, Tiziani Mancini and colleagues found that "the realm of digital migration studies is still fragmented and lacking an analytical focus" (2019, p. 1). Our understanding is limited as a result of (at least) five restrictions, that each require particular counter-strategies:

1 We digital migration studies researchers are trying to keep pace with a rapidly changing terrain and evolving group of relevant actors. In trying to do so, we face serious disadvantages. Challenges result from private companies that commonly take measures to limit access to protect commercial interests or government bodies that limit access to procedural details resulting from risk assessments, anti-terrorism measures or political sensitivity.
2 In pursuing the latest technological experiments, scholarly discussions overlook histories of migration and technological development. Migration has always been a mediated affair, constituted through storytelling and communicative exchanges. In addressing the impact of the proliferation of digital technologies on registering, administrating, identifying and controlling migration, greater attention on non-digital and early-digital pre-histories is needed.
3 Scholarly discussions largely develop in isolation within the confines of individual disciplines, in parallel to other fields and with little cross-fertilization. For example, it has been noted that "data science studies ...

consider 'migration' more of an application case, rather than contributing to the existing frameworks" (Salah et al., 2023, p. 5). We see specialized discussions happening in fields such as media and communication studies; migration studies; information and data science; ethnic, diaspora and racial studies; mobility studies; gender and postcolonial studies; anthropology; development studies; geography; border studies; urban studies; human–computer interaction; science and technology studies; and law and human rights. As a result, a wide range of specialized concepts have been proposed, including "connected migrants" (Diminescu, 2008), "migrant polymedia" (Madianou & Miller, 2012), "information precarity" (Wall, Campbell & Janbek, 2017), "digital diasporas" (e.g. Alonso & Arzoz, 2010; Gajjala, 2004), "smart refugees" (Dekker et al., 2018) and "digital borders" (e.g. Chouliaraki & Georgiou, 2022; Dijstelbloem, 2021), which are useful to generate knowledge on particular aspects of migration and the digital. We need to bring these varied approaches and accompanying methodological frameworks into dialogue. This is not an easy task.

4   In recent years, those of us pursuing digital migration studies have faced many rejections from conference organizers and journal editorial boards and peer reviewers. Editors of migration studies journals and organizers of migration studies conferences have rejected technology-oriented papers for being out of scope, while similarly, internet and media studies journals had trouble placing submissions focusing on questions of migration.

5   In tandem with the substantial degree of academic specialization, scholars have singled out particular (sub)groups of mobile people, such as refugees, asylum seekers, labour, queer or expatriate migrants. For each (sub)group, particular types of research frameworks and questions have become dominant. Dominant questions for each group include how refugees use smartphones during irregular journeys; how asylum migrants are datafied through biometrics and databases; how labour migrants keep in touch with loved ones overseas; how queer migrants express their identities across (digital) contexts; and how expatriates establish new homes. Research which compares various groups of migrants and research frameworks is scarce.

6   Although, over 25 years ago, Arjun Appadurai called for researchers to address the relationships between migration and digital technologies (1996), it took a long time for researchers to take up this call. In recent years, scholarship has proliferated, but only in the wake of the so-called 'European refugee crisis' in 2015–2016. The fact that this geo-political moment led to the establishment of a new research agenda is indicative of the common eurocentrism of digital migration research. The Covid-19 pandemic has also attracted strong scholarly attention, further

reinforcing a dominant preoccupation with Global North perspectives, stakes and issues. "Diversification and decolonisation" are urgently needed. As Claire Moran argues, "very few studies within the Digital Migration Studies field are written by non-Western scholars", and there is, for example, "very little research that engages with African case studies" (2022, p. 14).

In this book, we pursue a comprehensive, interdisciplinary and critical understanding of the relationships between migration and digital technologies. For this purpose, we take a relational view to:

- understand mobilities and migration as interrelated: migration results from the governing and politicization of particular mobile people, resulting in the mobility of some and immobility of others;
- understand how top-down governmental, security and corporate forces co-shaping the digital migrant condition and bottom-up digital migrant practices impact upon each other;
- demonstrate the overlaps and dissimilarities between various migrant groups to scrutinize the politics of categorization in light of datafication and digital mediation (including forced and voluntary migrants, transnational and internal rural–urban migrants, across the Global North and Global South);
- combine insights on the contemporary moment with insights into how migration and technologies have interacted in different periods in history,
- acknowledge heterogeneity and varieties of knowledge produced by specialized scholarly communities while also outlining the interdisciplinary common ground between various scholarly perspectives;
- acknowledge the pros and cons and ethical challenges of both large-scale and small-scale methodological approaches;
- give a critical account of how migration and digitization (re)produce unequal power relations as well as drawing on social justice perspectives to articulate possible alternatives.

To introduce the interdisciplinary research area of digital migration studies and its commitments, below we will review ontological, epistemological, methodological and ethical concerns. On the level of ontology, we are confronted with fundamental questions relating to the digitization, datafication and automation of human movements within and across regions, nations and continents. As 'migrants' come into being through spatial, legal and digital movements – such as border crossing, applying for work visas or refugee status determination, ontological and epistemological contemplation is needed. Finally, methodological and ethical reflection is needed about the opportunities and challenges related to digital-data-driven ways of studying human movement, as new corporate, governmental, security and academic datasets of movement are created.

A new ontology?

Ontology promotes philosophical reflection about an object of scholarly inquiry and invites researchers to give a systematic account of its existence. We can take ontology to reflect on the essence of what we as digital migration studies scholars may choose to examine. To date, migration and technologies have mostly been studied as two isolated and separated phenomena, which may incidentally converge in particular contexts. Here, however, we take as a starting point that migration in its essence is fundamentally co-shaped by media technologies. Migration does not exist outside technological development. Digital migrants are, for example, increasingly processed as data points in databases for asylum or visa verification purposes. Digitization, datafication and connectivity fundamentally co-constitute migrant being and existence. However, in trying to avoid being blinded by the contemporary spectacle of advanced technologies, we will also address whether or not migration has historically ever existed outside media systems. Vice versa, technology is not developed outside the social-cultural and political domain of migration. Rather, technological innovation is fundamentally tied to processes of facilitating and limiting human migration and mobility. For example, borders and refugee camps have become "testing grounds" to experiment with new surveillance, identification and payment technologies, including drones, lie-detectors, iris scans and blockchain (Molnar, 2020). However, testing new technologies on non-mainstream groups such as migrants does not come from a void. Here the question arises of what we can learn by thinking about the histories of human movement and the histories of technological innovation together (see Chapter 5, Histories).

With a relational understanding of digital migration, we thus move away from distinguishing migration and technology on the basis of their own unique substances, but rather we seek to address their mutual relations. The notion of digital migration proposed here thus presumes a relational ontology. It takes relations as the primary object of analysis and sees 'the digital' and 'migration' as ontologically inseparable. Relational ontology, for feminist philosopher Karen Barad, acknowledges how fundamentally inseparable relations between entities constitute "the basic units of existence" (2007, p. 333). We should therefore be less interested in seeking to study how 'the digital' and 'migration' have changed from an a-priori existence which was somehow less mediated or interrelated. Rather, here we shift our attention and consider how digital migration emerges in particular situated constellations. This relational ontology assumes that digital migration is unstable, locatable and reflective of power hierarchies. It is a product of particular entanglements, which results in particular entities and boundary-making practices (e.g. securing borders through so-called 'smart borders'). Consider, for example, how digital migration is entangled with rationalities of migration and technologies (see Table 0.1).

Digital migration is continuously (re)made in the interaction between two sets of hegemonic rationalities: the rationality of migration and well as technocratic rationality (Chouliaraki & Georgiou, 2022). These two rationalities together shape how contemporary borders and policies work to welcome some migrants and reject others. First, the dominant rationality of migration has emerged from the historical projects of colonialism, enlightenment, imperialism, racism, capitalism and nationalism, among others (Andrews, 2021; Madörin, 2022; Mayblin & Turner, 2021). These legacies continue to shape decisions about which bodies are allowed to be mobile, and which are rendered immobile, resulting in a persisting "good-versus-bad mobilities dichotomy" (Bruns, 2023). Across the world, this dichotomy shapes visa regimes, policies and recruitment schemes that allow for the movement of particular desirable migrant subjects to do particular work, or welcome particular groups of displaced people, and halt others. In extreme cases, the migration rationality informing border control, migrant detention and deportation in countries in the Global North distinguishes between which migrant lives matter, and which do not (De Genova, 2018). This is an example of what the political theorist Achille Mbembé describes as the racialized "necropolitics", or the politics of death, where governmental institutions have "the capacity to define who matters and who does not, who is disposable and who is not" (Mbembé & Meintjes, 2003, p. 27).

Table 0.1 Key features of migration and technology rationalities

Migration is...	Technology is...
reflective of the rationality of modernity	reflective of a technocratic, mechanistic rationality
seen as in need of governance and management, particularly through either humanitarianism or securitization	seen as efficient, objective, neutral and transparent
bound to particular hierarchical classifications of people to maintain a particular world order bounded by borders and channelled through passports, permits and procedures	a means to diagnose a problem and tackle it by dividing it into isolated components
shaped by histories of colonialism, enlightenment, imperialism, racism, capitalism and nationalism	a means to create an efficient solution to individual components and subsequently the overall problem

Second, migration is dominantly governed on the basis of a technocratic rationality (Oelgemöller, 2017). A technocratic rationality assumes human mobility can be approached as a problem that can be solved unidirectionally. Technologies are made to play important roles with the expectation that they will have a causal effect in solving problems. Technocratic rationality follows the logic of "componential thinking" (Fischer, 1990, p. 43), which first assumes that problems that are diagnosed can be neatly broken down and isolated in separate parts, and, second, assumes that for each of these parts there exist "one best technical solution" (ibid.). More specifically, the contemporary technocratic rationality revolves around a trust in "algorithmic reason" to govern the "self and other" (Aradau & Blanke, 2022, p. 3).

Particularly in recent forms of migration governance, such as the so-called 'European refugee crisis' (2015–2016, see Viola & Musolff, 2019) or the Covid-19 health pandemic (2020 onwards), we can see the embrace of technosolutionism: technologies are celebrated as a means to efficiently fix the problem of mobility of particular groups of people. However, technocratic migration rationalities are nothing new. By contrast, they can be traced back to the colonial era. For example, the Chinese Protectorate, set up by the British authorities in the late 19th century to govern workers in Singapore and Malaysia, institutionalized a racialized system to govern the residence and status of newly arrived Chinese labourers (Sai, 2021).

Although the rationalities of migration and technocracy are dominant, they are not all-encompassing. Alternative ontologies exist. In particular, the ontology of the "mobile commons of migration" (Papadopoulos & Tsianos, 2013), pursued by scholars who seek to address everyday mobilities and migration from the ground up, offers an inspiring alternative. This perspective moves away from discourses of governance, security and citizenship, to recognizing mobility in the broadest sense as an "ontological facet of the human condition, or indeed of human *being* as such" (De Genova, 2020, p. 172). Instead, it addresses the autonomy and everyday materialities of people who tap into informal digital networks while moving, despite borders and regimes.

Epistemologies

We can take epistemology to reflect on what kinds of knowledge are produced about migration and digitalization, why, by whom and for whom. Although this book focuses on scholarly discussions on digital migration, it is important to recognize that academics are not the only ones producing knowledge about migration and the digital. Very often they are also not the most visible or dominant one in the general discourse. Mainstream media, policy makers or corporations are often prominent. In this section, before discussing the main relevant academic frameworks, we will review which actors play a role in knowledge production about digital migration.

The digital has been taken as an entry point, stage and resource by a variety of actors to produce knowledge about migrants and migration. This results in a multiplicity of knowledges being produced: the digital has been mobilized to claim agency and share lived experiences about migration and migrants as well as to understand, monetize, control, attack, rehumanize and aesthetically capture migration. The non-exhaustive overview presented in Table 0.2 indicates how, in digital migration, both 'migration' and 'the digital' should not be seen as singular, homogeneous entities. Rather, they both mean different things to different actors. In this book, we centre epistemologies of academic knowledge production. Migration, mobility and digital studies are three major epistemological frameworks underpinning digital migration studies scholarship. We cannot do justice to the full history and internal complexities of these fields here. Below we briefly outline each separately by attending to histories and critical interventions that can guide us in deciding what knowledge we want to produce as digital migration scholars.

Epistemologies of migration studies

Migration studies came of age in the 1980s in the US, and in the 1990s in Europe, and has been institutionalized across universities, particularly in the Global North (Düvell, 2021). Conventional migration studies focuses on human movement across borders, putting on the agenda migration as a topic worthy of research and education. However, resulting from a combination of its originating contexts, funding scheme incentives, policy impact ambitions and polemic public discourse, its theories and methodologies reflect several biases. Most notably, migration studies commonly reflects state perspectives, producing methodologically nationalist findings (Wimmer & Glick-Schiller, 2002). Migration is dominantly analysed in relation to borders – territorial, continental, national, regional, urban–rural, legal, ideological, racial and digital. As a consequence, the human subjects crossing borders are politicized.

This framework has also socialized scholars into normalizing hierarchical categories. Through using categories, we scholars risk naturalizing essential differences between 'migrants' and 'non-migrants', particularly on the grounds of ethnic, racial, gendered, sexual and religious differences (Dahinden, 2016).

Table 0.2   Overview of actors and the type of knowledge about digital migration they produce

Actors	Type of knowledge production
Migrants	Digital as a domain to produce knowledge about routes, middlemen or policies, for example through the use of smartphones and social media platforms
Academics	Digital as an entry point to study bottom-up migration and migrants' experiences and top-down processes of recruitment, governance, securitization and control
Government actors (e.g. migration management and border guard agencies)	Digital used to produce knowledge for migration recruitment and management, border control, surveillance, deterrence, prediction, algorithmic decision making and verification of visa applications and asylum claims
Corporations (e.g. telco providers, hardware/software producers, consultancy firms)	Digital domain used to create and enter untapped market of migrant consumers' use of technologies (e.g. simcards) and digital services (e.g. digital wallets, remittances) and to have migrants enter the digital economy (e.g. coding schools or monetizing migrant labour through automation), as well as to facilitate recruitment, governance, management, securitization and/or deterrence of migrants
Non-governmental organizations (NGOs), such as humanitarian organizations	Digital domain to facilitate protection and service provision for migrant groups. New technologies, such as Virtual Reality installations, are deployed to make general audiences and donors aware of the plight of migrants, for example
Journalists	Digital domain as a way to learn more about migrant self-representations and digital voices as well as to trace broader sentiments about migration
Activists and social movements	Digital domain to circulate alternative knowledge about migrants and migration, for example by documenting and rallying against inhumane, violent and racist policies and practices worldwide
Artists	Digital domain as a stage and resource for creative interventions to share alternative imaginaries of migration
General public	Digital domain as a contested space where publics often polemically and discursively construct migration

Migration scholar Franck Düvell sums up why we should critically rethink the epistemology of conventional migration studies:

> the knowledge production of migration studies is haunted by a range of frustrations, including unconvincing definitions, lack of data, reductionism, short-range theories, often biased research funding practices, usually negative public and political discourse, and an underlying dominant perspective of the nation-state and thus an omnipresent sedentary bias. (2021, p. 215)

These caveats and biases might also impact our studies of migration in relation to digitization. Therefore, we should critically reflect on the definitions, frameworks and datasets we use in order to avoid stereotyping, reductionism and/or state-centrism.

Epistemologies of mobility studies

Mobility studies is a second important framework informing digital migration studies. Mobility is a means by which migration occurs, and migrants experience mobility. Mobility is not only a description of movement; as an analytic lens it invites us to probe particular aspects of migration. The "new mobilities paradigm" (Sheller & Urry, 2006) has gained traction since the mid-2000s. It promotes an alternative to the conventional understanding of migration as a fixed journey with a static beginning and clear end point (Cresswell, 2006, 2010). The term 'mobilities' invites a plural understanding of migration processes, as well as the recognition of the internal heterogeneity of migrant groups. In particular, the paradigm also made scholars more aware of the importance of addressing sedentariness alongside movement, advocating for a relational understanding of mobilities as inherently connected to immobilities. In contrast to migration studies, which is predominantly human-centred and politicizes human movement across borders, mobility research is concerned with all types of movements, including the mobilities of people, objects, money and ideas. The framework alerts us to the relations between human movement and the material cultures of objects, technologies and operating logics. Rather than people-centric accounts of migration movement, mobility studies prompts attention for human movement as circulation, but also, for example, transportation. It welcomes attention not only for long-term migration, but also for everyday and short-term mobilities, including tourism, international student exchanges or volunteer work. Its transnational approach does not centre state borders, but this means it is characterized by a certain utopianism, or rather elitism. In response, mobility scholars like Mimi Sheller have sought to account for how power shapes migration regimes, as is evidenced by the concept of "mobility justice" (Sheller, 2018).

Critical interventions

Scholars of critical migration, critical border, postcolonial and decolonial studies have made important interventions in migration and mobility studies. Critical scholarship on migration and mobility takes an explicit normative stance and seeks to be self-reflexive and face its own biases. Scholars seek to re-politicize stances on migration that have become de-politicized, normalized or taken for granted over the years. Examples include the dominant focus on migrants as 'others', which reinforces differences between societal groups (e.g. migrants and non-migrants), and the uncritical use of hierarchical labels and categories for particular groups of mobile people or studying the process of migrant integration without acknowledging the roles of other societal actors. This is done, for example, by questioning the relationship between academic researchers and policy makers or by foregrounding how human movement is fundamentally shaped by and reinforces power relations and racial, gender and class inequalities and violence. Illustrative works include *Humanitarian borders: Unequal mobility and saving lives* (Pallister-Wilkins, 2022), *Border as method, or the multiplication of labor* (Mezzadra & Neilson, 2013), *Crossing: How we label and react to people on the move* (Hamlin, 2021) or *Open borders: In defence of free movement* (Jones, 2019). Scholars in this terrain are thus outspoken about their political and ethical commitments. Such commitments guide their choice for critical, social-justice-oriented theoretical frameworks, participatory research designs and collaborative publication efforts (see Table 0.3).

Epistemologies of digital studies

Critical, theoretical engagement with technologies in migration is underdeveloped in migration and mobility studies. In the last few years, we could observe a "technology hype in migration studies" (Tazzioli, 2022, p. 237), although technologies are largely approached as static, singular variables. Publications oriented to migration studies particularly address methodological innovation and the challenges resulting from digitization, for example, *Migration research in a digitized world: Using innovative technology to tackle methodological challenges* (Pötzschke & Rinken, 2022). Leading theory-oriented introductions to migration, such as the fourth edition of the volume *Migration theory: Talking across disciplines* (Brettell & Hollifield, 2023), for example, do feature individual chapters on law, anthropology, sociology or geography, but do not feature chapters outlining the conceptual apparatus of technology, information or media studies.

Seeking to offer a corrective, in this book we address the digital not as a static entity or methodological challenge or opportunity. Rather, we conceptualize the 'digital' in digital migration studies by turning to branches of scholarship that follow a critical, constructivist perspective on mediation and a socio-technical approach to technologies. These frameworks, prominent in media and communication and in science and technology studies respectively, invite researchers

Table 0.3 Comparing migration and mobility studies

Migration studies	Mobility studies	Common ground
Commonly concerns international migration, taking cross-border movement as a starting point	Commonly concerns movements of people, objects or ideas	Focus on human movement in binary opposition to non-migration/immobility
Commonly assumes migration is based on permanence, longevity and lengthiness	Understands movement and stasis to operate in a continuum	Spatial dimensions are often considered, while temporal dimensions often remain implicit
Commonly reinforces pre-set categories that hierarchically distinguish between groups of migrants	With a historical focus on elite movements, it risks reinforcing binary distinctions between 'good' and 'bad' mobilities	Emerging awareness of the power of definition that scholars hold
Cannot be seen in isolation from migration industry and regimes, research agendas are commonly set by funders and studies are often policy oriented	In-decentring human movement, it risks glossing over power relations	
Has only recently begun to address the histories of colonialism, enlightenment, imperialism, racism, capitalism and nationalism	Until recently, it has commonly assumed a borderless world, which is a utopian aspiration and overlooks obstacles	Need for critical engagement with social justice perspectives of anti-racism and decolonial theory

to attend to the specificities of digital technologies, but not as isolated artefacts. Media and communication scholars turn to mediation theory to understand how standalone technologies do not fully determine any action; they do not have total linear, causal effects. From the perspective of mediation, we can address how technologies operate across the levels of institutionality, technicity and sociality (Martín-Barbero, 2006). By studying the reasons for developing technologies – the political, economic, social and material factors that shape technologies – and how they are used in pursuit of certain goals, we can capture, analyze and possibly contest the ideologies that technologies reflect (Hall, 2013a;

Williams, 1974). For example, from the perspective of mediation, we can critically assess contemporary digital borders as both material and symbolic products of cultural frameworks (Chouliaraki & Georgiou, 2022).

In science and technology studies, approaches to understand the socio-technical relationship between humans and technologies are prominent. Actor–network theory (ANT) offers a language and methodological tool for studying things in relation to their social contexts (Dijstelbloem, 2021), by investigating how they emerge as networked constellations (Latour, 2005). In this vocabulary, 'actors' include both humans (such as migrants, border officials or academic researchers) and non-humans (such as passports and patrol dogs). From the perspective of ANT, these actors cannot be understood in isolation. They only become meaningful as 'actants' (actors that act) in their interaction with other actors. In their interaction, they become 'actor-networks'. Furthermore, ANT offers a means to understand how the world is not a singular reality, but an evolving multiplicity (Mol, 2003). For example, from an ANT perspective, Yashar Mahmud investigates the multiple organizational making of refugees in Sweden, Finland, Greece and Bulgaria as an "actor-network that consists of people, their practices, supporting non-human actors, held together by a narrative" (2020, n.p.).

Bringing together critical concepts from migration, mobility and digital studies could establish new bridges between fields, as well as prompt reflection on dominant assumptions within fields. For example, with the concept of the "migration mobile", Martin Bak Jørgensen and Vasilis Galis draw critical attention to the "fluidity of the migratory space" (2022, p. 3). There is a constant (albeit controlled and contested) physical, portable and digital flow and fluid interaction between a variety of actors that, through high-tech and low-tech applications, "draw and re-draw lines of inclusion and exclusion" through borders, belonging and migration (ibid., p. 4). Insights from migration and mobility studies also offer a means to question dominant assumptions. To question the "dominant focus in the communication studies literature […] on mobility, movement and connectivity" (2019, p. 650), Kevin Smets brings in mobility and migration scholarship. He suggests that media and communication scholars can benefit from approaching mobility and immobility in a (digitally mediated) spectrum.

Methodologies

With the digitalization of migrant connectivity and migration management, a variety of "migration traceability" data (Diminescu, 2020, p. 77) is generated. The resulting large-scale human behavioural datasets are typically stored by companies that seek to extract monetary value from them or by governmental agencies that seek to use them to manage and predict migration. These digital datasets can be "re-purposed to address research questions for the social sciences" (Salah, 2022, p. 252). These sources can be of interest to both big data scholars using quantitative approaches and small data scholars using interpretative, qualitative approaches (Pötzschke & Rinken, 2022). For quantitative-oriented data scientists, computational social scientists and digital humanists, the empirical goal is analyzing human behavioural data using mathematical models to observe "patterns, trends, and associations" as well as explaining or predicting changes through modelling datasets (Salah et al., 2023, p. 6). Qualitative, interpretative scholars take digital data points as a starting point to draw a holistic picture and elicit meaning making of relevant actors, most notably migrants (e.g. Witteborn, 2021a).

A variety of methodological approaches can be used in digital migration studies. We can better understand these approaches along the spectrum of digital-media-centric-ness and non-media-digital-centric-ness as well as the continuum of migrant-centric-ness and non-migrant-centric-ness (see Figure 0.1).

non-digital-media-centric research ◄═══════════════► digital-media-centric research

migrant-centric research ◄═══════════════► non-migrant-centric research

Figure 0.1   Two continuums of methodological approaches observable in digital migration studies

Let us first consider the continuum of migrant-centric and non-migrant-centric research.

Migrant-centric research prioritizes the situation of migrants, thereby singling out migrants as a particular population segment. This research, for example, seeks to measure degrees of integration of migrants into societies or capture the layered life histories of migrant families.

Non-migrant-centric studies are interested in the power relations and contexts in which migration occurs. They do not assume migrants are a naturally observable group. They seek to avoid naturalizing and essentializing migrants as differing from non-migrants. For this purpose, they decentre their focus and go beyond ethnic-centric or nation-state-centric approaches, and, for example, study migrants and non-migrants together (Dahinden, 2016).

Second, we can consider the continuum of digital-media-centric and non-digital-media-centric research. Digital-media-centric studies isolate or prioritize more a focus on the role of standalone technologies. Non-digital-media-centric studies seek to understand the role of technologies as part of broader contexts of politics, economics, culture and ideology (Morley, 2009; Pink et al., 2016). In digital migration studies, a digital-media-centric study will address migrants as data: migrant behaviour can be studied on the basis of standalone digital data points in a database, for example mobile phone call records. The database could offer insights into patterns of human movements over space and time. A non-digital-media-centric study would approach digital migrant data as context. For example, researchers could study what is coded into biometric databases, by whom, how and for what purposes, to study how norms, values and ideologies colour data points. In recent years, many big data studies on migration have taken a digital-centric approach, whereas many small data studies have pursued a non-digital-media-centric approach.

There is potential for us digital migration studies scholars to take a position anywhere across these two scales, as long we reflect on the implications of prioritizing and isolating particular variables, such as technology or migration. For example, when we use a digital-centric approach and uncritically work with the data points we find in a database, we might essentialize and stereotype particular groups of mobile people. To invite further reflexive engagement, we address ethical considerations and commitments in the following section.

Ethics

Digital migration studies research ethics is a contested terrain (Sandberg et al., 2022). Studying migration poses several serious ethical challenges (Zapata-Barrero & Yalaz, 2020), which may be further compounded in digital contexts (Clark-Kazak, 2021). Researchers may, for example, operate in asymmetrical power relations with their informants. They have to establish trust relationships with people who may have experienced traumas, hardship, prosecution or exploitation. They are required to do so while navigating a wider landscape shaped by changing legal, social and political agendas. Besides the established virtues, such as empathy, and principles, such as voluntariness, minimizing harm and protecting personal information, research ethics in migration studies is increasingly relational and situated. This means that ethics are to be fine-tuned on the basis of the particular requirements demanded by the context of the study. Thus, studying the digital comes with its ethical concerns, which can become even more demanding in relation to migration. Classical ethical concepts that pre-date the internet era cannot be directly applied to the digital domain. For example, researchers need to re-establish in relation to the digital context the parameters of who/what counts as human subjects, personal data and informed consent. The entities, places and times of accessing, gathering, storing and processing information are ever-changing (Leurs & Witteborn, 2021; Tiidenberg, 2018). The intersections of migration and digital technologies have additional specific ethical implications that demand we reflect on our decision making. We will consider data privacy and the use of categories as issues to be confronted during our decision-making process.

Decision making: do no harm?

Ethical decision making is a thorny issue in digital migration studies. For example, 'do no harm' is a common ethical aspiration in decision making while planning, conducting, analyzing, reporting and valorizing research. Among migration researchers, it has become a standard, creating a stronger awareness of issues of access, asymmetrical relationships and privacy, particularly with vulnerable research partners. However, as Maurice Stierl argues, when "policy-friendliness" becomes a criterion for funding research, we risk becoming co-opted in state-centric regimes of migration management and governance. In particular circumstances, rather than 'do no harm', social-justice-oriented researchers are required to adopt the 'do harm' stance that is needed to pursue systematic change (Stierl, 2022, p. 1092). For example, researchers collecting testimonies of illegal 'push-backs' or the expelling of asylum seekers from territories are tasked with creating alternative (non-state-centric) knowledge about bordering, which "'pushes back' against the pushback regime" (Davies, Isakjee & Obradovic-Wochnick, 2022, p. 1). Alternatively, as an example of the "progressive politics of data for migration" (Taylor & Meissner, 2020, p. 286), researchers may make the argument not to use digital datasets for predicting migrant flows or risks, but rather to grasp the heterogeneity and complexity of human movement.

Throughout our research cycles, we make decisions that have consequences for the different actors involved. The critical question of "To whom and to what is research on migration a contribution?" (Sandoval-García, 2013, p. 1429) offers an important reminder to remain attentive to one's commitments to social justice. In operationalizing our studies, we can draw inspiration from ethics of care. Feminist sociologists Rosalind Edwards and Melanie Mauthner (2002) have proposed a set of questions which can guide us in our studies of digital migration:

- Who are the people involved in and affected by the ethical dilemma raised in the research?
- What is the context of the dilemma in terms of the specific topic of the research and the issues it raises personally and socially for those involved?
- What are the specific social and personal locations of the people involved in relation to each other?
- What are the needs of those involved and how are they interrelated?
- Who am I identifying with, who am I posing as different, and why?
- What is the balance of personal and social power between those involved?
- How will those involved understand our actions and are these in balance with our judgement about our own practices?
- How can we best communicate the ethical dilemmas to those involved, give them room to raise their views, and negotiate with and between them?
- How will our actions affect relationships between the people involved? (2002, pp. 28–29)

These questions help us to decide over the course of our research cycle who we can care for and how, and how we might want to push back or how we might do harm to oppressive procedures and infrastructures in pursuit of social change.

Data privacy

Data privacy presents us with a pivotal concern when making decisions in our research cycle. Industry, governments and humanitarian organizations are increasingly gathering, exchanging and triangulating data, each with their own incentive. While guidelines for handling personal data (e.g. informing subjects or obtaining consent) exist, the on-the-ground implementation of data collection, processing and sharing procedures often remains problematic (Latonero et al., 2019). A decade ago, Privacy International already expressed concerns about data privacy violations in refugee camps in Djibouti, Ethiopia, Kenya and Malaysia (Privacy International, 2011). During procedures, migrants, asylum seekers and refugees volunteering their data often lack clear information and instructions about their rights and obligations. Across government agencies and international NGOs, there have been several instances of breaches and hacks of datasets, but also various examples of so-called "function-creep" (Madianou, 2019a), where sensitive data collected for one purpose (e.g. refugee registration) is used for other purposes (e.g. surveillance). When digital migration studies researchers uncritically produce new insights using these datasets, they may exacerbate risks. For example, researchers have shown how aggregating and visualizing mobile phone call records uncritically may risk violating the data privacy of individuals on the move. Researchers might also be co-opted into producing a surveillance database of unaware individuals (Salah et al., 2019, p. 10). Therefore, Saskia Witteborn makes the urgent "theoretical and practical call to understand the concept of data and information privacy from the perspective of people who are legally and socially vulnerable" (2021a, p. 2303). In processing datasets, it is thus imperative to always consider migrants' perspectives and interpretations of their own data points – to include a grounded and community-centred viewpoint.

Categories

The use of categories and labels to describe the migrant people we produce knowledge on/with presents us with another important decision-making concern. In migration contexts, categories can protect, but also oppress. Categories are not neutral, objective or innocent; rather, they reflect particular legal, political, historical and cultural decisions, ideologies and power relations. The digitalization and datafication of migrant subjects is often presented as an efficient, neutral and effective process. However, as gender and technology scholar Kate Sim and digital anthropologist Margie Cheesman remind us, black-boxing categorization through digital systems obscures the power relations underpinning categorization: "de-politicised approaches to humanitarian digitalisation stabilise categorisation practices as objective, eclipsing intersectional issues about category-making, discrimination and mobility control" (Sim & Cheesman, 2020, n.p.). In producing knowledge about digital migration, we have to come to terms with the terms we use. It is ethically imperative to problematize the 'categorical fetishism' of migrants, refugees and asylum seekers, differentiating between people on the move as if these are naturally occurring groups (Crawley & Skleparis, 2018). Forced migrants are commonly perceived as vulnerable groups seeking survival, but we need to recognize that their quest is broader: to "create a life and not only to live" (Crawley & Skleparis, 2018, p. 58). We have to reflexively engage with how, in general discourse, the migrant has become a "stigmatizing label" (Scheel & Tazzioli, 2022). In the majority of categorization practices, mobile subjects have no say in how they are categorized. Therefore, following sociologist Ruha Benjamin, who argues that race functions as a technology of racialized stratification (2019a), migration can be seen as a technology which governs and stratifies mobile subjects along the lines of race, gender, sexuality, nationality, class, religion, age and ability, among others. It is, for example, virtually impossible to distinguish between voluntary and forced migration, and rather than sticking with dichotomies, we have to embrace non-linear, continuum and relational approaches. One way to do so is to draw on narratives of mobile people to develop new critical vocabularies, such as the analytic pair of "aspirations" and "frustrations" developed by Anja van Heelsum, based on narratives of Eritrean and Syrian refugees settling in the Netherlands (2017, p. 2137).

In her fieldwork with Iraqi families in Jordan's capital of Amman, media scholar Mirjam Twigt (2022) documented online and offline practices to offer a humanizing account of how her informants make do and stay hopeful amid legal marginalization and prolonged insecurity. In Tunisia, Algeria and Morocco, the anthropologist Amade M'charek argues that the Arabic word *Harraga* (الحراقة), which can be translated as "those who burn", is used to describe the activity of "burning" borders through mobility and expanding living spaces (2020, p. 418). In pursuing digital migration studies research, we have to decide which categories we use to describe our research informants and their activities and worlds. Does our terminology reinforce distinctions between deserving and undeserving groups? Do we, for example, speak of asylum seekers, or perhaps an alternative phrase, such as "life seekers" (Pallister-Wilkins, 2022, p. 62), is better suited? Who sets the terms we use? Are we sticking with categories we find in policy statements? In funding calls? In datasets? In legislation? In other research? In activism? In the arts? Or do the people who we write about also have a say in how they are represented? By highlighting common humanity, we can avoid further spectacularization, fetishization, othering, neutralizing and naturalizing of migrant research participants and emphasize they are fellow human beings with aspirations.

Outline of the book

In pursuing a comprehensive overview of digital migration studies debates, the five chapters that follow each cover a thematic entry-point: (1) infrastructures, (2) connections, (3) representations, (4) affects and emotions, and (5) histories.

To foster multiperspectival understanding, rather than being mono-disciplinary, each chapter presents a genealogy and reviews how particular thematic concepts are used across fields. Each chapter covers conceptual and empirical work with various mobile subjects conducted in the Global North as well as the Global South. Two 'Research Dialogues' accompany each thematic chapter. These Research Dialogues consist of questions and answers conducted with international colleagues who have made important contributions to the research area of digital migration studies, particularly with regard to the themes covered in the thematic chapters. These conversations with scholars versed in a variety of intellectual traditions offer insight on how autobiographies and intellectual interests have shaped research trajectories. They also offer practical advice and suggestions for future research directions. Together, the Research Dialogues are intended to provide inspiration to readers who are deciding about the theoretical and methodological frameworks of their own projects, as well as to offer reassurance, demonstrating that we all encounter obstacles and challenges in navigating challenging domains, such as digitization and migration.

Chapter 1: Infrastructures

Critical infrastructure scholars are committed to creating knowledge about the commonly invisible inner workings of technologies, systems and processes. Infrastructures enable and disable the circulation of people, goods, power and knowledge. In particular, research in this thematic area is committed to revealing the power relations which might be contained in 'black-boxed' infrastructures. Common infrastructures encountered by people on the move may include migration infrastructures (such as recruitment agencies), transportation infrastructures (airplanes, lorries, shipping containers) and communication infrastructures (such as smartphones or social media platforms). The digital workings of these infrastructures that enable, channel, govern and control mobility often remain totally invisible to most migrants (and most others). This chapter reviews how the concept of infrastructure is used as a tool to study (1) *brokerage* between various people involved in a migration cycle, a perspective developed in migration studies, (2) the *materiality* of social media platforms, their affordances and circulation, as proposed in media studies, (3) the *relationality* between human and non-human actors, as developed in science and technology studies (STS), and (4) the *imaginary*, as developed in cultural anthropology and sociology, to address the role of ideas, motivations, worldviews, expectations and frustrations that guide the caring and controlling functioning of infrastructures.

Research Dialogue I, with the social geographer Brenda S.A. Yeoh, draws attention to the multidimensional commercial, organizational and regulatory infrastructural assemblages that shapes how and why people move. Yeoh calls for greater attention to intersectional gender relations, care politics and forms of negotiation and resistance. In Research Dialogue II, science and technology scholar Huub Dijstelbloem invites us to reject infrastructures as a technocratic solution. We can do so by addressing infrastructures from the 'upside down' and 'inside out' approaches, by considering interactions between actors and materiality, and by realizing that infrastructures can never be grasped as unified wholes from the outside.

Chapter 2: Connections

The theme of migrant connectivity refers to scholarship addressing the abilities, qualities and conditions of being digitally connected across distance through the use of devices, platforms and networks. In this chapter, we overview the literature on digital migrant connectivity by focusing on the three themes of geography, information and rights. The theme of geography is considered to explore the analytic potential of working with the dominant geographical scales of local integration, transnationalism, a combination of both or alternatives such as translocality. The second theme of information draws attention to information practice, information needs and knowledge-making. We consider top-down perspectives on information provision, which alert us to the fractured information landscapes and information precarity faced by migrants. To balance this evaluation, we also consider agency-centric perspectives on information as a do-it-yourself practice existing largely outside institutions, corporations and civil society. Finally, we explore how migrant connectivity can both promote rights digitally as well as result in digital repression. These various perspectives allow us to grasp how and why digital migrant connectivity functions in multiple ways with paradoxical consequences.

Research Dialogue III, with sociologist Dana Diminescu, introduces us to the evolving digital sociology of migration. Diminescu discusses the concepts and methodological considerations relating to the complexity of how migrants switch and navigate between forms of digital existence. In Research Dialogue IV, with Amanda P. Alencar, we are reminded of the non-universality and normativity of the digital migration studies frameworks that originated in the Global North. Discussing work with Venezuelan refugees living in Brazil, Alencar advocates for the use of mixed methods to address translocal place-making with the communities under study.

Chapter 3: Representations

Chapter 3 addresses the digital politics of migrant representation, with a focus on how digital media representations become a battlefield over meaning-making of migration. The chapter is divided into two main parts. First, we explore how migration is represented top-down, by dominant actors such as mainstream news media, humanitarian organizations, governments and corporations. For this purpose, we deploy the analytic lens of representational regimes to address what aspects of migration news media, digital identity systems, data visualizations, virtual reality (VR) and diasporic media over- and under-represent. Second, we draw on the more 'people-centric' notion of representational repertoires to address how migrant actors digitally tell their own stories through digital voice, digital identification and personal digital archiving. The interplay between regimes and repertoires deserves further scrutiny, as well as the political economy shaping both domains.

In Research Dialogue V, media scholar Radha Sarma Hegde urges readers to combine attention to mediation, decoloniality and interdisciplinarity. This way, we can both be attentive to the weight of colonial histories on contemporary regimes of securitization as well as foreground digital practices and experiences of migrant meaning-making and contestation. Research Dialogue VI, with information and communication scholar Eugenia Siapera, invites readers to reflect on who benefits from our research. Thematically, she addresses how the relatively new modes of production of digitization and datafication reshape migrant representation.

Chapter 4: Affects and emotions

Affects and emotions are important analytic registers to produce knowledge about questions of embodiment in migration and digitization contexts. Affects and emotions are both products of migration and digitization, as well as constitutive of experiences of migration and digital technology use. Affectivity is a research lens which can yield insights into the process of migrants changing their bodily or mental state as a result of interacting with people or objects through digital technologies. Bodily changes, such as getting sweaty palms or goosebumps, are unconscious, and precede emotions. Emotions, such as fear, anger or hope, succeed affective bodily responses. They are consciously made meaningful through one's biographical trajectory, and can, for example, be expressed digitally. The chapter explores four key emergent themes of affectivity and emotions research in digital migration studies: (1) The political economy of affect considers feelings and sensations of elite and non-elite migrants in the context of neoliberalism and digital acceleration; (2) Digital intimacies refer to deep connections maintained digitally between subjects who do not live in close geographical proximity. We distinguish between public digital intimacies and private digital sexuality practices; (3) The affects, emotions and normative understandings of doing transnational family life are discussed by distinguishing between practices of care and surveillance; (4) The final section covers affective and emotional intensities of digital home-making, by exploring place-making, nostalgia and aspiration, political struggle and intersecting power relations.

In Research Dialogue VII, transnational migration and technology scholar Saskia Witteborn reminds us to examine affects and emotions as practices that enact links between the personal, social and political levels. She calls for future interdisciplinary and inter-methodological scrutiny of datafication and migrant labour. In particular, she locates gaps in our understanding of how immersive technologies such as virtual reality (VR) film commodify suffering as a mode of consumption. She also draws attention to how data privacy can be understood from the perspective of migrants' affective cultures of displacement. Research Dialogue VIII features media scholar Earvin Charles Cabalquinto, who alerts us to relationships between affective and emotional aspects of mobility and immobility in home-making and asserting belonging. Cabalquinto also reflects on using creative methodologies such as using Lego to visualize narratives and represent intimate experiences of mobility and immobility.

Chapter 5: Histories

Digital migration studies addressing contemporary, seemingly high-tech and advanced media and migration technologies, protocols, experiences and practices often take a 'firstist' perspective, assuming that what is happening is new and unparalleled. In this chapter, we explore the means to challenge the exceptionality and uniqueness of recent technological developments in the context of migration and mobility. We consider media archeological research as a means to excavate – in a literal, material sense as well as metaphorical sense – the *longue durée* of materiality, but also the accompanying procedures, protocols and practices of particular media technologies that enable support, govern, control, extract value from or violate migrants. We discuss historical approaches to migration infrastructures, connectivity, representation, and affectivity: (1) We historicize infrastructures by addressing the histories of social brokering of migration, materialities, relationalities and imaginaries of infrastructure; (2) Connections are historicized by considering the historical geographies of connectivity, as well as the histories of information practices and mediated rights and repression; (3) The politics of migrant representation is historicized by considering pre-digital and early-digital histories of representation regimes and self-representational registers; (4) To historicize affectivity and emotions, we consider the histories of the political economy of affect, intimacy, transnational families and home-making.

Research Dialogue IX, with media scholar Philipp Seuferling, informs us about the potential of de-centring and re-centring media in assessing the continuities and changes of how migration and the media have intersected across time and space. As we begin to see how contemporary migration and border regimes as well as artificial intelligence reflect historical projects of colonialism, slavery, eugenics, racism and fascism, there is a need to read against the grain of the archives. In this way, we can locate historically subordinated experiences, voices and forms of agency and reflect about which bodies have been excluded from the historical record. In Research Dialogue X, digital media scholar Łukasz Szulc reflects on his contemporary and historical research on transnational queer media. He emphasizes the importance of attending to contextual assemblages. Methodologically, he makes a passionate call to cruise the archives. Beyond systematicity, it is of vital importance to enable chance encounters by wandering around and following bodies in different archived times and places to ensure the proper contextualization of our research.

In sum, the thematic chapters offer scholars of digital migration studies various angles in which to view the workings of the migration–digitization nexus, including the general and contextually specific, top-down and bottom-up workings of power, transnational and local dimensions and their interrelationships. In the concluding chapter, we reflect on their overall analytic purchase, the added value of bringing these perspectives together and we discuss the limitations of the themes covered. In closing, we consider the emergent frameworks, topics and developments we may incorporate within our research agenda in the years to come.

NOTE

1 In this book, I use the first-person pronouns we and I. The first person singular is used when I'm discussing experiences I've had personally. The first person plural is used to invite an aspirational wider community of scholars and students to contribute to digital migration studies. I hope you - the reader reading this book - feel welcomed to join the exchange. Guided by feminist principles (e.g. Costanza-Chock, 2020; Haraway, 1988) I want to acknowledge that while this is a single-authored monograph, credit for the knowledge presented here is due to various migrant and scholarly communities and stakeholders including artists, activists, policy makers and practitioners. All responsibility for errors and flaws in this text is mine.

1

Infrastructures

The term 'infrastructure' has become a buzzword. It is popular in policy, security, humanitarian and academic discourse on digital technologies and migration. A variety of material and immaterial infrastructures can be said to support, sustain or control human mobility and immobility. People on the move may encounter migration infrastructures (such as recruitment agencies), border infrastructures (such as drones and patrol dogs), information and communication infrastructures (such as cell towers, mobile phone providers and smartphone devices), transportation infrastructures (such as airplanes and lorries), security infrastructures (such as fingerprint or body scanners), arrival infrastructures (such as language course providers) and deportation infrastructures (such as detention centres), among others. Digital components and/or datafied processes play an increasing role in all these forms of infrastructures. However, their inner workings are commonly invisible. Scholars working in this paradigm seek to look inside the "black-box" of infrastructures (Winner, 1993).

For digital migration studies scholars, the term "infrastructure" is a shorthand to refer to pervasive (digitally mediated) systems that enable a particular circulation of power, knowledge, meaning, people and goods, and restrict others. However, given the proliferation of the term, the question arises as to what we do when we study infrastructures. What exactly do we focus on when we research infrastructures in the context of migration and mobility? Infrastructural debates on digital migration have developed in several specialized directions. When we want to contribute to these discussions, we will encounter at least four different perspectives that each allow for a particular reading. We can distinguish between studying infrastructures: (1) as a form of *brokerage*, as developed in migration studies; (2) from the perspective of *materiality*, as developed in media studies; (3) from the perspective of *relationality*, as developed in science and technology studies (STS); and (4) from the perspective of the *imaginary*, as developed in cultural anthropology and sociology. Before we address these four particular perspectives in more depth we first consider what various branches of critical infrastructure studies have in common.

Finding common ground

In studies on technology, migration and mobility, the term 'infrastructure' has come to encompass a variety of meanings. Before looking at how we can deploy it to address the various dimensions of digital migration, let us first look at what studies of infrastructures may have in common. From the *Oxford English Dictionary* we learn that 'infrastructure' can be defined as the "collective term for the subordinate parts of an undertaking; substructure, foundation" (2021b). The *Collins English Dictionary* specifies that these subordinate parts play a specific role: "[t]he infrastructure of a country, society, or organization consists of the basic facilities such as transport, communications, power supplies, and buildings, which enable it to function" (2021). Infrastructures are thus based on a combination of parts, which are in turn required to enable a specific functioning of the infrastructure itself. In academic discourse, the concept of the infrastructure has travelled from engineering, planning and policy domains. Only in the last decade has it gained traction in critical humanities and social science scholarship. The infrastructural lens allows researchers to look inside technology. It invites researchers to address the myriad ways in which technology, politics and society co-constitute each other (Appadurai, 2015).

Across disciplines, critical infrastructural scholarship displays a number of shared commitments and aims:

- Infrastructure scholars generally seek to look beyond the input and output of technological processes. Instead, they scrutinize the inner logic of commonly taken-for-granted architectures of large- and small-scale systems (Holt & Vonderau, 2015).
- Infrastructures are commonly understood as a form of "techno-politics" (Dijstelbloem, 2021): infrastructures are assumed to play specific roles in maintaining uneven power relations, for example by controlling who can be mobile (Larkin, 2013; Winner, 1980). It is important to scrutinize how, why and for whom infrastructures co-shape "worlds in some forms rather than others?" (Haraway, 1997, p. 129). The black box metaphor appearing across fields reminds us that infrastructures are purposefully rendered invisible to subjects who are not in charge of their design and goals. This invisibility is problematic, because it hides power dynamics, makes forms of exclusion and exploitation possible and limits the means to accountability or contestation.
- Infrastructures are generally considered as a dynamic assemblage, which is actively and mutually constituted through top-down and bottom-up processes and practices involving humans, technologies, protocols and expectations (Boyle & Schneiderman, 2020).

People as infrastructure: The social brokering of migration

What might an examination of social brokering tell us about the role of the digital in migration? Social brokering considers "people as infrastructure" (Simone,

2004, p. 408), and focuses on how people act in the broader system of migration. Brokers fill the gaps between countries and places migrants are travelling to. For example, they volunteer or sell services to facilitate or impede migration and mobility. Considering the brokering role of infrastructures provides an "entry-point that illuminates broader contexts and processes from a particular position of mediation" (Lindquist, 2015, p. 874). Here we may add that this mediation is increasingly facilitated by digital networks. At various moments in migration and mobility, people can have agency and impact upon the process. Let us ground our understanding with a concrete example: the role of digital brokering in the lives of Chinese international students. Yang Hu, Cora Lingling Xu and Mengwei Tu (2022) documented how at the beginning of the Covid-19 health pandemic, these migrants had to turn to their own parents and international Chinese diaspora to navigate rapidly changing travel policies and personal insecurities. Before, with the "pre-COVID-19 infrastructure", main brokering responsibilities lay with the Chinese state and corporate agencies. Gradually, in their search for security, many international students turned to their own digital networks, preferring the immediacy of their responsive "family-mediated migration infrastructure" over institutions (Hu, Xu & Tu, 2022, p. 83, see also He & Zhang, 2022).

A focus on brokering can assist us in illuminating how in migration people enact roles in broader socio-political, economic, cultural and symbolic fields. These fields are shaped, maintained and constrained by agents (individuals, groups, communities, alliances) that are increasingly digitally networked. Such agents span domains and groups, including the state, markets, non-governmental organizations, social movements, informal facilitators and fellow migrants. The study of infrastructural brokering in migration and mobility was first developed in cultural anthropology, economic geography and migration studies. It has gained traction, in particular, as part of the "Asian turn" to infrastructures (Shrestha & Yeoh, 2018, p. 665). As one way of opening the black box of migration infrastructures, Johan Lindquist, Biao Xiang and Brenda Yeoh proposed to focus on brokering agents to study the "organization of transnational mobility" (2012, p. 7) as part of broader political economic transformation. In their definition of migration infrastructures, brokers play a central role in "the systematically inter-linked technologies, institutions, and actors that facilitate and condition mobility" (Xiang & Lindquist, 2014, p. 122). Both formal and informal brokers are proliferating in the contemporary moment as a result of neoliberalization and deregulation, alongside the proliferation of technologies in the broader contexts of deepening global inequality (Lindquist et al., 2012). These dynamics make critical scrutiny of the enabling, mediating and exclusionary infrastructural role of brokers in the digital domain conceptually and empirically urgent.

Informal and formal migrant brokers

For Tina Shrestha and Brenda Yeoh (2018), brokerage is a particular category of practice. The "migrant-broker" revolves around a "set of indeterminate and emergent practices unfolding through unpredictable encounters among diverse and transregionally located actors, bureaucratic objects, and impractical procedures contingent on institutional cultures" (2018, p. 663–664). Migrant brokers may include travel agents, smugglers, middle-men, social workers or engineers. Brokering takes place across various locations, including churches, training centres, charities and recruitment agencies. The broker – as the agent that intermediates – is not a fixed entity. The broker is socio-historically, morally, legally, politically and administratively ambiguous. Brokering is not stable or defined a priori, but is an outcome of administrative, bureaucratic, digital and datafied procedures. This process can thus only become known to us researchers when seen as a process resulting from and shaped by human actors encountering one another.

The lens of brokering can shed light on the roles of various formal and informal brokering agents involved in the migration industry, and how they draw on technologies to intermediate mobility. First and foremost, informal *migrant networks* broker know-how, remittances and technologies; a process based on ties, trust, emotional investment and altruism (see Chapter 2: Connections). Migrants themselves, be it in relation with activists, social workers and migrant organizations, become brokers in circulating care and solidarities. Researching brokering processes can make these invisiblized infrastructures visible. For example, previous research has illuminated how guest workers make do with precarious living conditions in the Islamic Gulf city-state of Dubai (Kathiravelu, 2012), or how solidarity is mediated between locals and newly arrived asylum seekers on the Greek islands of Lesbos, Chios, Leros and Samos at Europe's outer border (Fotaki, 2021). Asylum migrants in Hong Kong were found to gift mobile phones and data among the community as a way to expand social worlds (Witteborn, 2019, p. 765). However, informal, migrant brokering often does imply that there are costs involved in helping research with Cape-Verdeans in Cape Verde and the diaspora reveals how these costs are variously offset, including emotional and material rewards as well as through being indebted (Carling, 2016, p. 158).

Institutional brokering: State and legal practices

Brokerage happens in the 'middle space' between migrants and institutions, as mobile people negotiate immigration regimes, for example (Schapendonk, 2018). At the level of the state, we can address brokering by exploring how states dependent on remittances brand and train their migrant workers. For example, the Filipino state brokers a global view of domestic workers as iconic "super-maids", drawing on culturally essentialist gendered and racialized frames of docility (Guevarra, 2014, p. 130). In the legal domain, lawyers are also infrastructural brokers; with legal technologies expanding, forms of digital legal aid and services targeting migrants and refugees can be expected to grow. For example, "digital refugee lawyering" (Twigt, 2021) captures how, in the case of refugee protection in the Middle East, infrastructures are brokered through digital means. Alongside questions of access, power and privilege impact upon the already precarious negotiated practice of access to rights and legal aid.

Educational brokering

In the field of education, language teachers too are brokers. For example, second-language teachers broker Britain to newly arrived Syrian refugees through language instruction using mobile phones (Vollmer, 2019). In many countries, such educational brokering for migrants is under threat. Service provision for migrants, such as education, is increasingly privatized and outsourced. The market seeks to save costs and presents efficient digital solutions as a panacea to inclusion. As a result, neither general access to education nor quality levels are ensured (Leurs, 2022). Researchers have also captured how language-brokering within migrant families challenges intergenerational dynamics as younger people have to assist their parents. For example, young Karen humanitarian migrants settled in Australia have been found to perform "digital brokering" as a new type of intergenerational support (Worrell, 2021). Intergenerational brokering is also of particular importance in the context of ageing migrant families. Ageing and aged care routinely takes place in local spaces that are simultaneously globally and transnationally connected through digital kinship and "distant support networks" (Wilding & Baldassar, 2018).

Entrepreneurial brokering

A focus on entrepreneurial brokering can bring into view "the extraction of value from the transnational situations of migrants' lives" (Krifors, 2021, p. 148). Entrepreneurial brokering is embedded in formal and informal economies. On the level of the formal economy, international migration is commercialized variously by a growing "migration industry", consisting of brokers including entrepreneurs, firms and service providers who, motivated by financial gains, facilitate mobility, settlement, communication and remittances across borders (Hernández-León, 2013). Of particular interest to digital migration scholars, the "migration industry of connectivity services" (Gordano Peile, 2014) has emerged, consisting of travel agents and mobile telephone, transportation and money transfer companies that specifically target migrants. Through their products, services, practices and discourses, they broker connections between migrants and relevant stakeholders. Notwithstanding their profit-oriented motivations, these corporations also create alternative, potentially meaningful subject positions for migrants, for example as consumers, which differ from state-sanctioned categories of desired and undesired mobile subjects. However, little is known about migrant and mobile subjects' perceptions of entrepreneurial brokering. In particular, the digital experiences of illicit actors, such as smugglers and swindlers, who constitute the migration "illegality industry" (Anderson, 2014), are understudied.

A political economy (PE) perspective has the potential to offer a better understanding of the role of brokers in the economic, digital organization of migration and mobility, which might either reproduce or challenge intersectional power relations. However, research in this strand is also scarce, and the few existing studies demonstrate great relevance and urgency. For example, migration recruitment agencies have been found to cater to the demands of employees using digital platforms. In Accra, Ghana, agencies in their everyday brokering practices online and offline "produce ideal workers", filter and represent workers for overseas placements and cater to the local middle-class and expatriate market (Awumbila et al., 2019, p. 2655). Similarly, Thai migrant forest berry pickers and Indian migrant ICT industry workers in Sweden provide insights into how mobility and immobility as a form of "transnational interoperability" is based on the interplay between employer perspectives on supply chain structures and migrant experiences of mobility (Krifors, 2021, p. 161).

The 'gig-economy' is another important growing domain to consider here (Alencar & Wang, 2022). In the context of Braxil, training programmes for migrant entrepreneurs were found to change refugees into "on-demand migrants" (Zanforlin & Grohmann, 2022). Migrant labour brokers in the context of industrial decline have to adapt to neoliberal, networked practices. In doing so, migrant minibus taxi owners and transporters in Johannesburg, South Africa, reproduced patriarchal patterns as they felt their traditional masculinities were being challenged (Gibbs, 2014). Migrant personal shoppers, called *daigou*, engage in gendered digital labour for customers living in mainland China (Xie & Witteborn, 2020, p. 453).

Brokering precarity: Chutes and ladders

Across contexts, various groups of social brokers are linked in chains of social reproduction. Brokers are therefore deeply implicated in global, regional and national power relations. More attention is particularly needed for the human impact of the moral economies of 'flexible' employment and 'gig-work' on migrants and mobile subjects. Through so-called "pyramid subcontracting" (Wise, 2013, p. 436), the market down-sources responsibilities from global corporations to individual workers, putting migrant workers' rights at risk. In reviewing migration brokerage in the Global South, Priya Deshingkar notes that brokerage often results in making workers more precarious – through the "production of ideal migrant subjects" – but simultaneously she urges us not to lose sight of the positionalities and complex forms of agency felt among migrant workers (2019, p. 2639). Deshingkar gives the example of the upward mobility felt by Dalit workers in India who are brokered access to urban construction jobs. Based on research among migrant workers in Singapore, brokers reproduce precarity by both trapping migrants in "chutes" or setting them on the "ladders" of upward mobility (Wee, Goh & Yeoh, 2019). The interrelationships between digitized structures of exploitation and experiences of agency across local, national and transnational scales can be pursued more holistically in future research. Particularly by taking multi-stakeholder approaches, we can consider how various groups of people – as social brokers – together give online and offline shape to infrastructures of migration. In the following section, we shift attention from how people infrastructurally broker migration to how materiality infrastructurally produces migrants.

The material stuff of infrastructures

By focusing on materiality, we can study how things and objects come to matter in the infrastructuring of migration. Here we can draw on common definitions of infrastructure as the physical, non-human "stuff you can kick" (Parks, 2015, p. 356), which we can operationalize by researching the biography and circulation of objects (Appadurai, 1988). Illustratively, let us consider which material objects are used to register and identify refugee bodies. Here we can take cues from how the UN Refugee Agency (UNHCR) deploys analogue and digital technologies for the "fixing of persons of concern" for the purpose of gathering statistics and countering fraud. Fixing is done through material devices such as "visible or invisible ink", "wristbands", "tokens" and "biometrics" (UNHCR, 2003, p. 137). The recent example of "humanitarian wearables" (Sandvik, 2020, p. 87) is striking. These include devices that are inserted in or worn on beneficiary bodies that track, measure and represent these bodies digitally through various metrics. Material objects like wristbands look the way they look and fingerprint scanners function the way they function as a result of particular sets of decisions that reflect particular ideas, expectations, norms and assumptions. A material infrastructural perspective invites us to reflect on what these technical objects do, and what ideological values they represent.

Media and communication scholars and cultural anthropologists address materiality by scrutinizing which values and ideologies are embedded and baked into technologies (e.g. Bennet, 2010; Miller, 2005; Van den Boomen et al., 2009). Material objects thus have a specific radius of action. In a sense, non-human objects have agency or "thing-power" (Bennet, 2010, pp. 31–32), but it is up to people to accept, negotiate or contest these. Langdon Winner's classic essay "Do artifacts have politics?" (1980) offers inspiration to address the material dimensions of infrastructural politics. He posed this question to scrutinize means of transportation in New York City (USA): tunnels were designed for automobiles used by upper-class (mostly white) New Yorkers, and not for autobuses, so non-affluent populations (mostly African-American people) without access to cars could not visit parks. In the field of migration, with the notion of 'viapolitics', we can get at how the materiality of migration infrastructures, such as vehicles, ferries, roads and routes, enables mobility for some and results in immobility for others (Walters, 2015). Material infrastructures facilitate and impede migration. Across the spectrum from expatriate elite mobility to precaritized forced and irregularized migration, we can bring a great variety of objects, technologies and devices into focus. By focusing on the circulation and contestation of different material technologies, we can move beyond monolithic, acontextual or fetishistic understandings of the technologies that underpin migration infrastructures. We will organize our material understanding of migration infrastructures by focusing on platforms, affordances and circulation.

Platforms

Taking a platform approach to materiality can yield further insight into the infrastructural mediation of migration. The term 'platform' is common shorthand for digital media intermediaries, such as Facebook or WeChat, and encompasses at least four meanings:

- 'computation', in that a platform supports the design and usage of specific applications;
- 'architectural', or the physical, elevated structure on which people or objects can stand;
- 'figurative', referring to platform as a basis for action;
- 'political', referring to the political stage and political beliefs articulated (Gillespie, 2010, pp. 349–350).

Platform mediation happens at the interplay between bodies and technologies: "Both body and machine are considered platforms through which activities are mediated, yet the materiality of that platform profoundly matters: information is embodied as much as flesh is computed" (Van Dijck, 2004, pp. 367–368). What this means is that platforms enable certain user behaviours and limit others on the basis of a particular medium-specificity, genre conventions and normative frameworks. A platform approach allows for the specific demarcation of our analytical focus. The platform may be a specific place (digital or non-digital) which can be isolated to study the mediation of migration: "a focus on platforms highlights the complex and shifting landscape of actors, networks, materials and ideas that stitch together places to make migration possible" (Collins, 2021, p. 873).

In digital migration studies, an infrastructural focus on platforms may centre on the digital connectivity services targeted at migrants in order to get a better understanding of their marketing strategies and emotional appeals, as well as migrants' experiential meaning-making practices. Filipino migrants, for example, are addressed as a valued clientele on online remittances platforms such as Western Union, LBC: We Like to Move and BaLinkBayan: Overseas Filipinos' One Stop Online Portal for Diaspora Engagement. These platforms function as commercial infrastructures that construct a "platformed migrant subjectivity" (Cabalquinto & Wood-Bradley, 2020, p. 799). The prism of the materiality of digital platforms can yield additional insights on the infrastructural brokering of migrant gig-work labour. Across the world, platform capitalism strongly impacts many migrants' work conditions. Rural to urban internal migrant workers in China have moved into service sectors, including transportation, parcel and food delivery, conducting "platformed distinction work" (Sun & Zhao, 2022, p. 1) alongside migrant women gig-workers who work remotely on Upwork, one of the world's largest freelance platforms (Anwar & Graham, 2020).

As mentioned in the social brokering section above, while documenting precarity is important, it is also pivotal to remain attentive to how migrant gig-workers digitally maintain agency. For example, from the perspective of internal migrants in China, we can signal the digital tactics these workers have developed, including gaming the system and countering algorithmic service indicators as well as brokering offline relations between restaurant owners and clients (Sun & Chen, 2021, p. 19). From the perspective of irregularized migrants, researchers have also described the "route-work" of journeying, navigation, decision-making practices and negotiation of surveillance as "platform-work" (Sánchez-Querubín & Rogers, 2018, pp. 10–11). Through platform work, "alternative migration metrics" are produced, derived from the feedback ('likes', 'shares') circulating on social media such as Facebook, WhatsApp and elsewhere, about routes, the police and informal intermediaries like facilitators and smugglers (ibid.).

Affordances

The concept of affordances presents us with another entry point to understand the roles of infrastructural materialities in the lives of migrants. Coming from design theory, the concept of affordance refers to "the perceived and actual properties of the thing" that to some extent "determine how the thing could possibly be used" (Norman, 2002, p. 9). For example, "a chair affords ('is for') support, and, therefore, affords sitting. A chair can also be carried. Glass is for seeing through, and for breaking" (Norman, 2002, p. 9). So the research perspective of affordances allows us to obtain an overview of the possible ways things, devices, programs and applications are used in a given social context for specific actions or processes, on the basis of particular properties, shapes and scales of artefacts. Disaffordances refer to technological cues that block, constrain or halter certain actions. Disaffordances make us reflect on the discriminatory design of technologies, such as how a lock dissafords entry without a key, or a fence disaffords entry to a particular plot of land (Costanza-Chock, 2020).

Thus, in studying the lived experience of infrastructural materialities, digital migration scholars can ask the following questions:

- *What* forms of mobility do technologies afford and dissaford?
- *How* do technologies afford and dissaford mobility?
- *For whom* do technologies afford and dissaford mobility?
- *Under what circumstances* do technologies afford and dissaford mobility? (cf. Davis, 2020)

This way, the lens of affordances can provide new insights, for example in the constraining and enabling role of mobile technologies and social media apps in the lives of migrants. In refugee migration, the appropriation of media affordances is well documented (see overviews by Alencar, 2020; Gillespie et al., 2016): during refugee journeys, geo-location and GPS offer a means of navigation, but also increase surveillance; voice, chat and audio-message possibilities allow for the maintenance of transnational networks and the circulation of money and information. Rescue operations are often initiated by and with migrants; migrant deaths occur particularly in areas without mobile phone coverage; during protracted displacement, migrants engage in the strategic (non-) use of simcards, maintaining multiple accounts on social-media and video-chat platforms to enable the safe maintenance of emotional bonds away from surveillance as well as to document injustices; while during resettlement, administrative and locative functions allow for pathways to negotiate with bureaucracies (Alencar, 2020; Gillespie et al., 2016). It must be noted the refugee mobile phone and affordances scholarship is so far largely Eurocentric, and these insights are not universal. Previous studies have hardly discussed the African context (Stremlau & Tsalapatanis, 2022). In the Asian diasporic context, Sun and Yu demonstrate, in their book *WeChat diaspora* (2022), that context and the situated analysis of affordances are important. Illustratively, the WeChat Official Accounts broadcasting function, for example, has been taken up by Chinese migrant entrepreneurs in Australia to disseminate news within the Chinese diaspora (Yang, 2022).

Another strand of digital migration scholarship turns to affordances to research how migrants perform digital intimacies, do family and articulate queer sexualities. Scholars have teased out how aural, visual and haptic affordances of social media apps, such as WhatsApp, WeChat, Skype and Line, as well as dating apps like Gaydar and Grindr can stimulate positive and negative affects and emotions, co-presence and disconnection (Cassidy & Yang Wang, 2018; Dhoest & Szulc, 2016; Patterson & Leurs, 2020; Shield, 2018; Taipale, 2019). Affordance theories have also been further developed on the basis of studies on migration experiences. In her plea to avoid a technocentric perspective by exploring how technology operates alongside (gendered) norms, imaginations and discourses, Saskia Witteborn interprets the experiences of two women seeking asylum in Germany through the lens of "imagined affordances" (2018, p. 21). Based on her work concerning how Iraqi households living in Jordan experience and mediate hope and fear, Mirjam Twigt (2018) proposes that researchers need to further address the "affective affordances" of smartphones and social media. "Affordances-in-practice" is proposed by Elisabetta Costa to attend to how users enact social media and mobile phone properties within socio-cultural contexts (2018, p. 3641). The notion of "polymedia" is developed to account for how Filipino migrants choose and use specific channels for specific purposes and specific audiences, thereby exploiting various affordances alongside navigating moral, social, emotional and cultural registers (Madianou & Miller, 2012). These studies offer an important reminder: when we blindly trace materiality by looking at what technologies may afford, we might run the risk of reproducing a utilitarian understanding of media use. In other words, we should not blindly assume that affordances are taken up by migrant users with a specific aim in mind. Also, in migration contexts, entertainment, diversion and non-goal-oriented media use are meaningful and therefore important to address (Awad & Tossell, 2019).

Circulation

Finally, under the heading of circulation, digital migration scholars can map the biography of (digital-material) objects. To operationalize research on circulation, "we have to follow the things themselves, for their meanings are inscribed in their forms, their uses, their trajectories" (Appadurai, 1988, p. 5). People encode circulating material objects with significance, while, methodologically, the study of "things-in-motion" sheds light on their socio-cultural and political contexts (ibid., 1988, p. 5). Circulation has been theorized and operationalized as a lens to study how social orders are established and reified, a process through which particular ideas, norms and actors surrounding a material object become powerful, while others are excluded (Valaskivi & Sumiala, 2014). The circulation of audio cassettes as an infrastructure developed by exiled communities and other migrant groups to keep in touch across distance presents an important reference point in the literature in this strand. The "little medium" of the audio cassette grew in popularity from the 1970s for its affordances as a "two-way, grassroot medium which is reusable, durable, portable, and inexpensive" and was popular among Iranians in exile, among others (Naficy, 2011, p. 415). Also more recently, the audio cassette played an important role for the global Dinka diaspora, as it long remained the preferred carrier of choice to link with South Sudan, rooted in preferences for personal song making as well as cultures of pastoralism (Impey, 2013).

Approaching infrastructural materiality as circulation can be useful to develop an alternative understanding of the interdependent relationships between mobile people, commodities and information. For example, alongside the mobile phone or the migrant suitcase, the container box can be taken as an object to trace and think with. From the perspective of circulation, we can understand how this object has been transformed into an optimal, traceable infrastructure of "containerization" (Morley, 2017, p. 221), which includes questions of and struggles over packaging, mobility, security, transportation, borders, and its various offshoots, including the recent use of containers to temporarily house groups of refugees and migrants. Digital-born objects too are increasingly important to consider: maps and visualizations of migrant movement and journeys reflect specific ideological work. Analysis of the "migrancies of maps" (Presti, 2020, p. 911) shows that circulating cartographic conventions used in journalistic and policy visualizations of human movement – such as "arrows of invasion" (Van Houtum & Bueno Lacy, 2020, p. 196) – often reify historical racial and colonial power hierarchies between the centre and periphery, the Global North and the Global South (e.g. Allen, 2020, 2021; Risam, 2019). In the section below, we consider the perspective of relationality to address how human and non-human actors together shape migration infrastructures.

Infrastructures as relations

From science and technology studies (STS), we can find guidance to study the fundamental relationality of infrastructural "systems, assumptions and exclusions" (Lupton, 2019, p. 263). A case in point is the relation between built, technological and logistical infrastructures of "Operação Acolhida" (Operation Shelter), which was set up by the Brazilian government in the province of Roraima, bordering Venezuela. Through triage and processing, Venezuelan forced migrants in Brazil – over 220,000 in 2019 – were initially processed in two ways: at the police headquarters, temporary residence permits were instantly handled by police officials by making use of online computational systems, and asylum requests were all handled manually on the basis of a 12-page questionnaire. This questionnaire had to be completed by refugees and sent by mail to the National Committee for Refugees in Brasilia. In Brasilia, these documents were manually scanned by one contracted employee and two interns, which resulted in a backlog and long delays. The split bureaucratic classification of mobile subjects resulted from an ad-hoc infrastructure put in place to manage and enact migration control and humanitarian assistance to Venezuelans on the move.

Seen from a relational perspective, infrastructure is not absolute and cannot be clearly demarcated a priori (Law, 2010). Rather, an infrastructure can be approached as a moving target. Susan Leigh Star and Karen Ruhleder therefore famously asked not what, but "when is an infrastructure" to get at the fundamental relationality of infrastructural processes (1996, p. 112)? In a later work on "how to infrastructure", Leigh Star and Geoffrey Bowker specify that "the relational quality of infrastructure talks about that which is between – between people, mediated by tools, and emergent" (2002, p. 151). Based on analyses of categories and standards, and their socio-material articulation in infrastructures, scholars in this tradition have carved out a methodology of "infrastructural inversion" (Bowker & Leigh Star, 1999, p. 34). Through inverting infrastructures, turning them on their head, processes of invisibilization can be reversed, and empirical observations of relations become possible, "recognizing the depths of interdependence of technical networks and standards, on the one hand, and the real work of politics and knowledge production on the other" (ibid., p. 34). From this perspective, infrastructural analysis requires scholars to pay attention to and scrutinize the relationship between what political, ethical, social and economic choices have been folded into systems. This can be done by scrutinizing and problematizing which of these choices are transparent, and which are embedded and placed in the background (Pelizza, 2016).

For digital migration studies, a relational view on infrastructures can be helpful to disentangle the processes, architectures and systems of the processing, identification, classification, surveillance and selection of mobile bodies, as well as to scrutinize standard operating procedures (e.g., Bellanova & Glouftsios, 2022). Migrant bodies are increasingly transferred into digital data points, at borders and during visa application and asylum procedures (e.g., Trauttmansdorff, 2022). From an STS infrastructural perspective, we can address how this process of data collection "is actually a relationship, but it is a relationship that can be difficult to see" (Onuoha & Galvin, 2021, n.p.). Datafied relations are frequently uneven, the power often lies with the authority setting the terms and collecting the data. From a relational infrastructural perspective, we can scrutinize who, where and when is the object, and who, where and when is the subject in such processes of data collection on mobile people. STS infrastructure research on these themes has proved particularly powerful in opening up the black box of the "migration machine" (Dijstelbloem, Meijer & Besters, 2011) and especially European migration management and bordering (e.g. Dijstelbloem, 2021; Pelizza, 2020; Scheel, 2019). STS studies on migration infrastructures can be ordered on the basis of their different geographical foci. Below, we discuss national, local, transnational and translocal studies, and multiscalar approaches.

Infrastructuring the nation

In infrastructuring the nation, governments are generally seeking to find a balance in facilitating mobility for some, offering humanitarian protection for others and securing the state against yet another group of people who are deemed a threat. At the national level, we can study how mobile people are counted, processed and labelled in processes of datafication and digitization in relation to national policies and demographic or visa-status categories. For example, in the context of India, the Aadhaar national biometric identification system was set up to provide a digital identity to the 1.2 billion people of India. This infrastructure, which was established to benefit everyone, excludes populations such as migrants (and the homeless) who lack fixed verifiers such as home addresses (Shah, 2020). We can also research how, in defining and using digitized and datafied categories such as workers, international students, asylum seekers or refugees, statisticians working for national governments and universities contribute to policies that effectively reinforce hierarchical differences between mobile subjects (Boersma, 2020; Ustek-Spilda, 2020).

Localized infrastructures

At the local level, scholars can choose distinct sites to study infrastructural relations, including airports, train stations, hotspots and cities. For example, airports are crucial local sites that facilitate mobility for some and curtail mobility for most of the world's population. Airports can be scrutinized internally in distinguishing and selecting between allowed and forbidden passengers, and externally in distinguishing between visa regimes, airline carriers and airport operations. In his analysis of Schiphol International Airport in Amsterdam, the Netherlands, Huub Dijstelbloem (2021) articulates how these dimensions of infrastructural technopolitics, through "design, detection and detention", promise smooth passenger flows, optimal security and border control. Airport infrastructures, including procedures, scanners and checkpoints, outwardly display a "security theatre", offering reassurance to privileged mobile subjects (Browne, 2015). "Infrastructural whiteness" (Pugliese, 2010), coupled with a heteronormative and binary-gender gaze, disproportionally renders suspect non-normative bodies, including black and trans people (Browne, 2015). Airports and aviation more broadly can also be studied in relation to the wider system of "deportation infrastructures" (Walters, 2018).

In the so-called 'hotspot' of asylum migrant processing centres at Europe's borders, researchers have documented how infrastructuring happens through mundane logistical practices. For example, in the Moira camps on Lesbos, Greece, asylum migrants are processed by staff from various organizations by "filling out forms, taking finger prints, signing, and entering datasets along a chain" (Pollozek & Passoth, 2019, p. 606). Considering further bottom-up accounts and the experiences of local infrastructures is pressing. The digital and datafied hotspots at Europe's borders have been found to have been taken up by the asylum applicants themselves to "propose alternative chains of actors, data, and metadata that are more meaningful to them" (Pelizza, 2020, p. 262).

Urban cities, through the prism of "lively" (Amin, 2014) or "arrival" (Meeus, van Heur & Arnaut, 2019) infrastructures, mediate relations between newcomer and established communities. From below, migrants innovatively create intercultural and transnational relations while staying below the radar of surveillance, in public and digital spaces. For example, West African migrants living in Paris, France, reclaim the Gare du Nord train station as their "infrastructural hub". This rail transit hub is reclaimed to exchange information, build new relationships, find belonging and enable movement (Kleinman, 2019).

Transnational and translocal infrastructuring

Digital migration scholars can also address infrastructuring at the transnational (spanning across nations) and translocal level (connecting locations). When taking a top-down perspective on institutional infrastructural relations, we can address how supra-national organizations (such as the European Union or Association of Southeast Asian Nations) process categories of mobile people as units of economic productivity or flows to be governed (Ruppert & Scheel, 2021). This is done through data practices including "counting, calculating, cleaning, editing, extrapolating, ignoring, harmonizing" (Cakici, Ruppert & Scheel, 2020, p. 200). In managing territories, migration registration systems enact specific relations between categories, mobile people and technologies, thereby pursuing a particular "infrastructural construction of Europe" (ibid., p. 200). The establishment of European database systems, such as the Visa Information System (VIS), Schengen Information System II (SIS II) and the European Dactyloscopy Database (EURODAC), indicates a growing embrace of biometrics as a form of infrastructural migration management. These systems, in tandem with recent transnational 'DNA Data Exchanges' taking place within Europe, work to 'bio-border' between specific groups of people (Amelung, Granja & Machado, 2021). These systems facilitate the infrastructural processing of 'European-legible' bodies that meet infrastructural systems (Pelizza, 2020).

When we shift focus to infrastructuring from below, we can address how migrants develop transnational and translocal infrastructures, for example through circulating objects and sending money. A study on gift sending among Poles and Zimbabweans living in the United Kingdom, traces relations of trust (Burrell, 2017). Trusting practices range from packaging to shipping, comprising an infrastructure built on service personnel, formal and informal networks of couriers, and involving shipping containers and lorries, among others (Burrell, 2017). The sending and receiving of remittances further demonstrates how context matters and how people build the infrastructures they need, in relation to informal digital channels alongside official circuits such as formal banks and public services. Informal infrastructures from below also shed light on (the experiences and contestations of) power hierarchies. For example, the divergence of remittance costs, speed, routes, regulations and norms across African geographies illustrate asymmetrical regimes of mobility shape money transfers (Lindley, 2009; Pieke, Van Hear & Lindley, 2007).

Multi-scalar approaches to infrastructures

Relations *across scales* present us with an important avenue of future infrastructural research. Consider, for example, how the im/mobility of transnational migrants is tied to the "interoperability" of migration data (Pelizza, 2020). Movement is facilitated and limited on the basis of the degree to which governmental, humanitarian and corporate organizations are willing and able to share, process and act upon data generated by relevant partners. So far, infrastructural scholarship has prioritized top-down governmental infrastructural relations. However, despite the scope, breadth, force and rigidity of procedures and systems, mobile people themselves remain active agents in infrastructural relations (Scheel, 2019). As is noted in a review of infrastructural approaches to migration in the African context, prioritizing top-down approaches and forgetting to deploy infrastructure as a lens to study from below "runs the risk of underestimating or obscuring the ways in which migrants and other actors make alternative uses of existing infrastructure" (Kleist & Bjarnesen, 2019, p. 18).

Future research on the interplay between top-down and bottom-up processes, at the transnational and translocal scale, will increase our understanding of how, in the lives of mobile people, the availability of technologies and the construction of infrastructure do not simply result in a teleological compression of space and time.

Infrastructural imaginaries of care and control

Be it people, materials or relations, digital migration infrastructures are developed with a particular imagined goal or desired outcome. In this final section, we address infrastructures from the perspective of the imaginary. The concept of the imaginary is an analytic tool to research how the values and shared worldviews associated with one particular dominant group are able to see, rule or even marginalize another group in turn (Castoriadis, 1998; see also the review essay by Strauss, 2006). Twenty-five years ago, the cultural anthropologist Arjun Appadurai already proposed the concept of the imaginary to address how migration and digital technologies co-shape cultural globalization. "The work of the imagination", for Appadurai, "is neither purely emancipatory nor entirely disciplined but is a space of contestation in which individuals and groups seek to annex the global in their own practices of the modern" (1996, p. 4). When addressing infrastructural imaginaries in relation to digital technologies and migration, we can make an inventory of the ideas, motivations, convictions, aspirations, expectations and frustrations that lead to a specific "techno quo" (Benjamin, 2019b, p. 12) – a technological status quo mobilizing some and immobilizing others.

The situatedness of imaginaries

The technological status quo sustained through a particular dominant infrastructure is not neutral. Border agents imagine the role of surveillance cameras, finger printing or patrol dogs differently in comparison to expatriates or 'irregularized' migrants. Infrastructural imaginaries reflect uneven power relations. Imaginaries commonly:

- reflect a limited, specific cultural horizon;
- propose an instrumental, utilitarian functionality;
- connotate infrastructures positively (Sneath, Holbraad & Axel, 2009, pp. 5–6).

As a starting point, we should understand that "imagination is situated" (Stoetzler & Yuval-Davis 2002, p. 327). Therefore, following Therasa Enright, we should investigate "Who and what imagines infrastructure? With what effects?" (2022, p. 101). Migration imaginaries distinguish and legitimate mobility and immobility through caring for some mobile people and controlling others (Constable, 2020; Johnson & Lindquist, 2020). Technophilia, or the high hope invested in technologies as a means to solve major challenges, is an important stance within initiatives to care for migrants and control migration. For example, digitizing biometrics reflects a desire for the efficient registering of mobile people. Infrastructural imaginaries of technophilia are often wedded to nationalist state views, with modernist assumptions about state control over territories, borders and populations (Langenohl & Van Riet, 2020), or the supranational humanitarian desire of providing care to people on the move.

Infrastructural imaginaries of controlling migration

Focusing on forms of control, scholars have shown in detail how airports, train stations, ports and borders across the world are increasingly imagined to function as "filtering systems", offering a possibility for "triage", selecting between who gets "admitted to and rejected from a given national territory" (Balibar, 2004, p. 111). Increasingly, this triage is based on the digital identity profiles of mobile subjects. These data profiles are imagined to be neutral, factual, accurate and truthful. For example, eu-LISA, the European agency for the development and management of large-scale IT systems, in its development of digital infrastructure, encodes a particular vision of borders and security. In supporting EURODAC (a centralized fingerprint database for asylum seekers) and the Visa Information System (which gathers and controls the biometric identities of visa applicants), the agency displays a strong "sociotechnical imaginary" that transforms borders into a site of the "EU Schengen laboratory" (Trauttmansdorff & Felt, 2021).

Overall, at the state and institutional scale, the technosolutionist infrastructural imaginaries of control are most striking. These revolve around the belief that challenges and problems can be fixed through standalone disruptive technological innovations. Imaginaries of digital bordering display fantasies of efficient care and the circulation of desired mobile subjects, and concerns with safety result in desires for the total control of non-desired mobile subjects. In practice, states often see migration management as "technological testing grounds" (Molnar, 2020) to experiment with new, and often severely invasive, technologies.

Such "techno-humanitarian" (Morozov, 2012) imaginaries have predominantly been studied from the perspective of those in power. Beyond institutions, the 'vernacular imaginaries' of citizens too may reflect dominant conceptions of borders, migration and technology, as Georg Löfflmann and Nick Vaughan-Williams argue EU citizens imagine the border as an "information management" challenge (2018, p. 382). As Philippa Metcalfe shows in her study with migrants living in Athens, Greece, there is potential to account for the subjective dimensions of migration infrastructures from the perspective of imaginaries. She traces how being subjected to ink fingerprinting shaped alternative imaginaries in comparison to digital fingerprint scanning, which was imagined as more permanent (Metcalfe, 2022). Future research can document and amplify which imaginaries migrants develop, where, why and how, and how these challenge dominant imaginaries of, for example, migration infrastructures as signifiers of control.

Infrastructural imaginaries of caring for migrants

The perspective of care is a prominent one in scholarship on humanitarianism, solidarity and activism. In humanitarianism, technosolutionist imaginaries also characterize recent initiatives (Benton & Glennie, 2016). Seen as a way to bypass traditional humanitarian aid models, a "techno-hype" is invading "all spaces of humanitarian intervention" (Marino, 2021, p. 125). Strong hope is invested in technologies to alleviate crisis situations. Digital innovations include the delivery of digital services to displaced people, hackathons and apps for refugees. Across the world, we have seen how refugee camps have embraced public-private partnerships in pursuit of efficiency-driven technological innovation and disruption, including experiments with blockchain and payment through iris-scans, among others. Imaginaries of humanitarian technophilia can thus partly be understood as resulting from an increasing "philanthro-capitalism", as private, for-profit business are tapping into philanthropy as a new site for capital accumulation (Burns, 2019, p. 1101).

Besides a critique of capitalist extraction, digital humanitarianism demands thorough scrutiny of its fading "techno-legal consciousness" (Sandvik, 2020, p. 88). Caring technological infrastructures used by solidarity groups and activists reflect alternative bottom-up counter-imaginaries of mobility, state (maritime) territorial control and border configurations. For example, the Alarm Phone, a telephone hotline set up by a collective of European freedom of movement, human rights and migrant activist groups supports boats in distress in the Mediterranean Sea. Established in 2014, this digitally networked collective operates as a new nodal point in the "transnational underground railroad" (Heller, Pezzani & Stierl, 2017, p. 7). Using management software, calls from boats in distress are re-routed to volunteers from over 12 countries who work in shifts (ibid.).

When studying imaginaries from the bottom-up level of everyday migrant experiences, the emotional investments and aspirations projected onto devices like smartphones can be grasped as imaginaries of self-care. In the absence of family members, young people of Karen background, who were resettled in Melbourne, Australia, from a refugee camp on the Thai–Burma border, were found to construct a "family imaginary" to maintain family relations in the context of separation (Robertson, Wilding & Gifford, 2016, p. 225). Gifting phones or data, for some asylum migrants, creates a subject position of "aspirational mobility", to imagine oneself "beyond the bureaucratic asylum category" (Witteborn, 2019, pp. 754, 765). In navigating asylum bureaucracies, women asylum seekers have been found to develop specific digital practices. For women in a refugee camp in mainland Greece, awaiting refugee status, relocation and family reunification, tactical making do with displacement included seeking imagined sanctuary in nature photography (Greene, 2020) (see Chapter 4: Affects and emotions).

Although care and control are "two sides of a coin" (Constable, 2020, p. 327), so far they have been studied in isolation. We can take cues from the ethnographic study of Mark Johnson, Maggy Lee, Michael McCahill and Ma Rosalyn Mesina (2020) as to how to study their interrelationships. In their work on Filipino migrant domestic workers' relation to surveillance cameras in the home, they tease out the ambivalence of encounters between imaginaries of control and care. Filipino domestic workers remind us of the importance of addressing care and control not as binary opposites but as dialectic and being mutually constitutive.

From the perspective of the imagination, we can thus decentre technologies and centre subjective human perceptions of digital migration infrastructures in our analysis.

Conclusions

In this chapter we have seen how an infrastructural approach allows us to question commonly taken-for-granted, black-boxed processes in increasingly digitized and datafied environments. The four perspectives on infrastructures – brokering, relationality, materiality and imaginary – allow us to foreground specific aspects of infrastructures. A focus on brokering allows for the scrutiny of people as infrastructures. Besides studying particular subsets of migrant brokers in isolation, future work can address how these intermediaries, among themselves, are also digitally networked, potentially reinforcing and challenging unequal regimes of mobility. Infrastructures as relationality allow us to take relationships as an entry point to tease out what political, ethical, social and economic choices have been folded into the systems and processes of migrant governance, humanitarianism and securitization. Groundbreaking in this area is the scrutiny of the interoperability and transfer of relations across scales (multi-scalar research). The material approach to infrastructures as platforms, affordances and circulation stimulate various degrees of centring and decentring technologies and the perspectives of migrants in our critical analysis. Finally, infrastructures as imaginaries reject technocratic analysis by shedding light on how aspirations, hope and fears for care and control become embedded. Across the various sub-themes addressed under the heading of infrastructures, we can notice a strong emphasis on top-down forms of infrastructuring. Future studies can promote a more balanced understanding through attending better to the bottom-up, everyday experiences of infrastructural constructions and forms of contestation.

Research Dialogue I: Brenda S.A. Yeoh on studying care migration infrastructures

Brenda S.A. Yeoh FBA is Raffles Professor of Social Sciences at the Department of Geography, National University of Singapore (NUS). She is also the Research Leader of the Asian Migration Cluster at the Asia Research Institute, NUS. Her research interests include the politics of space in colonial and postcolonial cities, and she also has considerable experience working on a wide range of migration research in Asia, including key themes such as cosmopolitanism and highly skilled talent migration; gender, social reproduction and care migration; migration, national identity and citizenship issues; globalizing universities and international student mobilities; and cultural politics, family dynamics and international marriage migrants. In the last decade, Yeoh was a key contributor to the 'Asian infrastructural turn' (Shrestha & Yeoh, 2018, p. 665), which has inspired migration scholars across the world to approach migration from an infrastructural perspective. In particular, with colleagues from across various fields, she has offered a particularly strong impetus to research the 'migrant-broker' category (ibid.) conceptually and empirically.

1. **Can you offer us your history of how you came to work with the concept of infrastructures to address questions of migration and brokering in particular?**

   I came face to face with notions of migration brokerage and infrastructures largely because one cannot comprehend Asian migrations without giving attention to the commercial, organizational and regulatory aspects that shape how and why people move, and where they move to. My work on migrant domestic workers, for example, points to the important role of recruitment and placement agents operating both in the migrant-sending villages in Indonesia and the Philippines as well as in destination cities such as Hong Kong and Singapore (Wee, Goh & Yeoh, 2020a, 2020b). When working on the topic of marriage migration in Asia, international matchmaking agencies were vital in linking the trajectories of women from the less developed regions and those of men from more prosperous economies (Yeoh, Chee & Baey, 2017). As a social geographer interested in care migrations and gender politics, attending to the infrastructures that underpin human mobility in the region offered a methodological vantage point that has proven to be a productive move in enriching the Asian migration literature.

2. **Where would you situate your work on infrastructures in the broader research area of digital migration studies addressed in this book?**

In my work on migration infrastructures in the Asian context, I am interested in the non-migrant actors and socio-material arrangements that mediate and shape human mobilities as well as as the infrastructural processes that shape human subjectivites (Lin et al., 2017). I have not given sole attention to the digital sphere but, where relevant, take into account the growing significance of attending to transformative technologies that become part of infrastructural operations, such as the smartphone and the Internet as well as transportation industries (Xiang & Lindquist, 2018). With the growing digitalization and datafication of human mobilities as this book argues, there will be many more opportunities to focus on the increased reliance on digital platforms in migration regulatory regimes and migration brokerage, as well as the proliferation of digital social networks among migrants in border-crossing and transnational connectivity.

3. **What has been a key challenge or obstacle in studying migration and infrastructures for you and your collaborators?**

Methodologically, understanding migration infrastructures requires a careful consideration of relational approaches, assemblage thinking and attention to power asymmetries. The goal is not only to understand how migration infrastructures are produced but how and why they continually adapt and change in the light of frictions and fractures. This sort of work requires keeping in constant touch with the field and the multiple actors – not just migrants – involved in infrastructural processes at different sites. In the best of times, multi-sited, multidimensional fieldwork is a challenge for time-strapped researchers. Pandemic times and travel restrictions have no doubt raised these hurdles in studying migration infrastructures by disrupting travel infrastructures and hardening border control.

4. **In a recent paper with Kristel F. Acedera you focus on the 'care-triangle' of migrant-sending families in the Philippines (2021). To what extent would you consider caring as a digital migration infrastructure?**

We show that understanding the 'care triangle' among migrant parents, left-behind or substitute caregivers and left-behind children in sending villages requires an infrastructural perspective that shows how differential use and access to ICTs reflect 'hierarchies of care access' (Acedera & Yeoh, 2021). More generally, researchers interested in transnational care work have highlighted the importance of attending

*to the politics of gender, age and other subject positions in an era
when 'doing family' across national territory depends on digital communication while also being affected by border controls and increasing
securitization (Yeoh et al., 2020).*

5. **In reviewing infrastructural approaches to migration and digital
technologies, we explore the four perspectives of brokerage,
relationality, materiality and the imaginary. What is your impression of
this overview and do you recognize any additional angles?**

*The overview of infrastructural approaches covers much ground and
I found the division into four perspectives of brokerage, relationality,
materiality and the imaginary a useful intervention. If there are any
angles I would add, then I would say that an important line of inquiry
that could be also considered lies with the question of how migration
infrastructures dynamically and differentially shape migrant (and non-
migrant) subjectivities. Infrastructural processes often work to produce
conformity to some notion of the ideal migrant subject; at the same
time, migrants are not trapped by infrastructural power but are capable
of active negotiation and resistance.*

6. **Infrastructural scholarship has proliferated in recent years. What are
the recent dynamics that demand more of our attention?**

*As this book also argues, the conceptual and empirical links between
migration scholarship and digital communication research require
interdisciplinary scholars interested in bridging the gap. The role of
digital infrastructures and media technologies has become critical in
governing the way people care, communicate, live, work, study, mobilize and project identity across borders. This raises important new
issues around 'digital citizenship', which is likely to become an increasingly important research focus for migration and communication
scholars (Sinanan & Horst, 2022).*

Research Dialogue II: Huub Dijstelbloem on turning the notion of infrastructure upside down and inside out

Huub Dijstelbloem is Professor of Philosophy of Science, Technology and Politics and Scientific Director of the Institute for Advanced Study at the University of Amsterdam, the Netherlands. He works on the intersection of philosophy of science and technology and political philosophy. His research engages with questions concerning democracy and technology and the politics of border control and migration policies. Most recently, Dijstelbloem published *Borders as infrastructure* (MIT Press, 2021). In the book, the concept of infrastructures is developed into a critical vocabulary to scrutinize the mediation and technopolitics of borders.

1. **Can you offer us your history of how you came to work on questions of migration, bordering and infrastructures?**

    Borders and international human mobility express everything I am interested in: the exercise of state power, the use of technologies and specific forms of knowledge to include or exclude people, the building of structures and the creation of networks to circulate information, money, goods and people. I have a background in the philosophy of science and science and technology studies, but when I became increasingly interested in the study of the politics of technologies and the politics of knowledge in practice, I was struck by the lack of academic attention for issues such as violence, injustice and inequality in this field.

    Fortunately, much has changed since. My interest grew when an increasing number of techniques such as DNA-tests for family reunification, X-rays to determine the age of minors and fingerprints were applied in national migration policies. I came across the notion of 'infrastructures' in different ways. The work of historians of technology inspired me, but earlier studies, such as Bruno Latour's Aramis or the love of technology *(1996),* Sorting things out: Classification and its consequences *by Geoffrey Bowker and Susan Leigh Star (1999), the work of Paul Edwards (e.g. 2002) and, of course, Langdon Winner's seminal text* 'Do artefacts have politics?' *(1980) proved equally important.*

2. **Where do you situate your work on infrastructures in the broader research area of digital migration studies addressed in this book?**

    I see a strong connection with the work done in this book. One of the main points of similarity is the ambition to turn the notion of infrastructure upside down and inside out. With turning the notion of infrastructure upside down I mean that we consider infrastructures as the result of all kinds of circulations and traffic. Instead of taking a certain given infrastructure as a starting point, we look into the interactions between different kind of actors that shape the infrastructure: digital connections between migrants, families, banks and smugglers, relations between the material means of transportation and surveillance systems, digital security measures, visualization and images of migration. With inside out, I mean approaches that unravel the image of infrastructures as a unified whole or even contest the view that infrastructures can be pictures from the outside in its totality.

3. **Can you describe a key challenge or obstacle in understanding migration and border infrastructures?**

One of the biggest challenges was to develop a conceptual framework that does justice to the continuities as well as to the changes in border control. I aimed to develop a lens that is historically and institutionally adequate and covers a longer period, at least since the end of the Cold War, but that is also able to grasp recent migration developments and current techno-logical applications. Considering technology not only as an instrument but also as a kind of worldview, and understanding infrastructures as constel-lations that not only facilitate or complicate travelling but as moving enti-ties themselves, was an important step in my analysis.

4. **You hold a professorship (Philosophy of Science, Technology and Politics) at the University of Amsterdam (UvA) but until recently you were also affiliated to the Netherlands Scientific Council for Government Policy (WRR). To what extent is infrastructure a term to bridge (and/or translate) between critical scholarship and policy circles?**

The notion of infrastructure helps to clarify that borders are not just lines on a map or markers of territory that define the boundaries of states, but that borders are entities themselves that consist of a machin-ery of governing to manage the international mobility of people. The risk of the notion is that it is seen as a technocratic way to consider borders, or as an instrumental point of view.

5. **In reviewing infrastructural approaches to migration and digital technologies, we explore the four perspectives of brokerage, relationality, materiality and the imaginary. What is your impression of this overview and do you recognize any additional angles?**

Distinguishing different dimensions of infrastructures and perspectives to analyze them often results in combinations of methodological and conceptual approaches with suggestions to put more emphasis on particular aspects of infrastructures and the introduction of novel themes and topics. The four perspectives of brokerage, relationality, materiality and the imaginary are no exception to that. Taken together, they offer a very convincing and comprehensive innovative viewpoint. The focus on materiality and relationality is a methodological and conceptual perspective that is increasingly underpinning much of the research done in the field. The perspectives of brokerage and the imaginary are of particular importance and are extremely interesting contributions. The perspective of brokerage offers a variety of ways to study the forms of relationality and materiality, in migration practices as well as in state affairs and corporate settings. The perspective of the imaginary offers a crucial element to further the study of infrastructures, namely the way infrastructures are intermingled with international state power.

6. **What recommendations would you give those aspiring to study migration and border infrastructures?**

   You are likely to benefit from a conceptual lens that allows you to travel, to zoom in and zoom out, to follow continuities as well as sudden changes, and to combine the analysis of apparent structures such as nation-states with the emergence of new networks of people and technologies.

7. **Infrastructural scholarship has proliferated in recent years. What are the future themes, topics or dynamics that infrastructural researchers should pay more attention to, and/or do you see any limits to 'infrastructure' as a catch-all, academic buzzword?**

   The study of infrastructures undoubtedly will be affected by the consequences of climate change, future pandemics, and food systems. We will need to further incorporate notions of ecology, health surveillance, the circulation of non-human animals and the distribution of energy and food into our concepts of infrastructure. Connecting human mobility and infrastructures with nature, the environment, climates and ecosystems will be a crucial next step.

2

Connections

With migrant connections we refer here to the abilities, qualities and conditions of being connected across distance through the use of digital devices, platforms and networks. The three themes of geography, information and rights are most prominent in the cross-disciplinary study of migrant connections. These themes are intensely debated, and cover varied, and sometimes contradictory, claims and findings. The first theme concerns the question of what geographical scale to choose when studying migrant communication networks: the scale of local integration, the scale of transnationalism or can they be combined? The second theme concerns the use of communication networks for information. We will consider what we can learn when considering the precarious character of the information landscape, and we will attend to how migrants have created alternative, peer-to-peer networks of information exchange. The third theme concerns how migrant networks are mobilized in support of claiming digital rights as well as digital forms of state and non-state repression.

Geographies of migrant connectivity

According to the sociologist Dana Diminescu (2008), in our current era of increased mobility and digital connectivity, we can speak of the migrant figure as the "connected migrant", which escapes the opposition of presence and absence. This contrasts sharply with the pre-digital era, where migrants risked being doubly absent, both from their home and host society (Sayad, 1999; see Chapter 5: Histories). The speed and scope of digital means that migrants use to presence themselves in various social spaces is evolving rapidly. Migrants have been early adopters of modern communication technologies in pursuing "integration in host societies" and continuing "the struggle for the survival of their community" (Diminescu, 2008, p. 571).

In the current digital "polymedia" (Madianou & Miller, 2012) landscape, people can choose to connect via a large number of applications, platforms and devices to manage their relationships, strategically using the specific affordances of one technology to compensate for the limitations of others. The state of being digitally connected and co-present in host and home societies is strongly conceptualized but little empirically sustained. In her 2008 manifesto on the "connected migrant", Diminescu discusses "Rubin's vase" – a 1915 figure designed by the psychologist Edgar Rubin, which is sometimes referred to as 'The Two Face, One Vase Illusion'; see Figure 2.1) – to call into question the limitations of approaching connected migrants from a singular perspective.

When looking at Rubin's vase, viewers see either the silhouette of a vase in white or the profiles of two inward-looking faces in black. "[L]ikewise, in our analysis of the features of the migrant, we can see either the ruptures or the continuities" (Diminescu, 2008, p. 569). For Diminescu, 'continuities' refers to modes of transnationalism, while 'ruptures' refers to the previous expectation of having to rupture ties with contacts in order to integrate into a new setting.

Although the concept of the connected migrant invites scholars to move beyond a mutually exclusive binary understanding, divisions still strongly shape research on migrant connectivity (Ponzanesi, 2019). Studies commonly single out and pit against each other processes of transnationalism and communicative practices of integration. For example, either 'ethnic media', 'community media' and 'diaspora media' or 'intercultural media', either 'encapsulation' or 'cosmopolitanization' and either 'bonding capital' or 'bridging capital' are often used as parallel, mutually exclusive, analytic lenses through which to study migrant connectivity. As a

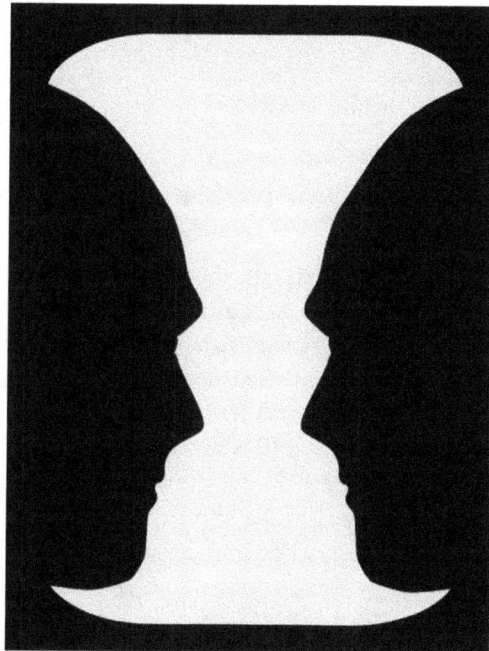

Figure 2.1 Rubin's vase (1915), illustrating the challenge of combining both the transnationalism and the integration paradigm in addressing migrant connectivity

Graphical representation by Nevit Delmen, 2011.

heuristic, below, we address the oppositional framing of integration and transnationalism, although the dynamics are largely transferable to the other binary understandings of migrant connectivity, discussed above.

Migrant integration

'Integration' is difficult to define. It is commonly taken to refer to the establishment of a common ground between diverse communities in so-called 'host societies'. The notion has become loaded with context and situation-specific political and normative views. Its meaning evolves as a result of various stakeholders, including policy makers, government officials, researchers and migrant organizations. Academics engaging with the term commonly focus on the goals of integration.

As indicated in Table 2.1, the goals of integration have evolved across time and place. They have moved between state-centric goals of 'assimilation' (the expectation that migrants will adapt and adjust) and 'multiculturalism' (the recognition of the value of cultural diversity). In addition, they have included community-centric goals of 'differentialism' (emancipation via the migrant's own group structures) or 'interculturalism' (intercultural contact as a strategy for communal forms of belonging) (Goksel, 2018; Scholten, Collett & Petrovic, 2017).

Table 2.1   Integration goals, from state and community perspectives

Integration goals	State-centric	Community-centric
	Assimilation	Differentialism
	Multiculturalism	Interculturalism

Integration is a dynamic process. In cultural psychology, the process is understood by acknowledging various "acculturation outcomes", including integration, assimilation, separation/segregation and marginalization (Berry, 1997). Integration processes range across various domains, including: (1) conditions of employment, housing, education and health; (2) citizenship and rights; (3) processes of social connection within and between groups; and (4) structural barriers to connection (Ager & Strang, 2008). Migrant connectivity scholarship is mostly concerned with the latter three, but we should not forget to consider the material conditions, such as access to devices and networks which are indispensable for migrants to connect.

Migrant transnationalism

Migrant transnationalism refers to the dynamics of maintaining social networks across borders among family members, households, communities and associations, a process intensified by new technologies, travel opportunities and financial mechanisms. The impact of transnational relationships spans across cultural, social, political, religious, familial and economic domains. Conceptually, trans-nationalism, seen from the 'bottom-up' perspective of migrants themselves, is taken to refer to a variety of processes, such as a cross-border morphology of social networking, a consciousness of being 'here' and 'there', the hybridization of cultures, flows of transnational capital and the creation of new in-between places (e.g. Vertovec, 2004a, 2004b, 2009; Waldinger, 2013; and for an overview see Tedeschi, Vorobeva & Jauhiainen, 2022).

The relationality of integration and transnationalism

The assumption that integration and transnationalism are necessarily at odds with one another is empirically and conceptually flawed, and should thus be problematized. In cross-cultural psychology, scholars found that migrants can successfully live in two cultures when they are able to balance cultural mainte-nance and host country participation (Berry, 2005). In migration studies, simi-larly, the 'push' and 'pull' of integration and transnationalism can be seen as a "precarious balancing of opening and closure in a translocal landscape of oppor-tunity and obligation" (Bude & Dürrschmidt 2010, p. 488). Migration scholars Marta Bivand Erdal and Ceri Oeppen addressed the complexity of these balanc-ing acts by presenting a typology (2013, p. 867). With the typology, they invite migration scholars not only to acknowledge the co-existence of transnational-ism and integration simultaneously, but to analyze the interactions between the two. They propose that this interaction can only be understood as place- and context-specific, and resulting from the many functional, emotional and prag-matic considerations of those involved. The basic premise for the typology is that integration and transnationalism is not a zero-sum game. They propose that interaction could play out in at least three ways: additive (the interaction out-come equals the sum of the two parts), synergistic (the outcome is greater than the sum of the two parts) or antagonistic (the result is less than the sum, or one cancels out the other).

We can add the category of 'overlooked' to this typology, to cover those studies which do not explicitly account for the relations between integration and transna-tionalism. We can transpose this multi-directional understanding of integration and transnationalism – as respectively overlooked, antagonistic, additive and synergistic – to foreground the variety of migrant connectivity practices (see Table 2.2).

The majority of studies on migrant connectivity single out either transnation-alism or integration. For example, reflecting on studies of information among migrants, Ramesh Srinivasan and Ajit Pyati note that "Most immigrant-focused information-science research has focused on distinctly local, place-based scenar-ios, while diasporic research on information behavior, in contrast, focuses mainly on issues of transnational identity online" (2007, p. 1734). Notwithstanding their limitations, studies that focus on either the geography scale of integration or transnationalism do offer valuable empirical and conceptual insights on specific elements of the digitization of migration.

Table 2.2 Typology of interactions between integration and transnationalism, adapted from Erdal and Oeppen (2013, p. 878) and Leppik (2020, p. 289)

	Types of interaction between integration and transnationalism			
	1. Overlooked	*2. Antagonistic*	*3. Additive*	*4. Synergistic*
Socio-cultural integration and transnationalism (emotional, cultural, social, religious)	Feeling of belonging and identification through connectivity in either country of origin or settlement is foregrounded, without attention to identification or belongingness in the other place	Feeling of belonging and identification through connections with one place result in a diminishing of feelings of belonging and identification in the other place	Feeling of belonging and identification grow through connections with country of origin and of settlement	Feeling of belonging and identification through connections in one place give confidence to further connect and develop belonging and identification in the other place
Structural integration and transnationalism (economic, political, legal)	Economic, political and/or legal dimensions in either country of origin or settlement is foregrounded, without attention for relations with processes in the other place	Demand for resources in one place limits an ability to meet demands in the other place	Citizenship and being economically active in country of origin and of settlement, often sustained through regularized mobility between places	Resources gained in one place (e.g. education, information, remittances) are sent and invested to develop further resources in the other place

For example, in the transnationalism paradigm, scholars have developed a strong, critical vocabulary to account for the complexities of the digital mediation of transnational lives. The concept of "transnational habitus" was developed in a study of Romanian professionals in Toronto, Canada, to refer to the everyday realities of digitally mediated, ubiquitous, simultaneous and immediate cross-border interaction and connectivity with "geographically distant and culturally distinct worlds" (Nedelcu, 2012, p. 1341); through live streaming on video culinary practices, transnational Italian families have been found to re-stage "family rituals at a distance" (Marino, 2019); the notion of "ambient co-presence" (Madianou, 2016, p. 183) theorizes how Filipino migrants in London, UK, negotiate a peripheral awareness of significant others living at a distance through ubiquitous media platforms and devices; and "transnational 'e-families'" points to dynamics of how Salvadorans mediate family life across borders between those who migrate and those who remain (Benítez, 2012, p. 1439). Similarly, integration paradigm research has developed robust frameworks to grasp, for example: "cross-cultural adaptation" and intercultural experiences of migrant groups in the United States (Kim, 2001, p. xi); the interactions between Chinese higher-education student sojourners and members of the Hong Kong host society (Jackson, 2017); how WhatsApp may be used by internally displaced persons in Nigeria to achieve greater societal inclusion (Dasuki & Abubakar, 2019); and the forms of agency experienced among refugees navigating information landscapes while being resettled in New Zealand (Díaz Andrade & Doolin, 2019). Besides the studies that overlook interactions between transnationalism and integration, a second branch of scholarship assumes an antagonistic relationship.

Antagonistic relationship between integration and transnationalism

It is also quite common for studies on migrant connectivity to assume or find a zero-sum relationship between transnationalism and integration. In this perspective, scholars argue that social media use among migrants can work as an "inhibitor to the acculturation process" (Mitra & Evansluong, 2019, p. 477). Migrants from various backgrounds in Sweden reported a growing sense of engagement, community and belongingness towards their host society when they received responses from local users on social media, whereas they felt more inclined to reaffirm connections with their home country networks when they received no responses on social media from locals (Mitra & Evansluong, 2019). Based on her ethnography with Korean transient migrants in Austin, Texas (USA), Claire Shinhea Lee contends that "if someone tends to consume homeland media dominantly, that person ends up decreasing hostland media consumption rather than reducing other leisure activities" (2020, p. 22).

A survey study on the use of social networking sites among international students and expatriates in the Netherlands found that home country relations strengthened social support. Those who keep in touch transnationally, however, also experience more loneliness and homesickness (Hofhuis, Hanke & Rutten, 2019). A longitudinal study of Facebook use by Muslim migrants in the USA found that increased contact with fellow migrants strengthened intergroup virtual community-building, but also strengthened negative perceptions and lowered motivations to adapt to the dominant culture: those oriented towards their ingroup are "using Facebook to strengthen ethnic ties, often at the expense of ties with the dominant culture" (Croucher & Rahmani 2015, p. 10). In a study on the social media use of Polish and Filipino migrants living in Ireland, Lee Komito (2011) argues that network connectivity reshapes the migration experience, but he also warns that staying in touch transnationally potentially slows down processes of integration and participation in host societies. International United Nations (UN) workers in Geneva, Switzerland, have been found to maintain expatriate bubbles, resulting in "geo-social encapsulation" (Jansson, 2018, pp. 73–74). In this process of encapsulation, migrants "nurture pre-existing social networks and communities" (ibid.), comprising a risk-free process of retreat, which does not require engagement with difference. Similarly, privileged Mexican migrants living in Europe were found to represent their mobile lifestyles on social networking sites as a form of "classed distinctions" (Nessi & Bailey, 2014).

In reflecting on these findings, we can notice that studies on elites, expatriates and sojourners do not commonly question the implications of a relative lack of local integration, in contrast to studies on refugees, so-called 'low-skilled migrants', ethnicized, religious minority migrants or postcolonial migrants that often include value-based judgements about the possible detrimental societal consequences of the transnational networking of these particular groups of mobile subjects. Although expatriates are commonly found to be 'least integrated' in their local contexts and highly connected to transnational communities, we should note the relative absence of privileged expatriate bodies in public discourse and the common politicization of highly visible migrant bodies such as refugees. It must be noted that as a result of changing labour dynamics under the Covid-19 health pandemic, working remotely has boomed, raising public concern about elite migrant practices. The 'digital nomad' phenomenon has grown (see Chapter 4: Affects and Emotions), leading to protests in 'digital nomad hotspots' such as Lisbon or Mexico City by local residents who are priced out of their homes as a result of gentrification (Gill & Baptista, 2022). The uneven consideration of how particular communities of mobile people impact upon societies and spaces warrants greater reflection in future migrant connectivity research.

Additive relationship between integration and transnationalism

Those studies that do combine integration and transnationalism in analyzing migrant connectivity most often take an additive approach. In migration studies, we can take cues from scholars locating migrants' "double engagement" and "double orientation". For example, through networks, Ghanaians in the Netherlands spend and invest both in Ghana (such as in housing, businesses, education and family, as well as paying for funerals) and in the Netherlands, where they invest on the level of the neighbourhood, city and the nation (Mazzucato, 2008, p. 199). With regard to digital networks, studies that show how transnational media practices provide migrants with a sense of reliability, trust, habit and routine, or "ontological security" (Giddens, 1990; see also Georgiou, 2013), as a solid basis for settling in a new context come to mind. Ontological security can be defined as "the confidence that most human beings have in the continuity of their self-identity and in the constancy of the surrounding social and material environments of action" (Giddens, 1990, p. 92). In the context of migrant connectivity, homeland media and networks are embraced as a substitute for the sense of security offered by the routines of one's family and one's home, which shape a sense of belonging (Georgiou, 2013). As such, digital transnational networks offer a potential "safe ground" (Elias & Lemish, 2009, p. 549) to migrants who are trying to settle into a new context.

For example, alongside feeling transnationally supported, teenage migrants from the former Soviet Union living in Israel reported using music websites like *Zvuki.ru* and chat and discussion groups because these offered opportunities for meaningful engagement with non-migrant Israelis. These migrants felt that these spaces provided both a "peephole" and a "fitting room" to respectively observe and experiment with new roles and codes of behaviour (Elias & Lemish, 2009, p. 548). Similarly, digital networks offered Karen Burmese youth in Melbourne, Australia, "digital escapes" that supported home-making in their new country as well as encouraging a sense of becoming a global citizen (Gifford & Wilding, 2013, p. 558). Sun Sun Lim and Becky Pham (2016), in their work with Indonesian and Vietnamese students in Singapore, found that social media communication facilitated "cultural silos that comprise only co-nationals", but also found that the students use social media for acculturation purposes, including gaining a better understanding of their host society and feeling better equipped to interact with fellow locals (2016, p. 2171).

From the additive perspective, scholars have documented how migrants seek to avoid "context collapse" between transnational and local communities. Young refugees in the Netherlands, for example, carry out strategic "digital care labour", where they maintain their contact lists and post content tailored towards specific audiences: they use platforms such as *Instagram* and *Snapchat* to share snapshots of food and nightlife and connect with peers locally, and they use Facebook to link with family and friends abroad living in hardship and civil war, thus maintaining separation in their lives (Leurs, 2019). Queer migrants might choose to 'stay in the closet' for some of their contacts on social media. As a way of navigating various online selves and roles (Dhoest & Szulc, 2016, p. 1), queer migrants, for example, use several browsers and create multiple social media profiles – one for transnational families and one for queer friends – or use specific platforms directed at specific audiences (Szulc, 2020a).

Synergetic relationship between integration and transnationalism

There is a scarcity of studies that explicitly assume and/or document a synergetic relationship between integration and transnationalism. Studies on queer migrant connectivity are exceptions: "New in town" gay immigrants in Copenhagen, Denmark, use the gay dating platforms *Grindr* and *PlanetRomeo* as a "cross-cultural social network" beyond sexual and platonic matchmaking, assisting newcomers with establishing friendships and accessing logistical support (Shield, 2017, pp. 258–259). The social chat application *LINE* was found to be used by local Chinese gay men in Australia as a way to bond with the diaspora and relate to gay men and their digital culture in Australia (Cassidy & Yang Wang, 2018, p. 852). In addition, the notion of "elastic mobility" was proposed to address how elite business people negotiate digitally transnational and local communication as well as home-making across contexts (Fast & Lindell, 2016, p. 447).

The question arises as to how far we can stretch our relational and synergetic understanding. What are the limits, and when should we move beyond focusing on integration and transnationalism? Based on research showing that refugees in New Zealand reshuffle "proximal and distant networks", Jay Marlowe argues that "social media is disrupting normative understandings of what refugee integration entails", as it is used to access opportunities to meet people and embrace openings, but also to close down other prospects (2020, p. 286). Similarly, in her work with Russian-speaking migrants in Estonia, Marianne Leppik (2020) addresses how a mediated transnationalism, for example through consuming Russian media news and entertainment, results in various forms of "segmented integration". Audris Umel addresses how digital practices allow Filipino migrants in Germany to navigate "spatio-temporal consructions", negotiating between past, present, homeland and hostland affiliations (2022, p. 1). These studies indicate that digital migrant practices demand us researchers to problematize and reconsider paradigmatic approaches to integration and transnationalism.

Translocality

Scholars worried about the limits of integration and transnationalism have proposed a number of alternative analytic lenses. In media studies, the analytic pairing of the "encapsulated Self", which nurtures pre-existing networks, and the 'cosmopolitan Self', which seeks to engage reflexively with other networks (Christensen & Janson, 2015; Jansson, 2018); in political science, the notion of 'differential inclusion' (Mezzadra & Neilson, 2013) were proposed as conceptual moves to overcome the dichotomy between inclusion and exclusion; in cultural anthropology, the term 'scalable sociality' is proposed as a definition of social media which allows users to decide on the scale of their sociality in communicating messages across an ecology of platforms, with various groups and various conceptions of secrecy, morality and privacy (Costa, 2016); finally, the notion of translocality is growing in popularity in migration studies to account for how multi-directional social relations across local, urban, regional, national and transnational scales may "shape transnational migrant networks, economic exchanges and diasporic spaces" (Brickell & Datta, 2011, p. 3; see also Anthias, 2020; Bayramoğlu & Lünenborg, 2018). As Melis Mevsimler (2021) demonstrates in her study with Somali, Romanian and Turkish migrant women living in London, the concept of translocality proves useful in addressing the paradoxical complexities of digital migrant networking. Below, we turn our attention to the information circulated in migrant networks.

Information practices

The second theme of migrant connectivity we explore in this chapter concerns information practices and knowledge-making. This theme highlights to what extent migration, networking, inclusion, participation and belonging is an 'information problem' (Caidi & Allard, 2005). The short answer to this question is yes: when unfulfilled, "information needs" might pose barriers to "socio-cultural adaptation" (Martzoukou & Burnett, 2018, p. 1104). Navigating a new environment "may involve satisfying information needs around, for example, language, employment, housing, health, education, transportation, banking and compliance with local regulations" (Díaz Andrade & Doolin, 2019, p. 147). To get a sense of the breadth and scope of the information practices of migrants, we can take cues from the information needs matrix proposed by information researchers Olubukola Oduntan and Ian Ruthven (Figure 2.2). They developed this matrix to distinguish between the various domains of information needs, based on the situated experiences of asylum seekers, refugees and rejected asylum seekers (2019, pp. 800–802).

When analyzing information needs and practices using this matrix, we can understand better how information for some migrants may work as an enabler, and for others is experienced as an obstacle as a result of strategically created information gaps that aim to deter some migrant populations. It is important here to recognize that information practices are not uniform across migrant populations and migrant trajectories, but also to acknowledge that migrants themselves creatively and strategically overcome information hierarchies among themselves, and with various actors, such as activists, solidarity groups, smugglers, job agencies or other migrant brokers (Udwan, Leurs & Alencar, 2020).

Studies with migrants commonly focus on "everyday life information seeking" (ELIS) media practices (Caidi, Allard & Quirke, 2010, p. 501). This social and phenomenological perspective allows researchers to address the quotidian, habitual, non-rational and multiple goals of information practices while also becoming attentive to how these are shaped by personal attributes and motivations as well as broader cultural contexts and societal structures (Savolainen, 2008). Information practices range from actively and consciously addressing

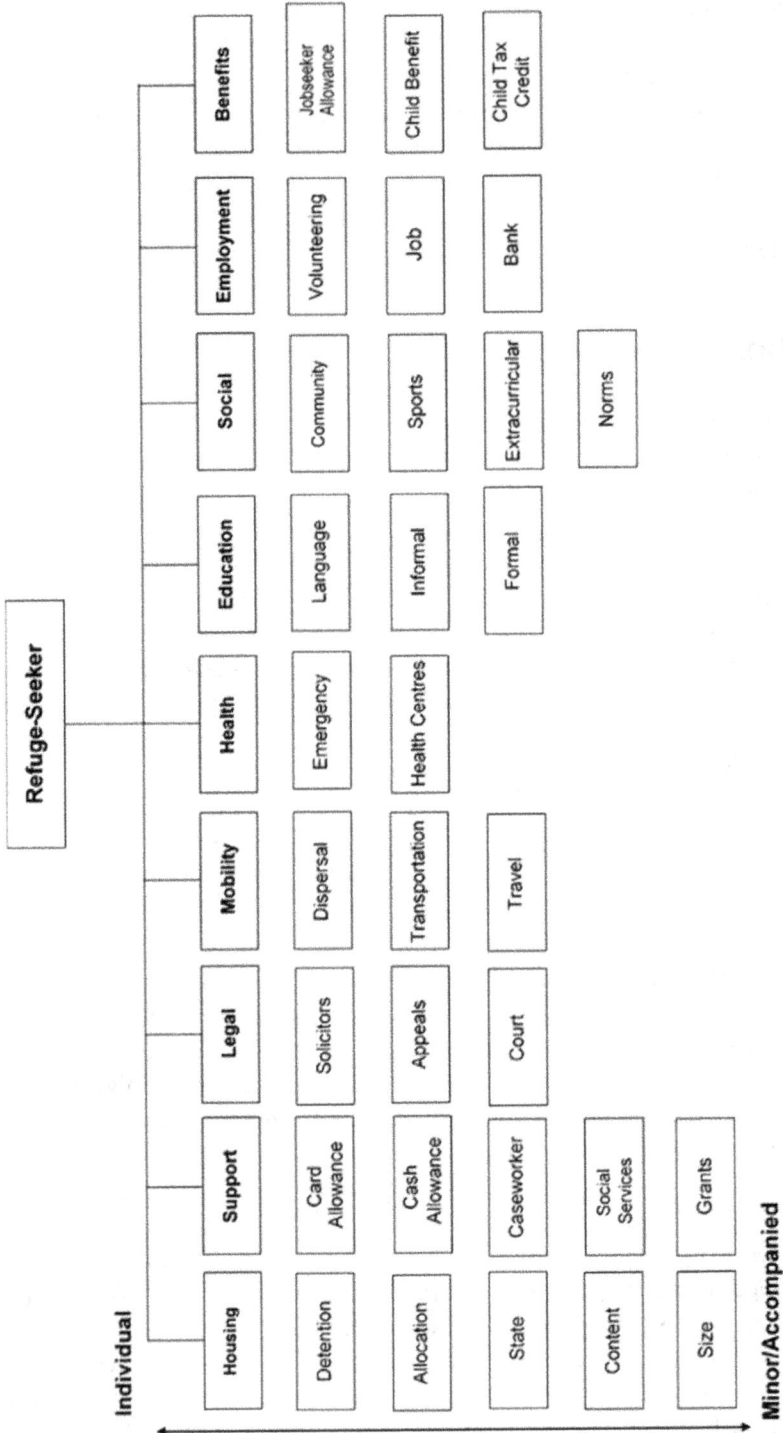

Figure 2.2   Information needs matrix (Oduntan & Ian Ruthven, 2019, p. 800)

recognized information needs as well as less directed activities, including entertainment, which also may become meaningful to seek, use or share information. For analytic purposes, scholars distinguish between information practices for the purpose of (1) orientation, (2) navigating problems or practicalities and (3) expressing oneself (Caidi et al., 2010; Díaz Andrade & Doolin, 2019).

Orienting information seeking can include monitoring current events through various formal and informal online/offline information sources, locating information on cultural, religious and/or political happenings and discussions, and accessing information about cultural identity issues and broader social contexts. This type of information may be meaningful for migrants to habituate and develop a sense of belonging to a new environment, as well as to negotiate stress and social isolation (see Chapter 4: Affects and emotions). Instrumental and problem-specific information seeking may span domains including language, employment, housing, health, legal, education, recreation, transportation, banking or professional associations, volunteering or community organizations. Many problem-specific information practices are similar to non-migrant mainstream groups navigating bureaucracies, but the process may be additionally challenging for migrants seeking to become familiar with an unfamiliar system in a new country and information environment. Expressive information practices refer to using and sharing information for social and communicative purposes.

Furthermore, information practices are specific to various moments in migration trajectories. Scholars, for example, distinguish between migrants' information needs in at least four, partly overlapping, stages (Caidi et al., 2010, pp. 505–506):

- pre-migration stage, which may involve gathering information through formal channels and informal migration networks;
- immediate stage, to address pressing needs to land and/or survive, to find shelter, language training or health support;
- intermediate stage, to navigate local systems and institutions for the long term;
- integrative stage, where needs revolve around desires for civic and political participation.

In the migrant information practices continuum, scholarship on refugees and asylum seekers is most prominent, although frameworks developed to address the experiences of refugees have been successfully applied to other groups, such as 'highly-skilled' migrants arriving in Australia (Sayyad Abdi et al., 2019). When placed in a broader spectrum, sharply contrasting claims about migrant information practices come into view. Overall, scholars on one side of the spectrum address how migrants experience fractures and precarity in information landscapes (Lloyd, 2017; Wall, 2020; Wall, Campbell & Janbek, 2017), while on the other side of the spectrum researchers address how migrants seek to overcome informational barriers on the basis of a radical migrant commons (Alonso & Arzoz, 2010; Papadopoulos & Tsianos, 2013; Trimikliniotis, Parsanoglou & Tsianos, 2015).

Information precarity in fractured information landscapes

On one side of the spectrum, the emphasis is on top-down institutionalized information landscapes and the possible consequences of "information poverty" (Chatman, 1996). In this strand, researchers theorize and empirically study how institutionalized information hierarchies might co-shape or further exacerbate the hardship of migrants living in precarious conditions; and how information is mobilized to deter migrant movements. The concept of "fractured information landscapes" (Lloyd, 2017) from the field of library and information sciences, provides a framework for scrutinizing the formal conditions co-shaping refugees' information practices:

> what enables and constrains knowledge construction, as well as considering areas related to how information practice and seeking behaviours are enabled and/or constrained in the context of marginality, transition and resettlement. (2017, p. 40)

The fracturing of information landscapes in part results from the complex interplay of varies actors (organizations, communities, officials) operating within and across jurisdictions and domains of information policy making, as illustrated in Figure 2.2 in the case of refugees. As a result of the involvement of a great variety of actors who often act independently and in parallel to each other, "it is not always clear which organizations have the responsibility or right, or even the capacity, to develop and enforce these policies" (Maitland, 2018, p. 210).

Information needs assessments studies reveal that fragmented information landscapes are common. For example, formal conditions, including expected resilience, self-management and individualized health literacy, have been found to result in fragmented knowledge which subsequently disrupts the settlement of refugees in Australia (Lloyd, 2014, p. 63). In Dadaab, in Northern Kenya, which hosts the second-largest single refugee population in the world in three camps, Ifo, Dagahaley and Hagadera, a survey found that 70% of arrivals lack basic information, such as registering for aid, accessing health care, contacting aid organizations or locating missing family members (Kivikuru, 2013). A study on the Karen refugee community living in camps along the Thai–Burma border, found that information needs are relegated as secondary concerns by the humanitarian sector (Jack, 2016, p. 98).

Seeking to intervene, Melissa Wall and colleagues understand information as a basic need, alongside food and shelter. They argue that insecurities among refugees grow as a result of what they describe as "information precarity" (Wall et al., 2017):

> the condition of instability that refugees experience in accessing news and personal information, potentially leaving them vulnerable to misinformation, stereotyping, and rumors that can affect their economic and social capital. (ibid., 2017, p. 240)

Working with Syrian refugees living in Zaatari refugee camp in Jordan, they observed that information precarity results from:

- limited technological and social access to information, which in turn is shaped by how power relations along the lines of gender, class, geography, and for example ability intersect;
- an understandable scepticism of official sources of information when coming from countries where information is controlled;
- an inability of some migrant groups to have a say over how they are represented;
- surveillance;
- disruption of social support networks (Wall, Campbell & Janbek, 2019, pp. 505–506).

Governmental provision and withholding of information is an area in need of further research, particularly when the logics of protection are used as a justification to conceal information from refugees in situations of humanitarian crisis (Jack, 2020, p. 201).

In addition, information campaigns are also deployed to deter specific migrant subjects. Sarah C. Bishop compared Australian, Norwegian and US Customs and Border Patrol government media campaigns, which seek to deter asylum seekers, showing how various groups of people who might aspire to move are collapsed into a single category of unwanted migrants (2020). For example, through private-public partnerships, the Norwegian government initiated a Facebook campaign entitled "Stricter Asylum Regulations in Norway". The reach of such campaigns can be tracked – an Australian Facebook campaign appeared on the screens of 11,500 people – but the effects of these campaigns cannot be measured (Bishop, 2020). These campaigns uniformly leave out information about migrants' human right to seek asylum, "thereby advancing strategic ignorance in their audiences" (Bishop, 2020, p. 1092). Furthermore, governmental information campaigns normalize and legitimize borders as places of death and violence, further separating citizens and non-belonging foreigners. This becomes apparent, for example, in the "Aware Migrants" (2016) campaign funded by the Italian government and managed by the International Organization for Migration (IOM) (Musarò, 2019).

Information hierarchies are also commonly addressed through the prism of the digital divide, in terms of ownership, access and participation. Digital divide scholarship commonly differentiates between a right side and a wrong side, in terms of technology and information 'haves' and 'have-nots'. However, here a word of caution is needed, in order for us to avoid reaffirming a digital connectivity bias skewed towards the Global North in our work on migrant networks (see Arora, 2019). Refugees, Linda Leung argues, across various contexts are part of a "global majority for whom technology access and use is neither assumed nor commonplace", and which includes women, non-English-speaking people, older people, people of low social-economic status, people in rural or remote areas, indigenous communities and people with disabilities (2020, p. 79). Instead of singling out digital exclusion as a "minority issue" or taking demographic approaches to digital inclusion and exclusion, Leung importantly calls for a "holistic approach to understanding differences in technology use and access" (ibid., p. 79) which privileges some and excludes other. An alternative approach to the digital divide addresses negotiations over what counts as legitimate digital practice and scrutinizes how digital privileges are reproduced (Sims, 2014, p. 670). Below, we shift our focus from top-down institutionalized information provision towards how information hierarchies are negotiated from the bottom up by, for and among migrants.

Information as a commoning practice

Migrant commoning refers to the cooperative production of non-proprietary and non-enclosed worlds outside public, private or civil society institutions. Alongside the maintenance of connectivity infrastructures, informal economies, coalitions and shared commitment to mutual care, for science and technology studies (STS) scholar Dimitris Papadopoulos and migration scholar Vassilis Tsianos, the "migrant mobile commons" consists specifically of:

> the invisible knowledge of mobility that circulates between the people on the move (knowledge about border crossings, routes, shelters, hubs, escape routes, resting places; knowledge about policing and surveillance, ways to defy control, strategies against biosurveillance, etc.) but also between transmigrants attempting to settle in a place (knowledge about existing communities, social support, educational resources, access to health, ethnic economies, micro-banks, etc.). (2013, p. 191)

The focus on commoning practices is part of a wider conceptual commitment to acknowledge moments of autonomy in the experiences of so-called "do-it-yourself" (DIY) migrants (Collyer, 2007, p. 674). Peer-to-peer, horizontal, bottom-up production and the circulation of messages through unofficial channels is central to the information commons, offering informal back channels of communication exchange. Information practices in the Basque digital diaspora, for example, have been studied as an activist commons: Basque "digital diasporas are a commons for the exchange of information, dissemination of personal or general news, re-creation of cultural memories, and new cultural activities. An Activist Commons for People" (Alonso & Arzoz, 2010, p. 69). The Diasporic Information Environment Model points to how such information networks may traverse multiple geographic scales, including the local, transnational and the global (Srinivasan & Pyati, 2007).

Migrant information practices have historically evolved from pre-digital forms of small media and community media (see Chapter 5: Histories). However, digital migrant information practices have attracted the interest of the broad public, especially in the wake of the so-called European migration crisis in 2015.

For example, a *New Yorker* story popularized private Facebook groups set up by refugees for refugees, such as "Asylum and Immigration Without Smugglers" as a 'Tripadvisor' for refugees (Schmidle, 2015). The pooling and sharing of information beyond gatekeeping institutions is particularly urgent during the "perilous navigation" of irregularized migrant journeys "when knowing is intrinsically difficult" (Mollerup, 2020, p. 95).

Information commoning may be seen as a form of democratizating knowledge, which itself is "a form of silent resistance against restrictive immigration regimes" (Dekker & Engbersen, 2013, p. 414). Social media platforms have become important channels to make decisions about migration, navigate challenging journeys (Zijlstra & van Liempt, 2017) and decide upon migrant destinations. With the notion of "smart refugees", sociologist Rianne Dekker and colleagues (2018) conceptualize information-based decision-making practices among Syrian refugees living in the Netherlands. In particular, existing social ties and personal ties are trusted, which was also noted in a study among Syrians in Egypt (Mansour, 2018) and in environmentally-related migrants' decision-making practices in Bangladesh (Boas, 2020). Furthermore, migrants and refugees develop various informal strategies to validate rumours from unknown sources circulating on social media. Strategies include checking and triangulation of sources as well as validating information with trusted social networks and personal experiences (Dekker et al., 2018).

Refugees connect with family, friends, activists and ideologically close "influencers rather than official, national, formal and state-funded institutions, including humanitarian organizations, mainstream media, government institutions and journalists which are generally avoided" (Gillespie et al., 2016, p. 76). Public libraries seem to be an exception, as they have proved to be essential in providing a means of access and offering ICTs and services (Koseiejew, 2019). In particular, community-oriented mobile libraries such as the 'Libraries Without Borders' Ideas Box' and 'Library-in-a-Truck' initiatives are promising (Easton & Wells, 2020). Information commoning practices, therefore, may enlarge logistical autonomy as well as enable one to coordinate organizational independence, as gender and cultural studies scholars Moha Ennaji and Filippo Bignami (2019) note in their study with refugee and undocumented migrants in the city of Fès, Morocco. A feminist analysis sheds further light on how the commons is not neutral, but power-ridden. The migrant commons is, for example, intrinsically tied to gendered, racialized and sexualized 'politics of care', as gender and political science scholar Carla Angulo-Pasel demonstrated in her ethnographic fieldwork on migration journeys with Guatemalan, El Salvadoran and Honduran women in Mexico (2018, p. 127).

The various roles, shapes and forms that information commoning practices take have not been systematically studied. Migration studies scholars argue that migration patterns evolve as a result of how the commons, as networked "migrant feedback mechanisms", develop. However, "there is little attention paid to the wide, and growing, array of forms of network that may be implicated in feedback mechanisms" (Bakewell, Kubal & Pereira, 2016, p. 6). In future research on migrant and refugee information practices, at least three partly overlapping "network effects" (Epstein, 2008) can be distinguished: "network externalities", which are the common resources gathered and vetted by previous migrants, support and solidarity groups, activists and migrant businesses; "social learning", which are the specific practices that can be adopted to reduce the risks or costs of migration; and "normative influence", which are the positive or negative sanctions that help shape people's views on the pros and cons of specific migration practices (DiMaggio & Garip, 2011, p. 1888). In addition, we can distinguish between how feedback operates directly, through assisting or hindering the mobile subjects that may follow, and indirectly, for example through the establishment of a migration industry (travel agents, employment agencies, smugglers, etc.) (Bakewell et al., 2016, p. 8).

Migrant commons networks have thus become a "'backstage' for migrants". However, through monitoring behaviour and targeting specific mobile subjects in deterrence campaigns, governments increasingly seek to "colonize" this informal resource (Brekke & Thorbjørnsrud, 2020, p. 61), a dynamic we will further tease out in the next section.

Rights and repression

The third theme of migrant connectivity we consider is how migrant connections may both promote migrant rights and may be used for migrant repression. Drawing on the vocabulary of critical citizenship studies, researchers consider how migrants, activists and solidarity groups may mobilize networks to digitally perform human rights claims and pursue forms of digital citizenship. Following political scientist Engin Isin and sociologist Evelyn Ruppert (2020), the digital pursuit of migrants' political subjectivity revolves around 'digital acts', such as linking, networking, blogging, photographing, vlogging, tagging, tweeting, emailing, etc. in pursuit of justice, recognition and rights, which configure the dialectics of openings and closings:

> Openings are those possibilities that enable the performance of previously unimagined or unarticulated experiences of ways of being citizen subjects, a resignification of being speaking and acting beings. Openings are possibilities through which citizen subjects come into being. Closings, by contrast, contract and reduce possibilities of becoming citizen subjects. (Isin & Ruppert, 2020, p. 57)

Whereas migrant activism may shape political subjectivity in pursuit of openings, migrant visibility, voice and data traces also offer new opportunities for closings, through forms of surveillance, monitoring, control and repression. When migrants exercise their rights to freedom of movement, states develop new counter-technologies to regulate migrant movement (De Genova, 2017). The focus on openings and closures juxtaposes migrant persons and collectives from the grassroots activism level against the level of the state, but also draws attention to the internal clashes and striving that happens within transnational communities and diasporic constellations. Digital diasporas, for example, hold a controversial role in conflict and post-conflict resolution, as they "have variously been described as war-mongers, peace-builders, or ambivalent in their influence on conflict" (Van Hear & Cohen, 2017, p. 171). Below, for analytic purposes, we discuss the perspectives of digital migrant rights and migrant repression processes separately, although in practice they must be understood as an inherently interrelated thorny issue.

Digital rights

Unlike 'Politics' (with a capital 'P') from the perspective of top-down institutions, a performative approach emphasizes the processual and active dynamism of making rights claims from the bottom up. This perspective allows for a critical recognition and understanding of the subjects who seek to claim what the political philosopher Hannah Arendt phrased as the "right to have rights" (1951/2004) through speech-acts, such as claiming: "I, we, they have a right to" (Isin & Ruppert, 2020, p. 12). This approach is particularly generative for digital migration studies. First, it offers a means to address the political subjectivity of migrants who are *de facto* or *de jure* excluded from national citizenship. The focus is on citizens not as subjects bearing sovereign rights, but as "performative rights-claiming subjects" (ibid., p. 12). Second, it proposes how we can conceive of digital acts, which include words, images, sounds, videos, links and all other actions that shape the conditions of "anonymity, extensity, traceability, and velocity" under which "digital citizens-yet-to-come" are produced (ibid., p. 12). Below, we discuss refugee rights activism, digital diaspora advocacy and queer migrant activism.

Analysis of bottom-up forms of performative migrant resistance is often conducted in conjunction with an autonomy of migration perspective (Nyers & Rygiel, 2012) and critical border studies (Stierl, 2020). For example, in political science, Kim Rygiel studied migrants' practices of citizenship in the informal refugee camp of Calais, France, focusing on "the ways in which migrants assert themselves as political subjects by making claims against certain perceived injustices and inequalities and through collective action" (2011, p. 6). Maurice Stierl similarly foregrounds and amplifies "the stories of people who subvert borders by crossing them, or who refuse to be crossed by them", recognizing, for example, (1) practices of dissent, including the confrontational protest of hunger strikes in refugee camps in Germany, (2) practices of excess, such as of those seeking to escape from lives in limbo in Greece, and (3) practices of solidarity, such as the 24/7 Alarm Phone transborder coalition that seeks to support precarious movement and end the massive loss of live in the Mediterranean Sea (Stierl, 2020, p. 1). Elisabeth Olivius (2019), in her work with Burmese women activists in

Thailand, documented how they perform acts of insurgent citizenship from their subject positions as refugees, ethnic minorities and women, *vis-à-vis* humanitarian organizations, the Myanmar government and exclusionary nation-building.

In recent years, attention has grown for the specific digitally-mediated means through which migrants may assert themselves. In particular, the prize-winning non-fiction book *No friend but the mountains: Writings from Manus Prison* (2018), by the Kurdish-Iranian Behrouz Boochani, strengthened public awareness of the inhuman offshore processing policy of the Australian government. Boochani spent six years in Papua New Guinea, mostly in the Manus Regional Processing Centre, during which time he wrote countless journalistic pieces as well as his book using smuggled smartphones to send WhatsApp text and voice messages to his translator Omid Tofighian. For Boochani, his writing is "first and foremost, an act of resistance" (Boochani & Tazreiter, 2019, p. 370). He explains: "We need our own kind of language – a free language – to represent our situation and to describe the [offshore immigration detention] system, how it works, and how life is under it" (ibid., pp. 370–371). With his writing, he aims to "show that refugees are people, just like you. Refugees are not angels, but they are not evil either. They are people. Simply people, like you and me" (ibid.). Through poetic reflections, for example, he represents everyday life experiences of this dehumanizing and extractive policy:

This is what life has become, after all … /

This is one model constructed for human life /

Killing time by leveraging the queue as a technology /

Killing time through manipulating and exploiting the body /

The body left vulnerable /

The body an object to be searched /

Examined by the hands of others /

The body susceptible to the gaze of others /

A program for pissing all over life. (Boochani, 2018, p. 228)

Media and communication scholars have addressed the various modalities of digital claim-making practices among various migrant subjects and groups across the world. Smartphone and social media practices of fellow refugees kept in Australian-managed offshore detention centres have been theorized to sustain "unmediated forms of self-represented witnessing" (Rae, Holman & Nethery, 2018, p. 479). The potential and limitations of "acoustic agency" through podcasting by Australian refugee detainees have also been explored, alongside the required practice of "earwitnessing" detention: a dedication to responsible and political listening to testimonies of injustice (Rae, Russell & Nethery, 2019,

p. 1036). With the notion "communicative acts of citizenship", media scholar Luděk Stavinoha (2019) analyses how refugees have mobilized media networks on the Greek island of Chios.

Undocumented activist migrants in New York City, share online and offline experiential, partial and oppositional stories that function as "digital reclaimant narratives", which offer a means of coping, self-actualization, responsibility and mitigation of uncertainty (Bishop, 2019, p. 108). Based on ethnographic fieldwork with low-wage immigrant workers in Los Angeles, Sasha Costanza-Chock developed the concept of "transmedia organizing" to understand how social movement media-making is linked to concrete opportunities for action and protest (2014, p. 50). Haitians who moved to Brazil after the 2010 earthquake were found to create "micro-spaces of autonomy and agency" in appropriating digital media to counter hegemonic racialized representations (Cogo, 2019, p. 82). African migrants in Johannesburg recorded videos with their smartphones to chronicle the neglect and abuse perpetrated by home affairs officials and circulated them on WhatsApp. In this way, they "shift surveillance from themselves to junior officials" (Mlotshwa, 2019, p. 235).

A parallel focus has been on collective mobilization, activism, civic engagement and diplomacy enacted through digital diasporas. Digital diasporas have been found both to support their homeland through diasporic nationalism, nation branding and reputation management and to hold homeland governments accountable. The Uyghur digital diaspora, for example, is "highly political", in contrast to the Uyghur digital presence in China, which is strongly self-censoring (Reyhan, 2012, p. 3). Uyghur communities in the digital diaspora mobilize Facebook groups and sites to articulate their political identity (NurMuhammed et al., 2016) and Uyghur citizen media is in competition with Chinese state media (Culpepper, 2012; Witteborn, 2023). Similarly, Nigerians living abroad act as citizen journalists, mobilizing their digital diaspora to respond to and help reshape Nigerian national policies (Kperogi, 2020).

Collective activism, protest and rallying has particular salience among conflict-generated diasporas. In the early days of the internet, BOSNET was set up by Bosnian diaspora IT specialists to pioneer forms of "digital diaspora diplomacy" (Hasić & Karabegović, 2020, p. 103). They had to resort to this channel to perform "unscripted, uncoded and unregulated" engagement such as collecting and sharing information and rallying for the independence of their homeland. In recent years, Tamil and Palestinian diasporas have established strong digital presences, which function as "transnational advocacy networks", for example through digital calls for self-determinization, autonomy and secession (Kumar, 2018). Through "infopolitics", Eritreans in exile digitally challenge the sovereignty of the Eritrean government (Bernal, 2014). These examples illustrate how migrant collectives do digital diaspora diplomacy and activism in the absence of regular diplomatic tools which cannot be used as a result of conflict, civil war or in fear of prosecution.

A final strand of digital migrant activism concerns the outward-oriented activities of migrant persons and collective queer diasporas who are in search of sexuality justice, through challenging patriarchy and the criminalization of homosexuality, and maintaining the community against the grain of heteronormativity and binary gender policing. In response to India's court ruling criminalizing homosexuality, the Indian "digital queer diaspora" engaged in online and offline public protests on December 15, 2013, "the Global Day of Rage", uniting people from 18 cities across continents (Dasgupta, 2017, p. 143). Through functions like live-streaming, the social media platform *Rela* (热拉) is used among Chinese queer women in the diaspora in Australia and elsewhere to manage intimate transnational relations and thereby critique the dominant normative expectation of heteronormative family life (Li, 2020). As a strategic silent form of "queer slacktivism" (Otu, 2021, p. 46), *Ghanaweb.com* is a news and entertainment website used to debate African heteronationalism among Ghanaians in the diaspora. Somali women living in Cape Town, South Africa, were found to use phones and social media to negotiate patriarchic and traditional social expectations of women (Brudvig, 2019, p. 152). The "radical queer epistemic network", established by queer Kurdish activists in London, shows how they connect homeland struggles over race and class with hostland struggles over the imagination of Kurdistan (Sandal, 2020, p. 81). These digital processes of rights-claiming have not gone unnoticed. As a result of gaining public visibility, these practices are also increasingly met with repressive state and community responses, which we address in the section below.

Digital repression

In general, it must be noted that so far studies in political science, migration and media studies have foregrounded digital rights rather than repression. Researchers generally "neglect to address how ICTs globalize regimes' methods of social control and impact anti-regime diaspora" (Moss, 2018, p. 265). This is an important lacuna that warrants greater critical scrutiny, as the few recently emerging studies on long-distance and "networked authoritarianism" (ibid.) that do exist indicate. Authoritarian states in the Gulf, Russia, Kazakhstan, Iran and China, among others, monitor overseas populations outside their own territories. The authoritarian state, through so-called "extraterritorial authoritarian practices", follows its populations abroad "and includes or excludes them, as subjects to be repressed and extorted, as clients to be co-opted, or as patriots to be discursively manipulated" (Glasius, 2018, p. 180).

For example, with the aim of countering the political opposition of labour migrants and exiled activists through surveillance, social pressure and detention, Uzbekistan extends its domestic repression beyond its national borders, establishing new illiberal transnational "spatialities of stateness" (Lewis, 2015, p. 155). When using the Russian social media platform *VKontakte*, post-Soviet migrants in Germany, for example, face the ideological discursive "soft power" of Russia. This includes encounters with Euroscepticism and the mobilization of pseudo-states in what is now war-torn Eastern Ukraine in their transnational net-working practices (Golova, 2020, p. 264). With an eye on remittances and educational opportunities, Tunisia, Morocco, Jordan and Turkey facilitate cross-border mobility as a developmental opportunity and simultaneously extend a "long arm of the state" and "securitize its diaspora policy" (Tsourapas, 2020, p. 351).

As a specific form of transnational authoritarianism, Turkey weaponizes its diaspora to monitor and surveil the exiled Gulen Movement (Baser & Ozturk, 2020). Research with pro-revolution Syrians demonstrates that anti-regime diasporas face increasing and divergent forms of "digitally enabled transnational repression", including systematic surveillance, threat and disruption by pro-regime agents (Moss, 2018, p. 277). Another example of the transnational repression toolkit includes "proxy punishment", to refer to the manipulation of activists abroad by abusing non-activist families at home (Moss, Michaelsen & Kennedy, 2022, p. 75). These developments further demonstrate the growing urgency to address the interplay of cross-border migration and security beyond the dominant focus of the Global North. Underlying these new developments we can discern patterns of digitized, extraterritorial state and non-state governmentality as well as community policing based on following the digital traces of migrants (Diminescu, 2020).

Alongside states monitoring and harassing diasporic populations abroad, non-state actors in the digital diasporas "can varyingly contribute towards peacebuilding processes or perpetuate conflict" (Toivanen & Baser, 2020, p. 47; see also Brinkerhoff, 2009). For example, overseas supporters of the Liberation Tigers of Tamil Eelam (LTTE) and the Kurdistan Workers' Party (PKK) have intimidated and spread fear among Sri Lankan Tamils in the diaspora and hegemonically-dominated international Kurdish communities, respectively. Such complex intra-diaspora-community dynamics can be teased out through the notion of participatory or "diasporic authoritarianism" (Adamson, 2020, p. 162).

Intra-community monitoring and policing also happens along lines of gender, sexuality and generation, among others. A heavy burden lies on the shoulders of "diasporic daughters', as Youna Kim found in her study of Korean, Japanese and Chinese women living and studying in the West. Their 'do-it-yourself' migrant biographies were questioned through media forums (Kim, 2011, p. 3). *Huaren.us*, a discussion forum popular among female Chinese immigrants to the USA shows a normative embrace of "re-feminization", where traditional gender roles that valorize domesticity and motherhood are foregrounded (Huang, 2020, p. 172). A similar intersection of patriarchy, Confucianism and migration impact upon some Korean transient migrant women in the USA as "every moment of their transnational lives seemed to be one of just waiting for a baby to materialize" (Lee, 2020, p. 97). The digital presence of Somali migrant women in Cape Town proved, for some, to offer only "false agency", as their personal autonomy about their body and decision-making were restricted through a reinforcing of a transnational gendered "burden of family honour" (Brudvig, 2019, p. 165).

Conclusions

In this chapter, we outlined debates on migrant connectivity by focusing on the three themes of geography, information and rights. Researchers disagree about the assumptions and consequences of these themes. Migrant connections have paradoxical results:

- Migrant connections generally span across geographies. Migrant networks should thus be seen as inherently including transnational and local integrative processes. However, scholars seldomly recognize the synergetic relations between the two. Most often their interrelationships are either ignored or addressed as antagonistic, or integration is added onto transnationalism and vice versa.
- Understandings of migrant information practices range from a fractured landscape characterized by precarity to a communal information landscape maintained from below on the basis of peer-to-peer exchanges.
- Migrant networking can serve grassroots digital rights claims from migrants themselves, but can also serve forms of digital repression from states or internal community forces.

Rather than approaching the two sides of each of these migrant connectivity debates as being mutually exclusive, we can draw on the term 'paradox' to move beyond the limitations of binary thinking. Through the paradox we can question "the monolithic" nature of a conceptual debate and address the disciplinary "politics of fragmentation" (Ponzanesi, 2004, p. xiv).

It might seem self-contradictory to acknowledge how, for example, migrant connectivity enables new forms of rights claims as well as forms of governmental and inter-community repression. However, through embracing this contradiction we can get a better understanding of how apparent oppositions are deeply relational and co-constitutive. Seen as paradoxes, we can begin to untie the conceptual knots in order to situate various relevant perspectives in a broader continuum, and also establish the grounds needed to acknowledge the complexities and divergent outcomes of many connectivity practices. This is not to say that in our work on migrant connectivity we should uniformly incorporate all the various perspectives listed above – that would be practically impossible. However, referencing digital integration scholarship in transnational communication journal articles, for example, is a simple way to recognize the multiplicity of migrant connectivity. This way, we can become more accountable in terms of how any foregrounded perspective offers a partial view. Additionally, besides its potential as a conceptual move to make ambiguities generative, the notion of paradox can also serve a purpose in countering public discourse (e.g. the dominant view linking transnational migrant media use to segregation and as an indicator of failed integration).

Research Dialogue III: Dana Diminescu on the connected migrant, e-diasporas, migration traceability and delayed presence

Dana Diminescu is an Associate Professor in Sociology at Télécom Paris Engineering School in France, where she coordinates the DiasporasLab. Diminescu's work is foundational for digital migration studies. With "The connected migrant: An epistemological manifesto" (2008), the sociologist Diminescu set the agenda for the study of migration and digital connectivity. Her large E-Diaspora Atlas research team pioneered methodological approaches. Most notably, the team developed the graph visualization software Gephi and generated important new empirical data about digital diaspora formation (see www.e-diasporas.fr).

1. What motivated you to write the connected migrant manifesto?

When I first developed my ideas, we were at the height of the transnational studies theories, and, at the end of the studies on migratory circulation, which Alain Tarrius first (e.g. 1995), then Michel Peraldi (e.g. 2001) and the whole Migrinter group (Poitiers, France, see http://migrinter.labo.univ-poitiers.fr), developed during the 1990s (for an overview of French theorizing on migratory formations, see De Tapia, 2010). I was very close to them, and they inspired me a lot. My first studies, devoted in particular to the migration of Romanians in Europe, were clearly part of this line of thought (e.g. Diminescu, 2002). Towards the end of the 1990s, I was seized by the field and by the arrival of mobile phones in the hands of migrants. That's when I took a different direction.

My positioning, if I may say so, is rather post-Sayad. I was inspired also by Nina Glick Schiller, with whom I had exchanges at the very beginning of her theory on transnational bonds (e.g. Glick Schiller, Basch & Blanc-Szanton, 1992). The theory of Abdelmalik Sayad was fundamental for me to explain the era of the connected migrant, which began 20 years ago and continues until today. In his famous article "Le phénomène migratoire, une relation de domination" ["The migratory phenomenon, a relationship of domination"] (1981), Sayad explains that studies on migration are studies on absentees and absences, hence the title of his book La double absence: Des illusions de l'émigré aux souffrances de l'immigré [The double absence: The illusions of the emigrant to the suffering of the immigrant] *(1999).*

I think, with Sayad, that presence and absence are like two sides of the same coin; that they are two constituent aspects of the migrant experience. Simply, with the arrival of ICT devices, the quality of presence changed considerably. We are faced with a connected presence: contact is instantaneous, potentially permanent and can be easily (re-)activated, often on a daily basis. For Sayad, immigration results in a presence and emigration in an absence; the paradox of the study of emigration is that it is a study of absence and of the absent.

This leaves little scope to grasp how presence may be possible in spite of absence, and that migrants may only be partially absent, even though their physical bodies may be absent. ICTs impact and change the picture: our body is always more (or more and more) involved in communication and presence at a distance. This is why I say that the uprooted person, as a paradigmatic figure of the 'absent' migrant world, is fading away. We can witness the emergence of another figure, which admittedly is still ill-defined, but which we can see corresponds to that of a migrant who may live a life following a 'logic of multi-level presence'.

2. **Where you do situate your work on the connected migrant, e-diasporas and migration traceability in the research area of digital migration studies?**

Yes, for me these three concepts are key concepts of a digital sociology of migration. Thank you for including them! Generally speaking, what I mean by digital migration studies is a field of study of migration in relation to information and communication technologies (ICTs). It is also a sub-field of digital sociology, in the sense of Dominique Boullier (2019) or Deborah Lupton (2014), for example. This branch of sociology uses the digital data of various social phenomena as today's raw empirical material. Whether it is traces from a digitized historical archive (e.g. migrants' letters from the eighteenth century) or indexical traces of logged social media use or smartphone activity, digital migration studies are fully situated in the field of digital humanities and computational social sciences.

Long before digital migration studies became a research area in its own right, for me it was above all a scientific, exploratory programme that was based on the epistemological manifesto that I wrote in 2003, published in French first (Diminescu, 2005), then in English (Diminescu, 2008). I say an exploratory programme because nothing had been demonstrated in this field before, and I spent quite a few years proving that, with the deployment of ICTs, there are fundamental, performative aspects that radically change the lives of migrants and that push us to question the vision and the whole epistemological and methodological approach that we previously used to deal with migrations before.

Now, reflecting on the methodology I used, yes, I have created, I realized later, a complex methodological framework (which included the use of algorithms inspired by data sciences) to analyze data from the different digital practices of migrants and their resulting data traces, but at the same time I have never abandoned the classic methods of investigation to capture the complex, situated and contextual worlds of migrants. Interviews, situational observation, etc. are all still valuable tools in my sociological work.

We cannot delegate all our research to machines. When it comes to big data – and you covered a lot of examples in your book – analyzing migrant digital trace data might indeed benefit from working with algorithms and artificial intelligence (AI). But even in this case, it is necessary to understand that the nature and the methods to collect this data are not neutral. There are situations when our own human analytical skills are more fair, humane and efficient than a machine. Often, machine-based methods are complementary, and traditional fieldwork remains a key means of validating the results obtained via algorithmic pattern detection or visualization. Note also that the data collected from digital platforms is increasingly inaccessible for academic researchers. Data produced by users of platforms has become a commercial property, a commodity owned by a company like Facebook/Meta or Twitter, who seek to monetize it. As a result, it is increasingly difficult for us to access them without paying. In your book, you have shown the complexity induced by ICT in the life of migrants and for research in migration, media and internet studies.

3. **In reviewing studies of migrant connectivity, we discussed the three main themes of geography (transnationalism-integration), information and rights. Do you recognize any additional important ones?**

Your breakdown is very clear. Particularly when considering that the spaces of connectivity are increasingly surveilled and militarized – think of the smart border – I can tell you what I think will be important to develop further in the future critical landscape of digital migration studies. If a student or an early career researcher asks me today by what approach she should study the connected migrant, and in general understand the issue of connectivity, I would suggest to her the field of complex systems. Today, no matter whether migrant or non-migrant, we evolve – largely invisible – in a digital universe. Digital technology places us in an environment, in a digital infrastructure that did not exist before. The migrant has learned to navigate and switch instantly between several worlds of existence. The challenge for future generations is to study and to account for this complexity.

4. **Geographical scale is the first analytic perspective discussed in this chapter. What is the explanatory potential of a geographical multi-scalar approach, in a context where digital practices and governmentality have both proliferated?**

The appropriation of ICTs by migrants has followed the evolution of digital technological innovation in all areas of life (including travel, policy and administration). Digital life is now supported by multi-media and digitally augmented to the point of saturation. If, for example, long-distance communication (with all the videocall technologies) was seen in a positive light because it responded to the compulsion for proximity that each migrant experienced, it is now performed as a duty, a duty to be present and online always. This has led to the configuration of an entire "alone together" community (Turkle, 2012). But this saturation does not call into question the central principle of my manifesto. Since what I wanted to show is this effect of preponderance of presence, even if this presence remains incomplete, the lines of continuity remain in the picture. Today, in my definition of the connected migrant I'm less 'rosy' (see Diminescu, 2020). With one my friends, the philosopher Bernard Stiegler, I think that the technology is pharmacological (Stiegler, 2013).

For Stiegler, all technology is pharmakon. It is at the same time poison and medicine. Just like medicine and poison, technologies do not act uniformly everywhere for everyone. Pharmakon is both something which allows you to take care and something to be aware of, to pay attention to: it is a curative power in the same measure as it is a destructive power. This 'at the same time' is characteristic of pharmacology, which comprehends both danger and agency. Thus, all technology is inherently and irreducibly ambivalent. From the point of view of a positive pharmacology, ICTs have met important, precise needs of migrants. First, they are taken up to fuel a compulsion of proximity which every migrant experiences. This compulsion seeks to alleviate negative emotions and to de-stress, to stay connected remotely, to find a new home, to integrate in society and culture, and especially to establish new networks and to find a job or education. Additional examples include the transfer of transnational remittances, as well as to better secure dangerous crossings and journeys and to connect with networks on the move. But at the same time, newly developed technologies also bring new constraints: tracking, privacy concerns, divergent patterns of digital literacy make it hard to navigate increasingly detached and impersonal administrative websites, new digitized forms of ghettoization and, finally, the emotional duty to be present, which weighs strongly on the shoulders of migrants.

5. **How do you understand the information practices of migrants?**

This is a very serious subject that we cannot summarize here. I will just emphasize one important observation. The so-called 'European refugee crisis' of 2015 has generated a kind of 'technophoria'. There have been many initiatives to find socio-technical solutions to the problems faced by refugees. We have identified more than a hundred initiatives, applications and platforms for refugees. We created a database detailing the content of the applications according to 16 indicators. In collaboration with the Simplon school, the database study was complemented with a field approach in September 2018, when refugees themselves evaluated 30 database entries. This allowed for an assessment of the performance, design and usefulness of the applications from the point of view of intended users. The evaluation revealed that refugees needed a wider offer of applications dedicated to language learning as well as allowing them to find information, including official information regarding their asylum application and integration in France. But what was also observed was that the vast majority of these applications are not and will never be used by refugees. Refugees use applications and platforms like everyone else (Facebook, WhatsApp, Google translation, Maps) that are not specifically dedicated to them (see also Bustamante Duarte et al., 2018; Nguyen & Nguyen, 2022).

6. **How do you understand the relationship between digital rights and repression?**

One of the striking features of the online migrant collective is their comet-like life. These peoples organize themselves and are active first and foremost on the Web: their practices are those of a community whose interactions are 'enhanced' by digital exchange. We are also talking here about dispersed collectives, a heterogeneous entity whose existence rests on the elaboration of a common direction, a direction not defined once and for all, but which is constantly renegotiated as the collective evolves. Activist or non-activist migrant collectives are unstable collectives because they are redrawn by every newcomer. They are self-defined, as they grow or diminish not by inclusion or exclusion of members, but through a voluntary process of individuals joining or leaving them – simply by establishing hyperlinks or removing them from websites or platforms. That's why I think that with all the software in the world, it's quite difficult to anticipate and trace the multiplicity of links between and activity of refugees.

7. **What has been a key challenge or obstacle in studying migrant connectivity for you and your team?**

In the early 2000s, when I started my research on the connected migrant, there was a kind of inertia in the field of migration studies. The figure of the uprooted migrant was still very dominant and uncontested. But I had real support from the Fondations de la Maison des Sciences de l'Homme, which in the early 2000s hosted and financed my research programme (a little); and later by Agence Nationale de la Reserche (ANR, the French Research Agency), and my digital school, Institut Mines-Télécom, now a school of the Institut Polytechnique de Paris. I also squatted at the beginning with other institutions, such as INA (National Audiovisual Institute) or Orange (telecom provider), both of which were not at all related to migration but were ready to experiment with me. Certainly, the most exciting challenge has been to prove scientifically what I launched in the manifesto: an epistemological renewal with an innovative methodological toolkit that goes with it.

8. **What practical recommendations would you give those aspiring to study migrant connectivity?**

I teach my PhD students to always start with a small inventory of terminals and the technical systems individuals navigate daily, as Dominique Boullier calls it (Boullier, 2015). So start with something that a connected migrant carries on their body which provides access to digital realms. Through this inventory, we can quickly understand their digital universe.

The environment can be located in the host country, in the destination country or elsewhere. The connected migrants carry their 'home' with them via their mobile phone, bank card, biometric passport, etc. These systems carry belongings to territories, institutions, banks, family, professional and friendship networks.

Once we know where connected migrants are browsing, we can also deduce where they leave digital traces, in which digital infrastructure, and ask ourselves by what method we can or cannot involve them and research logged data. Then we can start building our corpus according to our research questions and the findings of our explorations.

9. **What future themes, topics or dynamics of migrant connectivity should researchers pay more attention to?**

There are many interesting topics, but, for me, I think that a great task will be to define and understand presence at a distance (and also absence) that each migrant experiences today (and that what everyone experienced during the Covid-19 lockdowns). In particular, I'm trying to understand better what it is to live life in 'décalage', or delayed presence, which is the hidden misfortune of the contemporary hyperconnected individual.

Research Dialogue IV: Amanda P. Alencar on the socialities, spatialities and temporalities of digital connections

Amanda P. Alencar is Associate Professor in the Department of Media and Communication, Erasmus University Rotterdam, the Netherlands. Alencar has specialized in empirically tracing and conceptualizing how communication technologies shape the mobility and socio-cultural integration of refugees in various geographical contexts. She is Chair of the Intercultural Communication Division of the International Communication Association (ICA), Associate Producer of the *Migration Podcast*, hosted by the International Migration Research Network (IMISCOE), and she coordinates a digital training programme for students with a refugee background. For more information, see amandaalencar.com.

1. **How did you come to study media, migration and connectivity?**

   I spent most of my childhood and teenage years moving from one city to another because of my father's job. He was employed by a state bank. Every year, he was transferred. We moved to seven towns in under nine years. When I became acquainted with my new neighborhood, school and friends, my family needed to be back on the road again. Moving from one town to another in Brazil almost felt like crossing international borders. The communication technologies available in the 1980s made it difficult to stay in touch with people from a different city. Phone calls were very expensive and not all households had a landline phone. I used to write letters to friends and even managed to reunite with some of them years later. Feelings of distance and disconnection significantly impacted on my feelings and experiences of belonging as a child and teenager trying to fit in, and ultimately my understanding of place as an adult.

   I migrated from Brazil nearly two decades ago and had the opportunity to live, study and work in three different countries (the USA, Spain and the Netherlands). As a researcher, educator and a migrant woman from Latin America, I experienced discrimination but could also benefit from opportunities and privileges brought by research mobility. My trajectory and contradictory experiences of place-making have shaped my research as well as the way I position myself as a digital migration scholar.

2. **Can you situate yourself in the research area of digital migration studies?**

   My research interests lie in the intersection of digital communication technologies and forced migration. I combine methodologies and theories drawn from the social sciences and humanities to create cross-disciplinary research into how digital media are shaping refugee mobility and integration processes. In the past ten years, I have investigated the adoption of digital technologies among refugees and how this intersects with possibilities for integration and place-making in host countries. Through studies with Syrians, Afghans and Eritreans settling in Amsterdam and Rotterdam, the Netherlands, I mapped the role of individual and structural forces, including the network capital, policies and media perception of refugees, in the ways refugees engage in social media in their daily lives.

A very important aspect to be highlighted here concerns the specific meanings refugees assign to these technologies while experiencing challenges, as well as opportunities and barriers for social and economic participation. I have also studied the ways in which migrant groups engage with news media and how these practices reflect and shape their aspirations of acculturation in the Netherlands and Spain. Keen to understand refugees' adoption of ICTs in resource-scarce environments, I began to study technology appropriation in refugee journeys. Specifically, my research investigates the strategies Syrians have developed to sustain connectivity, establish social connections and avoid digital surveillance during their journey to Europe. This study further points to the overlooked material and psychological stressors influencing refugees' smartphone usage. More recently, I have combined data from refugees' technology experiences with an examination of digital governance and networks of refuge.

3. **In the chapter we address migrant connectivity as deeply situated and contextual. How would you compare digital migration research in the Global North and the Global South?**

In my recent work, I examine digital precarity in the context of Venezuelan forced migration in Brazil. In the so-called 'Global South', connectivity is still often described as an exceptional need. The idea of exceptionalism surrounding technology use among refugees makes it challenging to think of refugees as tech-savvy users who creatively and tactically engage with digital media technologies.

The needs-based approach to technology adoption contributes to reinforcing simplistic views of refugee populations as 'others'. At the same time, a perspective on needs when it comes to digital use in low-tech environments risks essentializing mobility and development processes in Southern contexts. Commonly, large humanitarian agencies and organizations in the Global North make decisions about the needs of refugees (and what constitutes their needs) and put in place digital initiatives to tackle the challenges of refugee protection and settlement. In many cases, these technological solutions are not sustainable in forced migration contexts, such as refugee camps and shelters, where access to connectivity is problematic.

Hence, the question of why connectivity remains a problem in these contexts is a very pertinent issue that continues to reflect normative understandings of Northern nations as promoting development, while failing to consider local communication infrastructures, and clashing with social imaginaries, cultures, traditions and literacies of refugee populations. For the most part, refugees in Brazil are not recognized as competent citizens with unique voices. This is not different from the refugee situation at border spaces in Europe.

In this regard, it is also important to highlight that diverse migration policies and digitalized responses from management actors have an impact on the place-making and integration experiences of refugees. For example, the Netherlands is an interesting case of restrictive migration policies but excellent digitalization support, whereas Brazil has less advanced digital infrastructures with progressive policies.

4. **What are the methodological challenges you face and how do you negotiate them?**

Mixing qualitative and digital ethnographic methodologies with participatory approaches has shaped my research on forced migration and technologies. The main methodological issues I encountered in using these methods concern their application and necessary adaptations, depending on the concerned population, as well as in the negotiation of ethical decision-making in different forced migration contexts. For example, limited access to connectivity and a digital device among Venezuelans in Northwestern Brazil required a very different research design compared to the methodological approaches adopted with refugee communities in Europe. Similarly, differences in migrants' digital literacies and appropriations required negotiations of research protocols that were more aligned with participants' circumstances and situations, and levels of research engagement.

The legal position of refugees can also play an important role, especially considering that the digital traces and data of people seeking asylum are being used by governments to assess visa applications. This certainly had an impact on refugees' engagements as well as on their perceptions of their participation in my longitudinal studies on technology and forced migration in Europe (the Netherlands, Spain, the UK). Refugees without legal status are hesitant to use certain social media platforms in fear of it affecting their possibilities to legalize their situation, or to have access to future employment opportunities. Therefore, I believe it is extremely important to engage in conversations with the populations studied before and during the development of the research design; these conversations should guide the decisions and protocols adopted. For example, in a WhatsApp research project I conducted (with Julia Camargo, researcher from the Federal University of Roraima, Brazil) with Venezuelans in Brazil, we incorporated multi-scalar methodological approaches (see Camargo et al., 2022). These allowed us to consider the different levels of digital mobilities experienced by participants, including negotiations of identity, belonging, well-being, expansion of social networking, digital literacies and livelihoods, and how these are produced and reconfigured across different scales in a spatial, social and temporal sense.

This multi-scalar approach allowed us to trace mobilities and connectivities, as well as their engagement with other actors and recurrent topics, interests and activities. Our digital ethnographic research was guided through the activities of participants – following the tenets of actor-network theory – while also tracing broader political and economic forces affecting their everyday lives. Important ethical issues had to be negotiated. Through an open and collaborative space, we collectively produced guidelines on how to share content and interact safely in the WhatsApp group. We designed an activity to discuss and produce ethical guidelines regarding (audiovisual) data collection with the participants. Risk assessment continued in the face of issues emerging along the research project, such as conflicts between participants and sharing of suspicious information in the group.

While this multi-scalar method has been particularly useful to understand the experiential and structural dimensions of Venezuelans' everyday lives in Brazil, there are important ethical, political and social challenges that need to be considered if we replicate this methodology with refugee populations in Europe or other contexts. Longitudinal mediated accounts of transformations and continuities in migrants' lives need to foreground these challenges.

5. **In reviewing studies of migrant connectivity, we explore the three main themes of geography (transnationalism-integration), information and rights. How do you relate to those themes and where do you see gaps in our scholarship?**

The notions of transnationalism and integration were developed by scholars of migration studies to conceptualize the processes by which immigrants build and maintain simultaneous connections between their societies of origin and settlement. Transnationalism and integration account for the persistence of nation-states as structural frames in the analysis of migrants' practices and bridge-building across borders. In my work, I focus in particular on the concept of translocality, which highlights the intersections that favour hybridity, diasporic relations and various cultural affiliations, while still acknowledging the importance of territorial borders, state actors and national identity politics.

This analytical perspective is particularly relevant for media and migration scholarship because it recognizes not only refugees' prior sense of belonging and attachment to places left behind and their related trauma. Translocality also highlights the agency of refugees in negotiating place and belonging through everyday digital practices, which also includes their ability to mobilize information to claim their rights (health, education, connections with individuals and institutions). Translocality also recognizes the importance of considering power relations beyond the direct sphere of influence of individual refugees, such as the case of top-down politicized and humanitarian adoption of technology in refugee protection and integration. Finally, the focus on translocality allows for mapping and assessing the different communities online around refugee issues as well as the ways in which these communities are connected in the digital space, both locally and transnationally.

6. What would you recommend to those aspiring to study migrant connectivity?

I believe that the study of migrant connectivity requires constant attention to the volatility of technology and migration processes. This is particularly relevant in a moment where digitalization, datafication and automation technologies and systems (e.g. Artificial Intelligence and Machine Learning) are increasingly shaping the experiences and governance of migrants. Further, it is also important to consider the unpredictability and uncertainty of mobility processes, especially in the (post) Covid-19 pandemic context. Changing technologies and mobilities affect research design, practice and ethics. Acknowledging the limitations and challenges of studying migrant connectivity, and working around them with responsibility, flexibility and sensibility, can contribute to generating research that is grounded and accounts for multiple ways of knowing, while also working towards social transformations and justice. Perhaps the most practical recommendation is the need to initiate and sustain collaborations with diverse stakeholders (community leaders, policy makers, practitioners, NGOs, humanitarian agencies) in your research. As we know, policy makers and practitioners *seem to have a very low tolerance of academic discourse. Yet, I think it is well worth the effort to establish these collaborations with suitable stakeholders in a way that is beneficial to them (e.g. avoiding a jargonistic style of communication) and that enables them to contribute and address their concerns, anxieties and interests, building bridges where they are needed to address refugee issues. This is fundamental for making progress in transforming practices of digital connectivity among migration governance actors, and that can benefit the concerned communities.*

7. **What future themes, topics or dynamics should digital migration researchers pay more attention to?**

Scholarship on digital connectivity and (forced) migration articulates the perspectives of migrants as individuals and publics, migration policy makers and practitioners and governance regimes, overlaid with a socio-technical approach to translocal and transnational networks as a socio-cultural, political and economic force. To develop a more holistic understanding of media and technology in the lives of migrants, it is necessary to integrate (digital) ethnographic methods of participation and observation into traditional research designs, as well as into big data analyses. This is very important to move away from the abstraction and isolation of media from migrants' contexts and practices of use.

Much uncertainty still exists about how different political contexts and priorities concerning immigration and integration, particularly in the Global South countries, impact differently on the intersection of technologies and refugee settlement. At the same time, there are still many unanswered questions about how differentiated digital governance infrastructures and policies impact migrants' experiences of settlement as well as how the attitudes and behaviours of the host society and host country's media towards migrants play a role in their digital practices.

3

Representations

Digital media, content such as selfies, music videos, memes, avatars, emojis, tweets, hashtags, dashboards or *TikTok* videos, may all represent migration and migrants. This chapter presents approaches to the study of digital representations of migration. We understand representation as the production of meanings through representational systems. Our particular focus is on the politics of representation, which invites us to study how representation becomes a battlefield over meaning-making of migration. *The British Dictionary* (2021) offers several useful definitions of the word representation:

1. The act or instance of representing; anything that represents, anything that is represented, a dramatic production of performance; a statement of facts.
2. The principle by which delegates act for a constituency; a body of representatives; an instance of acting for another.

In short, in the context of this chapter, representation refers to specific content that "stands in the place of" (Hall, 2013b, p. 2) particular migrant bodies through depictions, and particular actors who are in the position to "stand for" (ibid.) migrants. The interrelatedness of the dual character of representation becomes clear when considering the postcolonial theorist Gayatri Spivak's analysis of the problem of "speaking in the name of" oppressed people (1990a, p. 63), which often is the case for migrants. She draws on the double meaning of representation in the German language: first, in the sense of *Vertretung*, which means "speaking for", as in a political scenario where a member of parliament may represent her constituents in parliament, or a lawyer or journalist speaking for a particular group; second, in the sense of *Darstellung*, which means a "proxy or portrait" which can be made of someone or a group of people, and thus represent them in an aesthetic sense (Spivak, 1990b, p. 108). Thus, representation can be both taken to refer to *Vertretung*, or "speaking for", as in the case of politics when someone represents you by "stepping into your shoes", i.e. taking on a particular role that someone else has been doing. Second, *Darstellung* can be taken to refer to the aesthetics of the 'proxy and portrait' which can be made of you (Spivak, 1990b, p. 108). To get at the politics of representation, and the underlying struggles about who speaks about whom, why and how, and how misrepresentations can be challenged, these two sides of representation should be taken into account. For example, we may consider how representation works through *over-representing* some aspects (e.g. emphasizing racist, sexist or Islamophobic stereotypes in representing particular migrants groups) and *under-representing* others (e.g. ignoring the societal contributions or the vital roles of migrants in the economy). Below, we first theorize the politics of representation, before addressing how migrants are objectified in digital media representations, and consider digital self-representations as a site of potential migrant subjectivity and agency. The chapter ends with an overview and directions for future research.

The politics of representation

Following social and cultural constructivist understandings of representations, in line with post-structuralist and British Cultural Studies traditions, we here approach meaning-making as a dynamic, power-ridden and multi-directional, open-ended process. Representation, in its mediation of migration and difference, takes place in a dialectical relationship between media and society (Hegde, 2016; Siapera, 2011). Representation in this framework is assumed to result in certain discursive formations, which inscribe relations of power by articulating the parameters of "what is 'normal', who belongs – and therefore, who is excluded" (Hall, 2013a, p. xxv). No one actor can fully control the construction of meaning. There are hegemonic actors and gatekeepers who have the power to sustain particular monolithic and stereotypical representational "regimes of truth" (Foucault, 1977; Saha, 2021, p. 9), but whereas these regimes exclude and marginalize, there is always room for alternative systems of representation to challenge "discursive singularities" (Georgiou, 2006, p. 29). It is up to the scholar to read the instability of any representational conjuncture, as shaped by signification and contestation, but also the broader socio-cultural and material contexts. The literature, however, has largely reproduced the old divide in media and communications between studying media production and studying media audiences/consumption (Georgiou & Leurs, 2022).

In digital culture, this division is apparent from studies focusing on representation, on the one hand, and self-representation on the other. Below, representation and self-representations of digital migration are discussed, by pointing at how, respectively, regimes characterize institutionalized representational domains and how self-representation revolves around diverse repertoires. By attending to the multiplicity of representations of migration as regimes and repertoires, we acknowledge how access to and production of representation happens in a hierarchically structured terrain, dominated by privileged actors, which may help us to see why "certain representations belong to certain regimes" (Siapera, 2010, p. 132).

Media representation regimes

This first section discusses how migrants and diasporic groups are represented top-down by a selected, narrow group of more or less institutionalized gatekeepers. With the power to represent concentrated in the hands of dominant actors such as mainstream news media, humanitarian agencies, governments, corporations and community representatives, we can question which representations are made dominant, and which voices, identities and experiences are silenced. For this purpose, we can focus on how these actors, in making particular selections, give shape to specific regimes of representation. To specify, in their depiction of migration, the regimes of digital news media, digital identity systems, data visualizations, virtual reality and diasporic media can be said to perpetuate a "racialized regime of representation" (Hall, 2013c, p. 259). In other words, racial characteristics are often inscribed in the digital representation of specific subsets of mobile people. On the basis of binary oppositions, the complexities of particular migrant human beings are simplified and stereotyped. For example, refugees are typically reduced to unified masses with shared physical, phenotypical features and appearance.

Digital news media regime

The term 'digital news media' is used here as an umbrella term to describe mainstream, profit-driven multimedia news platforms. These represent migration in a broader political economy of attracting eye-balls and user clicks, in generating traffic and in pursuing virality. The racialization of migration in the digital news media is particularly evident in so-called 'crisis' situations where incompatibilities between groups are commonly reinforced for the purpose of containment and control, reducing complexity and denying legitimacy and recognition (Hegde, 2016).

First, the visual grammar of the 2015 European 'refugee crisis' (Georgiou & Zaborowski, 2017), for example, can be analyzed for how it reproduced fears by dehumanizing refugees as faceless zombies, as if EU countries and citizens were playing a video game to escape them (Zaborowski & Georgiou, 2019, p. 92). Furthermore, the smartphone wielding and selfie-taking refugee became a key trope. The refugee selfie was made into an ethico-political spectacle, which was found to function as a 'symbolical border' between deserving and undeserving refugees: rather than sharing refugee testimonies, voices or journeys, news stories included photos of refugees taking selfies as a means of distancing and estrangement (Chouliaraki, 2017, p. 78). The dichotomy of bodies that are naturalized into technology usage in digital news on refugees and the particular mobile bodies that are distanced from it betray the racialized and discriminatory regimes that digital technologies, despite their claims at neutrality, continue to reinforce (Leurs, 2016).

A second case in point is the racialized representation of mobile populations during the Covid-19 health pandemic (Hirata & Leurs, 2020). During spring 2020, anti-Asian discrimination grew as heads of state in the West used terms like 'Chinese Virus' and racist jokes like 'Kung Flu', which refer to Chinese traditional martial arts (Guardian Staff, 2020). These were seen to reinforce a 'Yellow Peril' theme, alongside representations of Asian migrants as a model minority, reverting back to the infectious disease epidemic of Yellow Fever (Shim, 1998) and portraying contemporary Chinese migrants in the UK, Europe and the US as unhygienic and dangerous aliens (Gao & Sai, 2021; Wang et al., 2021; Yu et al., 2020). In spring 2021, a new variant of the virus mutated in India and was dubbed the 'Indian variant' in digital news, which was similarly followed by a surge in anti-Indian racism against people of Indian descent in places like Singapore (Xinghui, 2021) and New Zealand (Ofren, 2021). Across these examples, the racist regime can be scrutinized by combining biological understandings of 'race' with cultural ones. These two instances, which illustrate the workings of the racialized regime of representation, are contemporary digital renderings of 'orientalism', a colonial representational system through which the West defined itself as modern and progressive and the Other as traditional, conservative, dangerous and backward (Said, 1979; see Chapter 5: Histories). As a sidenote, here we focused on popular, commercial news, but it is important to emphasize that publicly funded public service media (PSM), and in particular independent and investigative journalism, do remain important watchdogs, setting agendas for debate and holding governments to account. However, also in these domains, mediated solidarities are at risk of monetization and digital competition (Nikunen, 2019, p. 61). Besides popular news regimes, which stereotypically frame particular mobile bodies through racialization, social media platforms present us with another domain through which to study the digital politics of representing migration.

Social media regimes

With the growing popularity of social media platforms, media landscapes have become more complex and unpredictable. As an evolving "hybrid media system" (Chadwick, 2013), where old and new media logics interact, we can trace how power relations order this changing landscape: in contrast with mainstream news media, where power may be attached to a small group of more or less 'professional' actors, in social media power relations emerge out of networks consisting of 'professionals' and 'amateur' or everyday users. As a greater variety of people can publish their accounts (see the section on self-representation below), the hybridized media landscape results in a proliferation of voices and narratives. This development in turn impacts on the establishment of professional journalism, and the standing, status, access, influence and expertise of journalists. Besides studying the implications for professional journalism, there are various entry points to research the representation of migration on social media. Chadwick (2013), for example, urges us to consider the interrelated logics of social media representation of migration which include studying (1) the workings of the infrastructures that underpin journalism and the constitution, (2) how genres and norms of journalism are established and contested, (3) the behaviours of the content providers and users, and (4) the organizational contexts that set the contours of social media regimes.

The concept of networked publics was a dominant lens in the 2000s in the study of social media. This framework drew on an understanding of the characteristics of "persistence", "searchability", "replicability" and "scalability" of social media (boyd, 2010). Networked publics have been found to operate as regimes through the processes of networked gatekeeping and networked framing. On Twitter, elite and peripheral networks are shaped as a result of discursive markers such as hashtags, replies and mentions, alongside trending topics resulting from user traffic peaking in particular geographies and time-windows. The way social media regimes wield power can be teased out by studying the political economy, affordances and how ideas on social media circulate. For example, the power laws on Twitter work as follows: the top 10–20% of accounts, through their large following, disproportionally guide network discussions (Meraz & Papacharissi, 2016). Networked publics have been successful to a degree in impacting public debate and political agendas on social justice topics such as sexism (#metoo, e.g. Chandra & Erlingsdóttir, 2021), racism and police violence (#BlackLivesMatter, e.g. McIlwain, 2020; Sharma, 2013) and climate change (#FridaysforFuture, #climatestrike, e.g. Cole, 2021).

Social media have not had a similar impact on discussions about long-term migration and refugee justice. Anti-migrant sentiment has been fairly dominant, aside from short-term, intense, event-related outcries over migrant deaths and human right violations over push-backs, detention and family separation (#RefugeesWelcome, e.g. Siapera et al., 2018). For example, Farida Vis's research on the mediation of the death of 3-year-old refugee Aylan Kurdi on a beach in Turkey showed how the virality of the image (20 million views in 12 hours) momentarily changed the language of the debate on migration (Vis & Goriunova, 2015). In parallel to the news media regime, crisis situations can therefore compound stereotypes: during the Covid-19 pandemic scholars have shown how social media regimes amplify and counter anti-Asian and anti-Indian hate against migrants, where users assert themselves alongside bots (Ziems et al., 2020). To attend to the specificities of our changing hybrid media landscape, which is shaped by a growing distrust of information, an economy dictated by ever shorter attention spans, content saturation and gamification, digital anthropologist Crystal Abidin (2021) suggests that we shift attention from networked publics to "refracted publics" and attend to the key conditions of contemporary social media: "transience", "discoverability", "decodability" and "silosociality". Additional understudied terrains include the workings of algorithms in amplifying specific visuals and networks, and the functioning of automated and human content moderation (Jiménez Durán et al., 2022). In the next paragraph, we look at the institutionalized governance of migrant bodies through digital identification.

Digital identity regime

Institutionalized digital identity systems targeting migrants and refugees are commonly seen as a crucial 'enabler' for access to health care, education, food and other essential services. Recent initiatives, such as the global, public-private ID2020 Digital Identity Alliance and the World Bank's Identification for Development (ID4D), demonstrate trust in digital systems by governments, agencies and businesses for the purpose of "closing the identity gap" (ID2020, 2021). These initiatives reflect Sustainable Development Goal (SDG) 16.9, which covers the aim to provide legal digital identification to people globally by 2030. However, digital identification – understood here as the "conversion of human identities into machine-readable digital data" (Masiero & Bailur, 2021, p. 1) – is a double-edged sword that serves competing and unevenly addressed interests. Top-down digital identity representations are promoted under the banner of efficiency, knowability and provision (see Chapter 1: Infrastructures), but they are also inherently reductionist, fixing complex individuals and groups into specific patterns and categories of data points. Thus, although digital identity systems promise refugee sovereignty, they form a regime by reinforcing "monopolistic" state roles of classifying and sorting people (Cheesman, 2022, p. 137) on the basis of an exclusionary "bureaucratic bias" (Latonero et al., 2019, p. 23).

To capture the two-sidedness of digital identity regimes, we can draw on the concept of data justice developed by feminist, critical data, legal and STS scholars. From a standpoint of anti-discrimination, co-liberation and reflexivity (D'Ignazio & Klein, 2020), data justice seeks to attend to "fairness in the way people are made visible, represented and treated as a result of their production of digital data" (Taylor, 2017, p. 1). Socially and historically situated forms of "agency in action" recognize how, for example, non-mainstream populations from the margins and multiple "global souths" appropriate and resist data practices (Milan & Treré, 2019, p. 328). For example, drawing on a data justice framework, refugees in Lebanon, Jordan and Uganda experienced little agency over having their personal data included in the digital identity systems used by humanitarian organizations. Simultaneously, refugees were found to negotiate these digital identities and associated statuses to maximize access to services, employment and mobility (Schoemaker et al., 2021). Similarly, through a data justice lens, the digital identity regimes of displaced Rohingya populations in Bangladesh reveal that their exclusion is effectively baked into the IDs provided (Martin & Taylor, 2021).

Data visualization regime

Digital maps, data visualizations, infographics and interactive dashboards promising neutral, objective, distanced and rational accounts of migrant movement have become omnipresent representational repertoires across news media and governmental and humanitarian agencies. The data visualization regime is chiefly based on dataism, or the ideological "belief in objective quantification" and "trust in the (institutional) agents" that gather, analyze and share data (Van Dijck, 2014, p. 198), which often underpins their ideological orientation. However, critical cartography and critical data scholars have revealed that there is no such thing as an objective or neutral map. Every map, visualization and dashboard results from choices made during the gathering, cleaning, analyzing, selecting and presentation of datasets. We can critically question data visualizations by asking what information is selected for compilation, and why? What is shown and what is left out? Every map, visualization and dashboard thus projects its own worldview.

For example, maps made by Frontex – the EU's border agency – have been found to contrast sharply with the principles of contemporary geography. Instead, they reflect traditions of "propaganda cartography" (Van Houtum & Lacy, 2020, p. 196). From the perspective of critical cartography, maps of migration can be explored as evocative visual scripts: "iconotexts", as mediators of emotions, "iconobjects" and "actionable objects" that connect certain actors involved in migration (Presti, 2020, p. 911). From the perspective of media studies, the political dimensions of online migration data visualizations can be brought to the fore by addressing their "conventions" for example by collecting data through Google Image Scraper (Allen, 2021). From the perspective of journalism, the narrativity of data visualizations can be studied by addressing how people and movement are translated into data points, including the map axes, shapes, colours, projections and size of the visualizations. As is evident from Wibke Weber's analysis of the data visualization "Mass exodus: The scale of the Rohingya crisis", in the case of moving images, the editing, sequencing and the accompanying sound can be studied by focusing on the role and function of the voice-over alongside the volume, pitch, duration, tempo and rhythm as well as background music (2020, p. 303). Migrant data visualizations tell specific stories about migration, and future research on these representations should further counter the "god trick" (Haraway, 1988, p. 584) that is commonly played. Data visualizations do not come from nowhere. We scholars should more firmly situate them in their ideological, cultural, historical, material and symbolic contexts.

Virtual reality regime

Besides data visualizations, virtual reality and serious (video) games are storytelling genres that have become popular in recent years, particularly as part of experiments with immersive journalism and the multimodal communication strategies of humanitarian agencies (Etem, 2020; Gruenewald & Witteborn, 2022). These genres combine shared aims to stimulate embodied experiences. Virtual reality (VR) is commonly heralded as an 'empathy machine', building on an experiential regime of becoming close and intimate or immersing oneself into the point of view of marginalized bodies (Clark, 2021; Raessens, 2019).

Examples of VR storytelling on refugees and migrants include applications of three and six degrees of freedom (DoF). Notable examples of 3DoF (rotation of the head to the right and left, side to side, backwards and forwards) include the 360-degree video *Clouds Over Sidra* (Milk & Arora, 2015), a virtual tour of the Zaatari refugee camp in Jordan by 12-year-old Sidra, who serves as guide, and *Trafficked* (BBC, 2016), an animated film about Maria, a Nicaraguan mother trafficked as a sex worker to Mexico. 6DoF combines 3DoF and movement of the body up and down, to the right and left, backwards and forwards, and a key example is the Alejandro González Iñárritu's *Carne y Arena* (Flesh and Sand) (2017), which is about migrants crossing the border into the US and their arrest by border patrol agents. VR representations can be studied for their employment of non-fiction genre conventions that create an "illusion of presence", including the assumed realness of people, locations and intentions, alongside their reception, editing, voice-over, and other indexical claims to reality (Studt, 2021, p. 175).

The genre of serious (video) games can be studied for its potential of challenging the de-contextualized, narrow representations of refugees that are dominant in typical mainstream media as well as the dominant emotional discourse of pity and compassion, by prompting reflection on the historical, political and socioeconomic factors of refugee decision making and experience (Morrissette, 2017; Sou, 2018). Studies of such games show various levels of success. For example, several online games in the 'virtual saviours' genre were found to reproduce trafficked people as ideal victims, without agency, individualizing problems and overlooking overarching structural problems such as uneven access to safe mobility (O'Brien & Berents, 2019). Serious games about refugees and migrants include, for example, *Banopticon* (Marmaras, 2013), *BAN Human Trafficking* (Balkans Act Now!, 2019), *Papers, Please* (Pope, 2013), *(Un) Trafficked* (FFunction, 2017), *Against All Odds* (UNHCR, 2007), *My Life as a Refugee* (UNRIC, 2012), *Missing: Game for a Cause* (Missing Link Trust, 2016), *The Migrant Trail* (Williams, 2013), *Darfur is Dying* (Ruiz, 2006), *Cloud Chasers: Journey of Hope* (Blindflug studios, 2015), *Zaytoun: The game* (Riklis, 2013), *On the Ground Reporter: Darfur* (Radio Darfur, 2010), *Food Force* (WFP, 2005), and *Frontiers: Welcome to Fortress Europe* (Gold Extra, 2008).

Besides audio-visual elements, researchers can study the procedurality – the flow and rules of a game which result from a host of decisions made by game programmers. Also, it is revealing to study who initiated and produced such games, as makers include commercial for-profit private companies, humanitarian agencies, non-profits, artists and activists as well as researchers. Whether or not refugees and/or migrants collaborated in co-designing these games (Çatak et al., 2017), and whether games receive recognitions and awards, such as the Games for Change awards, are also elements worthy of researching. Further research on video games, augmented reality (AR) and VR is needed for a balanced assessment of their potential contribution to (inter)cultural and racial literacies versus their appeal in terms of distanced, voyeuristic exploitation of suffering as a form of entertainment (Shanneik & Sobieczky, 2023).

Diasporic media regimes

Digital diasporic media are the media "for and by" diasporic, exiled, migrant, refugee, expatriate groups (Ogunyemi, 2017, p. 1). These constitute a regime of their own, as a selection of actors within these communities control plaforms and get to prioritize identities, topics, foci and frames (Trandafoiu, 2013; Bozdag, Hepp & Suna, 2012). Digital diasporic media draw on longer lineages of cinematic media production, including Third Cinema, cinemas of exile, migration, diaspora, feminist cinema, accented cinema, transnational cinema and postcolonial cinema (see Chapter 5: Histories; Ponzanesi & Waller, 2012). Recent digital media production initiatives targeting migrants and diasporic communities include a myriad of fiction and non-fiction genres, various audiences and aims. This complexity demands a multiplicity of analytic approaches. Most importantly, scholars have addressed forms of community bonding. For example, iROKOtv, as an example of the 'performative digital Africa', offers a subscription-based streaming service and social media platform featuring content from the Nigerian film and TV industry known as Nollywood. This platform reaches an audience spread over 200 countries where particularly African-born and African-descended individuals can "inhabit Africa – digitally" (Arthur, 2020, p. 216). AfroLandTV is presented as a 'Netflix for the Global Pan African Diaspora' showing TV shows and movies that are African, African-Amercian, Black-European, Carribean and Afro-Latino. Bridging diasporic communities across difference, the platform's chief branding officer, Brittin Maponga, notes that AfroLandTV "is our response to bridging cultural discrepancies within the global Black community". Besides the Black community, "the stories featured on AfroLandTV are universal stories told from an African/Black perspective [...] for everyone" (Edwards, 2020, n.p.). Latino and LatinX media produced in cities in the Global North can be studied for their transnational reach, and whether they "homogenize communities" (Retis, 2019, p. 115) across geographies.

In addition to entertainment, informal and professionalized forms of diasporic journalism present another point of entry (Oyeleye, 2017). For example, the 30–144 million Russian speakers living outside the Russian Federation are variously targeted by Russophone diasporic journalists living outside Russia, providing a new lens onto how media makers negotiate the economic and power loci of their countries of residence and countries of origin (Voronova, Voronova & Yagodin, 2020). With the Russian invasion of Ukraine on February 24, 2022, this has only become of even greater importance, particularly given the state censoring of war coverage on domestic Russian media. For example, after it was blocked by the Russian censorship bureau, the Russian-language independent television channel TVRain (*Dozhd* in Russian) started broadcasting from Amsterdam, the Netherlands, from the summer of 2022. In addition, journalistic diaspora media can be studied to provide a 'window on the world', offering information and alternative views on conflicts, and as a 'mirror', reflecting and offering additional backgrounds (Ogunyemi, 2017). The digitally mediated displacement, conflict and political reconstruction of Somalia, for example, has been thoroughly documented by Idil Osman (2017), drawing on journalistic experience and critical media analysis. Similarly, the political significance of digital mobilization is evident from the Eritrean diaspora's deployment of digital media (Bernal, 2014).

Self-representation repertoires

Whereas representations produced by a selection of actors on behalf of larger groups inherently leads to reduction, hence the above focus on regimes, self-representation promises a broader base of people who can speak for themselves (Thumim, 2012; Dahlberg & Siapera, 2007). For us to get an overview of the varied practices of self-representation, in this section we take a repertoire-oriented approach. Focusing on media repertoires, we can understand self-representations as patterns of behaviour or use and as meaningful practices (Hasebrink & Domeyer, 2012). Furthermore, the media repertoire perspective assumes a 'user-centric' perspective, which takes an individual's relation to media as a starting point. It is oriented towards grasping media practices in their "entirety" and it is committed to "relationality", acknowledging the interrelations of the cross-media landscape (Hasebrink & Hepp, 2017, p. 367). Here, we take self-representations as a way to understand the various modalities that migrant and mobile people have embraced to tell their own stories.

Repertoires of digital voice

The study of digital migrant voices emerged in response to the growing popularity of internet discussion forums and online message boards in the late 1990s and early 2000s; it researched how and why communities claimed spaces for themselves online. Increasingly adopted from the early 1990s, message boards are interactive, largely text- and icon-based technologies that reflect the digital cultures of the 1970s dial-up bulletin board system (BBS), newsgroups and electronic mailing lists. Theorists have argued that voice is embodied, plural and processual (Butler, 2001; Couldry, 2010). "Giving an account of oneself" through narration is fundamental for the social construction of the subject (Butler, 2001, p. 22) as well as the collective; as postcolonial theorist Frantz Fanon famously stated, "a community will evolve only when a people control their own communication" (cited in Kahn & Kellner, 2007, p. 17). Furthermore, voice reflects and shapes socio-political, economic and cultural processes. It is an important element of the struggle for power and recognition. Subordinated people are ignored, silenced or marginalized in the mainstream public sphere. Again, we can turn to Spivak (1988), who raised the important question "can the subaltern speak" to reflect on how structures of colonialism and patriarchy deprived brown women of the epistemic and political position needed to assert their voice.

When transposed to the digital, the critical analytic lens of voice allows us to study whether, how and why online spaces can be taken up by migrant groups to express themselves and to call out those in power, resulting in either acknowledgement or further silencing, and for various migrant groups to form alliances in their shared struggle (Mitra, 2001). In this spirit, scholars have conducted case studies on repertoires of voice on message boards. Media, communication and cultural studies scholars as well as linguists have focused on, among others, Chinese migrants in the UK (Parker & Song, 2006), Asian-American, Mexican-American and African-American communities (Byrne, 2008), Indian migrants in the US (Mallapragada, 2006), South Asian women (Gajjala, 2004; Mitra, 2001), Eritrean people in the diaspora (Bernal, 2014), and Russian LGBTs and queers in Israel (Kuntsman, 2008). These studies collectively add to the framework of voice, showing its analytic potential to research the material, symbolic and political implications of who speaks, who is silenced, who is listened to, who is recognized and who is ignored.

For example, the role and workings of dedicated message boards – such as *AsianAvenue.com*, *BlackPlanet.com* and *MiGente.com* – which are frequented by marginalized groups, have been compared to 'hush harbors', a notion previously used to describe spaces in which slaves gathered away from the supervision of their white masters, to maintain identities, group cohesion and community knowledge (Byrne, 2008, p. 17). While still popular for some groups, message boards have also been replaced with forms of multimodal digital storytelling. From message boards onwards, scholars now ask "can the subaltern tweet?" (Trillò, 2018). For example, recent grassroots digital storytelling projects of refugees and migrants show how self-representations fall between the binary of hegemonic mainstream media and organized, citizen-led social media movements. This grey area warrants further critical and empirical scrutiny as it "constitutes a space where the subaltern might not just speak but might also occasionally be heard" (Georgiou, 2018, p. 56).

Digital identity repertoires

Digital identity repertoires refer to the digital media practices of self-identification, which contrast with institutionalized, top-down digital identity regimes. Following feminist post-structuralist theories, we can scrutinize the performative process of digital identification (Sundén, 2003). By doing so, we not only research what identities are visible online, but more specifically how they are executed (Cover, 2012; Leurs, 2015). By publishing a story, selfie, video or status update, people perform actions that bring their identities into digital being, while always having to relate (through citing or countering) normative expectations of gender, age, sexuality, race, generation, ability, migration status, among others. Digital identity performativity is a "way of doing things" (Nakamura & Chow-White, 2012, pp. 8–9), of presenting oneself online through expressions while having to relate to pre-given platform structures, interfaces, affordances, categories and technological standards.

Digital identity repertoires have been studied on the basis of case studies of the use of distinctive platforms to perform identity work. Consider, for example, the use of the video sharing platform *TikTok* among Hispanic migrants in Spain and the US (Jaramillo-Dent, Alencar & Asadchy, 2022) or by the Chinese diaspora (Sun, 2021), the use of the social network *LINE* by Chinese migrants living in Australia (Cassidy & Yang Wang, 2018), or gay migrants' use of the dating app *Grindr* in Denmark (Shield, 2019). A second strand of research has foregrounded how migrants assert themselves against the grain of either hegemonic mainstream culture or the dominant forms of diasporic normativity. As debates about modernity, normativity and tradition are commonly "staged over women's eyes and bodies" (Hegde, 2016, p. 19), media practices of digitally doing gender and sexuality are important entry points.

For example, a study of Indian diasporic daughters living in Australia saw how they challenged traditional community gender roles by performing 'good' gendered identities on Facebook and Instagram alongside 'bad' girl identities (Volpe, 2021, p. 177). However, the dominant dichotomy of studying digital identity performativity among migrants as either a form of subversion or a form of abiding with hegemonies should be reconsidered. For example, Łukasz Szulc (2020a, p. 5444), in his research with queer migrants (Polish LGBTQs in the UK), demonstrates the urgency of understanding particular digital identifications and disidentifications of gender 'in situ', as they may be strategic and contextual as well as sometimes forced, simplified, protective or unwanted, among others. Along the lines of this third strand, scholars have sought to account for how migrants, particularly young migrants, articulate hybrid identities, combining historical collective 'roots' and contemporary orientations 'routes' (Gilroy, 1993) while asserting in-between selves. Norwegian immigrant youth, for example, were found to represent themselves on the local social networking site *Biip* through combining axes of difference, including race, ethnicity, gender and religion, in order to detach themselves from "stable and essentialist" identities (Mainsah, 2011, p. 190). In my own work with Moroccan-Dutch youth and refugee youth in the Netherlands, I similarly observed hybridized workings of digital identity performativity. Informants signalled a multiplicity of affiliations in messenger nicknames, combining and showing a variety of page-likes on profile pages, and articulating nuanced biographical statements on their profiles (Leurs, 2015, 2017).

Personal digital archiving repertoires

Personal digital archives have proliferated in recent decades, but they remain undertheorized and empirical scrutiny is sparse. Personal digital archives – as technologies, artefacts and networks – are repositories consisting largely of two types of records: self-logged and automated data (Kaufmann, 2018). Self-logged archives include those digital records consciously created by posting on social media platforms and making, circulating and/or saving texts, images, sounds and videos on digital devices like smartphones. Automated data refer to those digital traces resulting from sensors and trackers in smartphones (geographical positioning, connectivity), alongside corporate and governmental forms of tracking, monitoring, surveillance and data collection (at airports and borders, as well as during visa and asylum procedures). As 'records of the past', both dimensions of personal digital archives are vital to mobile populations to secure collective memories, but also to aspire for just futures:

> For migrants, more than for others, the archive is a map. It is a guide to the uncertainties of identity-building under adverse conditions. [...] This living, aspirational archive could become a vital source for the challenge of narratability and identity in contemporary times. (Appadurai, 2019, pp. 558, 563)

In particular, self-logging data show how mobile populations mediate, curate and archive lived and embodied experiences through self-representation. To a degree, although *ad hoc* and often unstructured, these archives are testimonies and autonomous records of the migrant gaze (Georgiou & Leurs, 2022).

On the level of the collective, personal digital archives can provide insight into shared experiences, such as the often-convoluted place-making practices of irregularized migrants. For example, Miguel Fernández Labayen and Irene Gutierrez (2021), over the course of 11 years of collaboration with migrants from the sub-Saharan region living in Ceuta, a Spanish enclave in Northern Morocco, established a database of over 200 videos gathered from personal digital archives. As self-representations of place-making at the border between Morocco and Spain, North Africa and Europe, the videos were found to play profound roles of "camera-witnessing ('if I die, I want at least the world to have these images from me')" and "camera-dissidence ('we will make it, you will see')" (Labayen & Gutierrez, 2021, pp. 673–674).

Across the world, marginalized migrants have sought to mobilize their archives to fight injustices and claim their human rights, including refugees documenting the atrocious Australian offshore processing regime (Rae, Holman & Nethery, 2018) or refugees contesting Europe's bordering in Chios, Greece (Stavinoha, 2019) (see also Chapter 2: Communications). On the level of the individual, personal digital archives reflect how (im)mobile people document their own experiences, feelings and frustrations. Along these lines, smartphones can be understood as personal pocket archives, as material objects carried on the body, containing a variety of ego-documents (Leurs, 2017). For example, refugee women awaiting resettlement in Greece found diversion in capturing and storing scenes of nature to divert their negative thoughts (Greene, 2020).

Conclusions

Migration is a key but painful example of the exclusionary workings of the politics of representation. Mobile subjects, as the objects and the subjects of representation, embody this intense battleground over meaning-making. The various bodies of scholarship we have combined suggest that mobile bodies straddle regimes of representations that seek to establish hegemonic reductionist understandings of migration with repertoires of self-representation that allow for the negotiation, exposure and countering of these expressions. In striving for simplicity, order and efficiency, the largely institutionalized and top-down workings of the regime of migrant representation showcase how every representation is a reduced rendering of complex reality. Choices made in digital news, data visualization, VR representations and in how people are digitally identified indicate that this regime is inherently racializing migrants. Power relations between societal groups are installed and perpetuated, by reducing mobile people to homogeneous and essentialized entities. The diasporic media regime seeks to intervene, but also risks replicating inherently exclusionary workings by virtue of having a selected tiny minority of actors speak on behalf a great variety of people. Self-representational digital media repertoires offer fundamental insight into the multiplicity and heterogeneity of migrant experiences from the bottom up, as we can discern in digital identity performativity, personal digital archives and initiatives to record migrant voices online. Future research on representations can address further the interplay between regimes and repertoires, its political economy as well as the implications of migrants' personal digital archiving.

Research Dialogue V: Radha Sarma Hegde on researching the mediation of migration as an active process of meaning-making with material consequences

Radha Sarma Hegde is a Professor in the Department of Media, Culture and Communication at New York University, USA. Her current research interests include the global spread and mediation of the English language, as well as current practices of bodily politics at the border. Her monograph *Mediating migration* (2016), anthologies *Circuits of visibility: Gender and transnational media cultures* (2011) and *Routledge handbook of the Indian diaspora* (with A. Sahoo, 2018) offer digital migration studies scholars the conceptual vocabulary, historical depth and contextual sensitivity needed to grasp the material, the symbolic and affective consequences of media, migration and representation.

1. How did you come to the study of media and migration?

Questions concerning mobility and circulation have long been areas of interest to me and, no doubt, are intertwined with the autobiographical. Both growing up in postcolonial India and my diasporic positionality in the United States made me intensely aware of living between cultures and between social worlds and nations. This meant an acute awareness and visceral knowledge of the idea of the West and its power to marginalize. It is these lived experiences of difference and migration that drive my scholarly interests in the politics of migration and the broader concerns of transnational mobility.

My education and abiding interest in literature and in the humanities also contributed to shaping my scholarly views, interests and perspectives about migration. My early undergraduate and graduate education was in English literature and that was a very formative experience in India. It was after a brief stint as a journalist that I decided to pursue doctoral study in the United States. For my dissertation, I turned to study the communicative worlds navigated by the South Asian diasporic community in the United States. My activist experience with South Asian women in situations of domestic violence also greatly influenced my continuing interest in the gendered politics of diaspora and questions of intersectionality. Being immersed in these contexts has no doubt shaped my perspectives and the questions I ask.

The intellectual impetus and inspiration to think through questions of representation, Otherness, the West and the non-West came from postcolonial and critical race scholarship. I am also an avid reader of literature that is born out of the diasporic imaginary and try to integrate that in my teaching and research. My scholarly interest in this area is also driven by the belief that research should be responsive to the politics and contestations that are taking place globally.

2. **How do you define and operationalize mediation in the broader context of the politics of representation?**

Yes, considering the broader context and perspective is key to this question. How one views the politics and study of mobility and migration is central to how we approach the subject of our research and, in turn, define concepts we work with. The point of departure to your object of study, as it were. I begin from the view that transnational mobility involves a complex assemblage of factors, including the material challenges of adaptation, rituals of admittance, ideologies of inclusion, resentment and exclusion. Each of these takes different social and political twists and turns, depending on the context. Most importantly, all of these layers are nested today within media and communication environments and diverse practices of representation.

'Mediation' is a term that has been variously defined across disciplines. In the context of migration, a focus on mediation serves as a generative point of entry. I find it most productive to think of mediation as the active process of meaning-making that has material consequences. To begin to understand a complex, multi-sited, multi-layered subject such as migration and its intersection with media cultures, we need to keep our conceptual vocabularies supple. So, in order to be able to do the analytical work required I argue for a broader and more encompassing view of mediation as meaning-making processes that bridge, create and transform social and cultural worlds. In other words, to reiterate, we need to understand the constitutive connections between media forms, practices and the dynamics and politics of migration. Putting mediation and mobility in the same frame enables us to see how migrant identities, diasporic formations and social meanings are activated, enabled and disabled by and within media systems.

As Edward Said and Stuart Hall have eloquently reminded us in their scholarship, systems of meaning and representations do not just happen, but arise within a political context (e.g. Said, 1997; Hall, Evans & Nixon, 1997). The task before us is to unravel the complexity of what migration means today through complicating mediation rather than streamlining the concept.

3. **In reviewing studies of representation, we address the two main themes of media representation regimes and self-representation registers. How does your work speak to these themes?**

What you offer is an extremely helpful conceptual framework to attend to the multiplicity of regimes and registers of representation. As you state in the chapter, there is a battle over meaning-making when it comes to migration and it is indeed important to distinguish and emphasize the reductive hegemonic narratives from diasporic self-representations. Working from a feminist perspective and committed to the production of decolonial knowledge, I do believe that it is of utmost importance to represent voices that have been evicted from dominant discourse. So, bringing these voices and forms of representation into our research archive and academic discussion is vital.

At the same time, while these two forms of representation, top-down regimes and bottom-up registers, diverge, they are also deeply intertwined in terms of the politics and conditions of articulation. Consider, for example, the narratives that some refugees have to create as 'acceptable' horror for their asylum appeal. I am thinking of women who have to recreate the violence in their life in a manner that will mark them as eligible or, in other words, deem them 'worthy' victims by the state. Their language, their narrative and the form allowed to them are all already dictated or subsumed by dominant structures. While incommensurable and even polarized on one level, the dominant and other narratives are already entangled, and this constitutes the conditions of possibility. I have always attempted to be attentive to the contradictions and contestations within the layering of these multiple narratives, in order to open up the complex space of migration.

4. **With the accelerated digitization and datafication of migration, where do you see gaps in our scholarship on migrant representation and what topics do you think we should pursue further in the future?**

Our task as scholars is to ask questions, examine spaces made opaque or inaccessible both by contemporary regimes of securitization and, of course, the weight of colonial histories. With regards to the digitality of the present, we have to resist celebratory views of technology and data as having the potential to solve, rectify or restore. We are surrounded by this discourse, and it creeps into our research as well. While we need to understand the place of data in the experience and control of migration, the story has to zoom out and be contextualized both globally and historically. This is a challenging terrain to work on and a mere focus on the here and now barely does justice to the complexity of the migration condition. Hence it is also important to remind ourselves that it is not the next shiny object or digital innovation that matters. Rather, we have to address the role and place of technology and data in creating the conditions of mobility and increasingly precarity. Ultimately, the focus is on understanding the poignancy and humanity of the migrant drama that is playing out around us.

The current pandemic moment has introduced new turns in the study of media and migration. The spread of the Covid-19 Coronavirus has once again exposed deep structural inequities and has also reopened questions concerning the complicity of digital infrastructures with processes of precaritization. Rising levels of aggressive resentment towards immigrants and the manipulation of information and digital systems are having deep repercussions on the lives of vulnerable populations, especially migrants. There is no dearth of questions and issues to study at the intersection of media and migration. In fact, the challenge is to respond quickly to the changing global landscape of migration. The study of representation becomes meaningful, in my opinion, when it leads to or is accompanied by rich and deep ethnographic analyses of how these meanings are embedded in or shape the contours of migrant life.

5. **What practical advice would you give to aspiring digital migration scholars?**

The intersection of migration and media is not a traditional field of study by any means. First, it is a shifting terrain affected by the fluctuations of political and economic life and, as we well know, comes into public view most often represented as crisis or catastrophe. We need to remind ourselves that it is not a stable, static field but one that is volatile yet embedded within global, historical and contemporary currents. In order to be responsive to the moment, our work has to draw on intellectual resources from across disciplines and maintain an epistemic focus on decolonial knowledge. This, in turn, will hopefully bear on our methodological choices. This is not always easy in terms of the institutional and academic borders that we have to navigate even as do we our research and publish. However, the intellectual pull to study migrants, mobility and media is all about finding imaginative and innovative ways to study a complex convergence of factors that extends across bodies, geographies and time periods. Thank you, Koen, for the opportunity to participate in this exchange.

Research Dialogue VI: Eugenia Siapera on the ethics of studying digital and datafied representations of migration

Eugenia Siapera is Professor of Information and Communication Studies and Head of the School of Information and Communication at University College Dublin, Ireland. Siapera's research and teaching interests include digital and social media, gender, race and the media, digital journalism technology and social justice. Her books *Cultural diversity and global media* (2010) and *Understanding new media* (2018) offer digital migration scholars important conceptual and methodological tools to scrutinize media representations, gender, race and migration.

1. How did you come to the study of media and diversity, gender and race?

My intellectual journey paralleled my personal journey in many ways. My undergraduate degree is in social psychology, which I studied in London. At the time, prejudice and discrimination in the context of social psychology were seen as individual attitudes or group-based responses, such as in-group favouritism. During my degree I came across the theory of social representations by Serge Moscovici (e.g. Moscovici & Duveen, 2001) and Discourse and social psychology *by Jonathan Potter and Margaret Wetherell (1987) – these made very clear that understandings of social groups, communities and identities are socially constructed and that communication and language play a crucial role in these constructions. Focusing on the media, and in particular on the area known as audience effects, was the next step in my intellectual journey.*

As a migrant from Southern Europe, I experienced prejudice, a few 'hard' racist incidents and what we would now call micro-aggressions based on my ethnicity, while as a woman I experienced the ill-effects of patriarchy. Needless to say, I also witnessed these around me, not only as first-hand experiences. I became very interested in the ways in which the media reproduce racist constructions and on the impact these have on audiences. When I embarked on my PhD I shifted the focus towards media workers, and in particular journalists, studying the press corps in Brussels. At the time, in the late 1990s, the question of Europe was at the forefront: was Europe going to succeed in replacing the nation-state? Could a supranational European press and media contribute to the construction of a different kind of identity?

At the time (and now!), I understood the nation-state, and the chauvinistic, exclusionary attitudes it inculcates, as part of the problem. Nationalism was very evident to me as a migrant in the UK of the 1990s, and the media and popular culture were an integral part of it:

from the Spice Girls' Union Jack dresses to 'cool Britannia', from naïve pride in and admiration of the Empire in various films and period dramas to continuous stories about criminal foreigners in the tabloids and 'British values' – all these were constructed as sources of pride for the British but actively excluded, marginalized and othered certain people and communities who did not and would never be allowed to belong.

In making sense of these, I was influenced by the great British tradition of media, culture and race scholars, and in particular by Stuart Hall and Paul Gilroy. Both Hall (e.g. Hall, Evans & Nixon, 1997) and Gilroy (e.g. Gilroy, 1993) were keen to identify and highlight the agency of racialized and othered communities and their active, world-building practices. This has been at the forefront of my own thinking and writing about the media, gender and race: identifying the limiting and constricting structures, institutions and practices while paying attention to the active ways in which these are resisted and the means by which communities open up new avenues in their pursuit of equality, justice and freedom.

2. How do you define and operationalize mediation in the broader context of the politics of cultural representation?

I derive my understanding of mediation from the works of Roger Silverstone. For Silverstone, mediation was the process by which the media are shaping other institutions and social life, while at the same time the media, as technologies and messages, are themselves shaped by social practices (e.g. Silverstone, 1999). It is this dialectic that interests me in particular – Marx had also highlighted a version of this in his famous saying "Humans make history but not under circumstances of their own choosing" (Marx, 1852): the constant struggle between power that is consolidated institutionally, structurally and politically and bottom-up or outsider attempts to upset, widen, change, undermine or fight these structures. This is therefore how I understand mediation: as a dialectic in the sphere of the media, which includes all media processes (production, representation, reception and use, regulation, identity), along with the struggles that take place within and across these media processes.

3. In reviewing studies of representation, we address the two main themes of media representation regimes and self-representation registers. How does your work, for example on gender hate online or networked publics around refugees, speak to these themes?

As readers will have gathered from my previous answers, representation as a key media process is always under tension and perpetually contested. The two themes of my research, online misogyny (e.g. Ging & Siapera, 2019) and hashtag or networked publics around refugees (e.g. Siapera et al., 2018), bring this out very clearly. The broad feminist consensus we had achieved in Europe in the 1990s and early 2000s is currently actively contested by the far right and its political allies, alongside new ideological formations around anti-feminism. These contestations lead to new resistance practices and more struggles over representation and meaning, which have a direct impact on women's lives. The same with the refugee issue, which really is about race and ethnic 'otherness': Fortress Europe is contested both in the streets and in social media. I don't mean here that we can be complacent because contestation will teleologically arrive, but the exact opposite: that social labour and energy has to be invested in actively contesting representations that seek to control, exclude, subjugate and exploit othered communities and that in many ways it falls upon all of us to do so and to call out such representations.

4. **With the accelerated digitization and datafication of migration, where do you see gaps in our scholarship on migrant representation and what topics do you think we should pursue further in the future?**

This is a very important question. For the most part, migrant representation is a media process in the sense that it follows logics, routines and norms of media production, narrative constructions, genre conventions, and the like. We have been studying these for some time, and we have developed a set of tools to help us with criticisms and with picking them apart, exposing their faults and contradictions. But the relatively new processes of digitization and datafication operate with different modes of production, different norms and practices, which are often opaque or hidden from us. These are likely to lead to different forms of representation through data, which may make contestation harder. This is because they evoke an aura of science, facticity and a kind of materiality that is difficult to contest or, rather, you can contest mainly through the same tools (e.g. data methods) but these may not be accessible to most of us.

So I think that we need to adapt our strategies and develop new approaches to the ways in which data is used for representations, and ultimately for political decisions and for policy development in the field of migration. In my view, there are least two fruitful avenues of inquiry. The first is to focus on the labour practices involved in the production, processing and reporting of data on migration. Who produces the data, who processes it and for whose benefit? Who is exploited and what form does this exploitation take (Madianou, 2019b)? The second avenue concerns the values that are embedded in data systems: what are the ideologies and values that drive the development of data systems that apply to migrant populations? There is already a developing body of work on data colonialism (Viera Magalhães & Couldry, 2021), data justice (Martin & Taylor, 2021), and in general on critical data studies (Iliadis & Russo, 2016; Milan & Trere, 2019) that has laid strong foundations for further explorations.

5. **Your research is commonly interdisciplinary and you have conducted several mixed method studies. What are, for you, the pros and cons of combining perspectives and bringing together quantitative and qualitative data?**

   I am definitely not a purist when it comes to methodologies. I tend to use the kind of method that is more likely to help me answer the kinds of questions I have. I find big data studies fascinating because they allow research at an unprecedented scale. I am intrigued by computational methods and I am very interested in working with computer scientists because it is a great learning opportunity. For example, I am now working with computer scientists in applying a topic modelling approach to social media data concerning the far right. When it comes to nuance and depth, I think qualitative methods are more suited. So we would be looking to combine topic modelling with discourse and frame analysis. Combining both is ideal in theory, but in practice they operate with different assumptions and this does not always work.

6. **What practical advice would you give to those aspiring to study media and questions of diversity, race, gender and migration?**

   My usual advice to researchers is to be persistent, reflexive, curious and open to new learning. But for students of diversity, race, gender and migration I would also add to actively engage with questions of who stands to benefit from your research. If this does not first and foremost include racialized communities and minoritized people, think again and reframe your research. For all researchers, but especially for those in our areas, ethics, values and principles are very important and should guide the research process. Strong ethics lead to strong research.

4

Affects and emotions

The concepts of affectivity and emotionality are important lenses in the production of knowledge about feelings migrants might have when interacting with digital technologies and systems. Addressing affects (embodied sensations, such as goose bumps that are not consciously registered) and emotions (feelings that are consciously registered, such as happiness) enables researchers to shed new light on migration and digital mediation (e.g. Khorana, 2023; Oiarzabal, 2020). Moods, feelings, passions and frustrations cannot be reduced solely to meaning-making or materiality. In comparison with the study of underlying infrastructures, connectivity practices or performances of identity, as outlined in the previous chapters, affect and emotion foreground the study of contextually situated embodiments of migrants in relation to media practices, activity routines and accompanying digital traces (e.g. Alinejad & Ponzanesi, 2020). Only recently have scholars started to take this register seriously as a mode of inquiry. A research gap between the study of migration, technology and emotion currently remains. The economic and rational factors that influence mobility are often the primary scholarly foci, and emotions have remained of secondary importance (e.g. Alinejad & Olivieri, 2020). More research is needed to understand how affect and emotion mediate connections and disconnections among migrants. Seeking to offer a corrective, this chapter provides entry points to study the digital transmission and intensities of affect and emotion in migration contexts. For this purpose, first we define digital affectivity and emotionality. We then explore how we can deploy these analytic registers to describe sensations and feelings as situated in broader, power-ridden spatial and temporal contexts. Subsequently, we discuss transnational families and care, the digital mediation of intimacy, home-making and the constitution of subjectivities.

Affects and emotions in migration and digital contexts

In the context of digital migration studies, the research lens of affectivity can offer insights into the process of migrant bodies attaining a different bodily and mental state, resulting from interacting with people or things through digital devices, social media platforms or networked technologies. Let us consider first how we can distinguish affect from emotion. Affect precedes emotions and consciousness. Affects thus refer to bodily changes, such as getting sweaty palms, that are pre-emotional. Emotions like embarrassment or anger succeed affect and are biographically registered (Massumi, 2015). 'Digital emotions' refers to how affective changes in one's state are consciously made meaningful through forms of digital expression. Before discussing how we can deploy affectivity as a lens of critical digital analysis, we will pause for a moment and reflect on the emergence and travel of the concept across fields.

The word 'affectivity' borrows from the Latin *affectus*, which referred to a "mental or emotional state or reaction (especially a temporary one)". Its meaning, furthermore, can be traced back to the Old French meaning of desire, passion and state of being (Oxford English Dictionary, 2021a). In academic literature, the term 'affectivity' is used to address a broad variety of concerns. Recent affectivity research includes attention to the feelings, energies and intensities that grow in bodies in response to certain stimuli and seeks to address how moods are displayed through gestures, postures, facial expressions or tone of voice. As a result, assumptions about affect differ widely. One dominant model assumes affectivity is universal (observable in strands of psychology and evolutionary biology), whereas another model maintains that it is culturally specific as a site of power struggles (observable across strands of anthropology, sociology, feminist theory) (Stark, 2019). Here we follow the latter model, drawing particular inspiration from critical, feminist and queer theorists who put the cultural politics of affectivity on the research agenda. Below, we provide further definitional groundwork and explore how affectivity is approached in studies of digital culture and migration.

The French philosopher Gilles Deleuze (1988) theorized affectivity in the context of bodies encountering images. He stated that affectivity involves the process of bodies moving, or passing, from one emotional state to another as a result of interacting with a stimulus, such as an image: "these image affections or ideas form a certain state of the affected body and mind [...]. Therefore, from one state to another, from one image or idea to another, there are transitions, passages that are experienced" (Deleuze, 1988, p. 48). Seen this way, affects capture the subtle or not so subtle changes in the experiential state of an individual body or group of people resulting from a relational encounter (Gregg & Seigworth, 2009). Affects are "visceral perceptions" (Massumi, 2002), which include, for example, physiological shifts like shivering, feeling a lump in one's throat, or feeling breathless after hearing bad news. Emotions refer to how those pre-cognitive passages are interpreted and concretized through one's own biography. The work of Sarah Ahmed, a feminist, queer and race studies scholar, is particularly helpful in understanding how affects are embedded in ideological cultural practices. Affect provides insight into how bodies are made to move (or not) as they engage in relationships with communities or construct boundaries between nations.

For Ahmed, affect "circulates", and "accumulates" value the more it circulates, and thereby "endures" over time and space (Ahmed, 2004, pp. 45–46).

For digital migration studies scholars, it is important to recognize the fundamental relationality of affectivity. Affective intensities can be positive and negative (see Ngai, 2005), which offers a window into why and how individuals, through affective practices, may or may not align with others: "they involve (re)actions or relations of 'towardness' or 'awayness' in relation to such objects" (Ahmed, 2004, p. 8). Cultural practices become "archives of feelings", as affect is encoded and transmitted through texts (Cvetkovich, 2003). This archive does not function in isolation; it can only be understood in relation to actors involved in their production and their reception. Feelings range from the extraordinary, resulting, for example, from emergencies, to 'ordinary affects' that give a quality of continuity to everyday life (Stewart, 2007). Finally, affectivity is power ridden. The feminist scholar Sneja Gunew (2009) urges scholars to recognize that the degree to which specific people may be able to display affect and emotion highly depends on their social status, and cautions researchers to move beyond Eurocentric assumptions of emotionality.

Before addressing affectivity in digital migration studies, let us consider the main threads in migration studies and studies of digital media. In migration studies, affectivity and emotion are seen both as the products of mobility and as constitutive of experiences of mobility (Mai & King, 2009). Following the emotional and affective turn, both the feelings and experiences of the mobile subjects themselves and the impacts on sending and receiving communities are studied (Boccagni & Baldassar, 2015; Boehm & Swank, 2011; Conradson & McKay, 2007). For example, the sociologist Grace M. Cho has researched the role of the often unspeakable traumas of emotional and physical violence during the American–Korean war among members of the Korean diaspora. She found an affective spectrum of shame, sadness, grief and rage that unconsciously haunts this diaspora (Cho, 2008). Another key theme in migration scholarship is the scrutiny of affective dimensions of labour migration. This perspective is used to document the experiences of South East Asian workers in Hong Kong and Singapore (Piocos III, 2021) and Latin-American domestic workers in Europe (Gutiérrez-Rodríguez, 2010).

Affect scholarship has also addressed space-making and sensorial experiences of temporality. The prism of affective becoming, for example, was used to research the bodily sensations of Gazan refugees in Europe. Reflecting on journeys where temporalities and spatialities often contradict, in their migration process participants negotiated feelings of desire, despair, hopefulness, fear, guilt and loss. Researching affective sensations, in sum, can remind us "how migration experiences do not begin and end with their physical relocation and settlement but, rather, are a dynamic and ongoing emotional and embodied relationship across time (before, during, after travel) and (physical and digital) space" (Thorpe & Wheaton, 2021, p. 923). Finally, affect theory has been further developed to address how belonging and boundaries are relationally produced at the transnational level. Sociologists Amanda Wise and Selvaraj Velayutham have proposed the concept of 'transnational affect' to address the "circulation of bodily emotive affect between transnational subjects and between subjects and symbolic fields which give qualitative intensity to vectors and routes, thus reproducing belonging to, and boundaries of, transnational fields" (2006, p. 3). With the notion of "affective mobility", researchers have called for greater attention to be given to the role of emotions in experiencing mobility and immobility, hope and despair (Glaveanu & Womersley, 2021). Thus, migration scholars commonly foreground the affective and emotional practices of migrant bodies in their situated, power-ridden contexts.

In studies of technologies and digital culture, affectivity has prompted scholars to move beyond focusing either on the disembodied material or the social characteristics of technology (Hillis, Paasonen & Petit, 2015). Several strands of studies can be discerned that address how typed, aural, visual and haptic modes of digital communication circulate affect and emotions. Foremost, scholars examine the visceral engagements of social media users, content, workers and capital (Sampson, Maddison & Ellis, 2018). It is in the relation between technologies, affordances and users where affective, bodily transitions happen. Platforms and apps sustain affects of hope of connectivity and fear of dis-connectivity in various ways. For example, we can think back to the delayed presence, or "décalage", that Dana Diminescu discussed in Chapter 2 (see Research Dialogue III). Illustratively, "the three dots shown while someone is drafting a message in iMessage are quite possibly the most important source of eternal hope and ultimate let down in our daily lives" (Abolfazli, cited in Sundén, 2018, p. 74). On the level of political economy, there is a growing focus on affective capitalism, or how technological innovations, including affective computing, sentiment analysis and social robotics, seek to recognize, measure, modulate and/or monetize affectivity (Karppi et al., 2016). Focused on politics and governance awareness, scholars address the disruptive potential of affective contagious virality (Sampson, 2012) and growing misinformation, populism and extremism as social media affects (Bösel & Wiemer, 2020). In sum, this strand of scholarship has provided deeper insights into the affective co-constitution of bodies interacting with technologies.

The legacies of migration and digital studies inform research directions on affectivity in digital migration studies. In the sections below, we will discuss the political economy of affect, intimacy, transnational families and home-making – the four emergent key themes of affectivity and emotionality research in digital migration studies.

The political economy of affect

In this section, we consider affect from the perspective of political economy (PE) to understand the spectrum of migrant feelings in the broader context of neoliberalism, which is often accelerated through digital developments. Before being able to combine affectivity, political economy, migration and the digital in our analytic frame, let us consider each element separately. A political economy perspective addresses the interrelations between the political and the socio-economic structures in which people live, and critical PE scholars focus on how power hierarchies impact upon these relations. In migration studies, political economy scholars address the underlying political and economic causes and consequences of migration, for example by studying the impact of globalization on migration on micro, meso and macro scales (e.g. Talani, 2015). Affects like fear and hope can, for example, work to push and/or pull people to act and move or stay (Griffiths, 2020). In media and communication studies, political economy scholars focus on the incentives and constraints of media institutions; how powerful those involved are and the roles the different people have in the making, circulating and distributing of media (e.g. Mosco, 1996). Affect offers an important framework for studying the political economy of migration in relation to digital technologies. Political economy studies of affect, for example, demonstrate how capitalism and governance through technological developments create and limit possible bodily responses (Clough, 2008). In sum, the "economy of affect" can be a generative entry point to study how migrants' feelings play a role in mediating systemic power hierarchies (Raiño-Alcalá, 2008).

Two research strands reveal how migrant affective economies play out differently for different types of migrant and mobile subjects. For elite migrants, the political economy of affect reflects a side-product of their desired mobile lifestyles, which they are expected to cope with through the use of technologies. Second, for non-elite migrants, including labour migrants, displaced people, refugees and asylum seekers, the political economy of affect offers insights into how migrants make use of technologies to negotiate the emotional obstacles they face.

Elite migrants

Regarding elite migrants, mobilities scholarship is starting to question how elite mobile subjects, professionals and international students navigate the emotional toll of their international, digitally-connected lifestyles (Cranston, 2014). In the contemporary moment, internationally mobile subjects, such as expats, are expected to embody a neoliberal, ideal-type "entrepreneurial self" (Heidkamp & Kergel, 2017, p. 99). The systemic "emotional precarity" of international lifestyles is not often discussed (ibid., p. 102). This lack can also be explained because international expatriate mobility is often presented as smooth and friction-free. Elite migrants are expected to deal with the emotional intensities of their lifestyle through individualized forms of self-care and self-development. However, the tension between mobile lifestyles and feelings demands greater attention, as Anthony Elliott and John Urry urged us:

There is a kind of in-built tension or contradiction between the global mobile economy, which privileges speed of movement and fast rational calculations, on the one hand, and the sociocultural order of intimacy in which personal and familial relationships become increasingly ordered around short-termism, episodicity and communications at-a-distance, on the other. (2010, p. 110)

Consider, for example, the political economy of affect co-shaping the lives of digital nomads. Digital nomads are a category of workers who have moved to tourist sites with costs of living lower than the Global North, including Chiang Mai in Thailand, Bali in Indonesia and Medellín in Columbia. They are commonly young, relatively resourceful professionals who value autonomy, flexibility and the ability to travel internationally, where they choose to work remotely. Their lifestyle is often imagined as one of general freedom, where work and leisure boundaries are overcome. News reports on digital nomads pursuing opportunities to work remotely resulting from the Covid-19 pandemic often emphasize how they 'ride out' the pandemic, combining digital labor with a laid-back leisure lifestyle (Matthes, 2022).

However, in-depth research reveals that digital nomads are part of a competitive gig economy. They can only sustain themselves through strict self-discipline, including strict time-management, managing their life-work balance and maintaining their own working conditions. Furthermore, digital nomads predominantly travel solo. Behind the façade of freedom and autonomy, the challenges of transnational communication and the lack of meaningful local contacts may result in feelings of loneliness and isolation. In addition, the stereotype of the digital nomad as a white, western, middle-class 'bromad' hints at masculine, heterosexual norms that shape the uneven affective terrain of elite mobilities (Cook, 2020).

Non-elite migrants

Regarding non-elite mobile subjects, critical media and migration scholars have taken economies of affect as an entry point to grasp bottom-up, everyday experiences and top-down corporate and governmental incentives. On the one hand, this framework is used to uncover how less privileged and marginalized migrants seek to establish a sense of community, normalcy and routine in adverse and challenging circumstances of "protracted uncertainty" (Biehl, 2015; Galhardi, 2022). Seen this way, affect and emotion can play an agentic role, as a form of capital, alongside traditionally recognized forms of capital, including economic, social, cultural and symbolic capital (Bourdieu, 1986). For example, the notion of "transnational affective capital" was developed to account for how young Somali people stranded in Ethiopia pursue transnational communication with parents and family who have migrated onwards, from internet cafés in Addis Ababa. They connect with their loved ones abroad to create a sense of temporary digital togetherness, which helps them reduce their anxieties (Leurs, 2014). Engaging with aural, visual and haptic (touching the screen) affordances can act as affective stimuli, altering the emotional state of the bodies of migrant technology users. Research with Iraqi refugee households in Jordan shows that they make life more bearable by using "affective affordances" and the utilities of digital platforms and devices to reorient themselves to places and people abroad (Twigt, 2018). Asylum migrants in the Hong Kong Special Administrative Region contribute to an alternative affective economy by gifting one another digital data and devices, thereby countering social and technological isolation (Witteborn, 2019). Underpinning these analyses is an understanding of the media as extending and/ or replacing human senses.

On the other hand, governments and humanitarian agencies seek to contain and manage mobility through "techno-affective practices" as the digital border dehumanizes particular subjects not only through geo-political and bio-political but also through emotional registers (Chouliaraki & Musarò, 2017, p. 536). Corporations seek to monetize the informal local and "transnational affective economies" of migrants (Cabalquinto & Wood-Bradley, 2020, p. 787). For this purpose, corporations, agencies and service providers, such as remittance platforms, construct a "platformed migrant subjectivity" based on an ideal type of desirable emotional, transnational and digital migrant transactions (ibid.). In addition, for marginalized and racialized mobile subjects, the "security theatre" (Paige, 2021) of highly visible airport and border security measures trigger affects such as fear, insecurity and uncertainty. No Fly lists, full body scanners, sniffer dogs, random searches and facial recognition are measures that are meant to make privileged travellers feel safe. For others, they are sensed as an affective form of governance through control and deterrence. With the term "racial baggage", Simone Browne emphasizes how security theatre at airports, including pat down, hair searches, cameras and x-ray machines, allows some (read white, CIS-gender male bodies) to travel lightly, while it affects and weighs down on those travellers who are for example racialized as Black (2015, p. 131). Additional research is needed into the political economy of affect underpinning the security theatre at airports, train stations, and at land and sea borders, as it risks the further marginalization of ethnic, racial, religious, sexual and gender minority bodies on the move (Hasisi & Weisburd, 2011). In the next section we shift our focus towards the affects and emotions of digital intimacy.

Digital intimacies

Intimacy is a "close, affective relation" (Sadowski, 2016, p. 47) maintained in specific contexts, such as families, friendship circles, communities and between romantic partners. In the context of migration and mobility, digital intimacies can be taken to refer to the deep, affective connections between bodies who do not live in close geographical proximity, and who are sustained through processes of digital mediation. When considering digital intimacy as a frame-work of analyzing affectivity, it is strongly advised that we move beyond the dominant hetero-normative model of the 'western couple', and address intense bonds between people regardless of socio-cultural categories like race, national-ity, gender and sexuality. In addition, while digital intimacies revolve around a shared "technology of propinquity (temporal and spatial proximity)", they are not universal, but differ widely depending on individuals, communities, spatio-temporal contexts, situations and the technical settings involved (Hjorth & Lim, 2012, p. 477). To account for this dynamism, we can build on sociologist Lynn Jamieson's two-fold definition of intimacy as "the quality of close connection between people and the process of building this quality" (2011, p. 1). The quali-ties and processes of affective intimacies can be considered as those practices that are performed, through which "habits, rituals and everyday pastimes that aid us in achieving a certain emotional state" are maintained (Scheer, 2012, p. 209).

For digital migration studies scholars, digital intimacy provides insights into the processes and goals of how mobile subjects, in lieu of physical proximity, maintain mobile relationships through digital acts of "intimacy-at-a-distance" (Elliott & Urry, 2010, p. 850). This is of particular urgency for various migrant and mobile subjects who, depending for example on their migration status, have to negotiate a situation of "emotional precarity" (Awad & Tossell, 2019, p. 613). Digital intimacy research is concerned with how affective registers and dynamics oscillate and result in connections and disconnections between bodies and tech-nologies (Hynnä, Lehto & Paasonen, 2019). Intimacy routines – for example, lovers living at distance exchanging selfies in a particular rhythm throughout the day – are affective practices that offer "the body's movements a kind of depth that stays with it across all its transitions – accumulating in memory, in habit, in reflex, in desire, in tendency" (Massumi, 2015, p. 4). Digital intimacies thus offer a means to understand the complexity of the emotional consequences of mobility as they may reveal the ambivalences of maintaining deep relations across space and time.

Public digital intimacies

Existing scholarship concerns itself mostly with *public* forms of digital inti-macy (e.g. Dobson, Robards & Carah, 2018). For example, Punjabi migrants in Manila in the Philippines negotiate their "double consciousness of intima-cies" by using certain apps to maintain contact with their diaspora and others within their local communities (Cabañes, 2019, p. 1662). Public displays of digital intimacies require affective practices which may be quite intense. Italians living in London mediate food preparation, cooking and dining through their screens, which Sara Marino argues makes people feel emotionally close. Simul-taneously, the process may strengthen feelings of nostalgia (Marino, 2019). To navigate the affective intensities of maintaining an intimate public pres-ence online, Earvin Cabalquinto found that Fillipino overseas workers living in Melbourne, Australia, strategically embraced social media affordances such as limiting the visibility of posts to particular audiences: "behind every customised post lies the tears, strain, and constant struggles of separated family members to perform and reclaim a satisfying and intimate relationship beyond borders" (Cabalquinto, 2018, p. 260). Queer migrants have been found to compartmentalize queer intimacies either away from specific platforms, and act on it only on specific dating sites or apps, or to maintain several profiles on one platform. These are strategies to avoid content circulating beyond targeted audiences (Szulc, 2020a) (see Chapter 2: Connections). Illustratively, in the context of internal rural to urban migration in China, the dating apps of choice among mobile gay men – such as groups identified as Blued and Aloha – was based on *suzhi*, a Chinese term reflecting affect, desire and class-based distinctions (Wu & Trottier, 2021).

Private digital intimacies

Following calls to consider *private* forms of digital intimacy, including personal relationships and sexuality (Costa & Menin, 2016), digital sexuality emerges as a second important thread in digital intimacy research. In general, digital sexuality reflects intersectional power relations and charged histories. Consider the dating practices of digital nomads, the subgroup of expatriate, location-independent workers introduced above. A study with a group of self-identified digital nomads, all 'strong passport'-holders, found that in their digital dating they feel they all have to position themselves *vis-à-vis* the dominant stereotypes of the nomad as a "digital bromad", "a privileged, heterosexual white male, located on the beach next to his laptop and surfboard, and who stays in Thailand where his socio-economic status empowers him" (Yuen Thompson, 2019, p. 78). Experiences of the digital dating scene of the Chinese diaspora in Australia show how digital sexuality is a battleground of Orientalist and Occidentalist fantasies of courtship, femininity and masculinity, based on an underlying system of white racial entitlement (Chen & Liu, 2021). It is also notable how the digital sexualities of mobile subjects reflect and invoke the gender politics of sex tourism, gap-year volunteerism and histories of white male colonial hetero-patriarchy. The specific digitally mediated erotic rituals allow for an improvising and experimenting with sexual intimacy practices at a distance. Emergent research with mobile subjects demonstrates that these are highly ambiguous experiences. Digital practices of sexual intimacy among young expatriates living in Amsterdam, the Netherlands, were found to offer intense, temporary embodied feelings of connection and warmth, although the absence of physical touch may also strengthen feelings of absence and distance (Patterson & Leurs, 2020). Nonetheless, digital sexuality practices pioneered by mobile populations became the 'new normal' for many during the extended periods of physical isolation resulting from the lockdown measures of the Covid-19 health pandemic in 2020, 2021 and 2022 (e.g. Watson, Lupton & Michael, 2021).

Overall, studies of digital intimacy have focused on researching how intimate relations that pre-date mobility are sustained digitally. Future research can explore further how these digital intimacies of maintaining relations can be juxtaposed with how mobile subjects establish new ties across geographies and affectively negotiate "stranger intimacies" (Koch & Miles, 2021, p. 1379). In the next section we discuss what we can learn about how family life is maintained across borders from the perspective of affect.

Transnational families

Transnational families have become a key research site in studies on affect and emotion. It is only a recent development that researchers pay attention to the experiences of migrant families in Latin America, Africa, South-East Asia and China compared to over-researched Global North contexts (Acedera & Yeoh, 2018). This is long overdue, especially when we for example consider the situation of an estimated 3–6 million Filipino, 1 million Indonesian and 500,000 Thai children who live without at least one parent as a result of migration (Mazzucato & Dito, 2018). Transnational families can be defined as those nuclear or extended families that live most or some of the time physically separated from each other, while holding together feelings of familyhood or a collective unity across distance, including across national borders (Bryceson & Vuorela, 2002). Transnational families question traditions of western, heteronormative family life that correlate "bonds of place, country and family" (Beck & Beck-Gernsheim, 2014, p. 13). As connected migrants, it is common for mobile subjects to maintain relationships with family members living at distance or living abroad. This way of 'doing family', which differs from dominant norms, has remained "marginalized in family studies debates" (Reynolds & Zontini, 2013, p. 234). This is an important research gap, particularly when considering that the non-normative family life of transnational families, particularly of non-white mobile subjects, is surveilled and policed (Turner, 2020).

The circulation of affect and emotions is foundational to transnational family life. Digital Technologies are recognized as the key tools to support the processes of "digital kinning" or the maintenance of a web of social relations through the digital (Wilding et al., 2020, p. 639). Scholarly accounts have so far mostly focused on how the transnational maintenance of family bonds stimulate positive emotional outcomes, affects and sensations, such as joy, relaxation, confidence, enthusiasm, energy, reassurance and security. For example, scholarship mapped new technologies and the new opportunities of transnational communication to show the resilience of refugees, expatriates, domestic workers and internal migrants. Despite living abroad, technologies like *Skype*, *Zoom* and messaging, promise mothers living away from children to remain 'ideal mothers' to their children (Peng & Wong, 2013). However, recent research has highlighted how transnational family connections might trigger negative affective intensities, such as fear, shame and guilt (e.g. Cabalquinto, 2018; Leurs, 2019). The two dimensions of care and surveillance are helpful in bringing out the multi-sidedness of digitally-mediated transnational family life. Care and surveillance are interrelated processes, but for the purpose of clarity we consider them separately below.

Transnational families and care

Particularly in the field of migration, "care is the dominant theoretical tool for analyzing transnational families" (Walsh, 2018, p. 27). Digital care in transnational families includes hands-on practical activities of "caring for" family members, through assisting with household chores, homework or sending remittances, as well as "caring about" them, by offering emotional support, for example through digitally-mediated rituals such as sending frequent updates through family group chats, having deep conversations or the periodic sharing of meals on screen. On a more abstract level, care refers to reciprocal, multi-directional and asymmetrical practices, experiences and affects that circulate across distance (Baldassar & Merla, 2014; Parreñas, 2005; Skrbiš, 2008; Yeoh et al., 2020). A focus on the affective circulation of care enables researchers to map the actors involved in care-giving (which include migrants as providers and receivers of care), the activities of care themselves, as well as the balancing of sensed duties of care and possible care deficits and obligations. Care in transnational families can only be understood as contextually embedded in the socio-political, economic and cultural contexts of sending and receiving societies (Acedera & Yeoh, 2021), and in the normative gender, sexuality, age, generation, religious, etc. expectations that are maintained in the digital diaspora (Candidatu, 2021). Furthermore, the circulation of care in transnational families is approached as dynamically changing over the life course (Sinanan & Hjorth, 2018).

Transnational families need to be sustained by performing digital care labour, which is a combination of emotional labour, care labour and digital labour (Leurs, 2019). The digital labour of managing and communicating affective intent takes place in a "polymedia" landscape, a concept proposed by Mirca Madianou to understand how Filipino migrants negotiate an expanding environment of digital platforms and devices to keep in touch with their family members (Madianou, 2016). For mobile and migrant subjects, expectations to be 'always-on' and available for care labour can be quite taxing. In an era when transnational connectivity is possible, the emotional consequences of feeling that one always *has to be* connected (practically 24/7) with loved ones living at distance can be substantial. For example, fieldwork with young refugees in the Netherlands shows that they may struggle with "keeping face" while being part of a constant, but unequal, circulation of care. They have to process and respond to a continuous flow of calls, audio, image, video and text messages to be reassured of the health and safety of family members and friends living in precarious circumstances, including war, deprivation and devastation (Leurs, 2019, p. 641).

The ambivalence of digital care labour is not only evident among underprivi-leged or marginalized migrants. Similar affective experiences shape the migra-tion for education of middle- and upper-middle-class households in East Asia. The emotional labour performed by Chinese 'study mothers' (*peidu mama*), who accompany their school-going children to pursue education in Singapore, is felt as a double burden: in maintaining digitally connected lifestyles they felt con-stantly reminded of their familial responsibilities as wives, daughters, sisters, as if they had never left, while they felt they could not always attend practically to the pressing needs of their kin in China (Wang & Lim, 2021). When studying how emotional care is done as a form of digital labour, we should realize that the promise of connectivity does not equal intimacy and silences do not equal distance (Acedera & Yeoh, 2021). The digital practices of second-generation Turkish–Dutch migrants, who were born in the Netherlands and migrated to Istanbul as adults, maintain a "careful co-presence": informants carefully selected between particular platforms with distinctive emotional affordances, while being "care-full" in how they circulate care in transnational families (Alinejad, 2019, p. 2). Additional research is needed on how transnational families develop "pro-cedures and practices through a process of reflexive negotiation" (Beck & Beck-Gernsheim 2014, p. 171) to deal with misunderstandings, anxieties and disputes over transnational obligations.

Transnational families and surveillance

Like care, surveillance also connects times, spaces and bodies. As a near ubiqui-tous, normalized and yet often clandestine process, surveillance unconsciously impacts upon everyday life (Ellis, Tucker & Harper, 2013). Alongside caring, transnational family life also involves practices of surveillance. Unlike the mass surveillance of the state or a broader diasporic community, here surveillance revolves around intra-familial and micro-level forms of observation, policing and control (see Chapter 2: Connections). In this sense, as an asymmetrical form of circulation of emotion and affect, with the lens of surveillance we scrutinize the power dynamics of transnational families, particularly around the axes of generation/age (parents-children) and gender/sexuality (partners). Parents living at distance, particularly mothers, have been found to monitor their children remotely. Illustratively, the notion of the "mediated family gaze" can be used to tease out the mobile media-based two-way – but often hierarchical – negotiations of control in diverse family and parenting arrangements (Chen, 2020, p. 133). Among non-migrant or 'left-behind' children in China, technologies were experienced not only to function as a vehicle to convey affection, but also to 'cage' in lifeworlds.

Illustratively, Chinese migrant parents living in London noticed that their son was playing truant on the basis of his *WeRun* app (an application that is part of the *WeChat* platform which calculates and publishes how many steps a person takes), which registered his limited physical exercise, and parents living in Van-couver found out that their daughter had a boyfriend by reading her blog posts on *Qzone* (Chen, 2020, pp. 141, 143). Parental aspirations of caring for their children may often be affectively felt as forms of surveillance. Young international students living in Amsterdam, the Netherlands, reported feeling controlled and limited in their autonomy by their parents, as parents would ask questions about their activities when observing bank account expenses (Patterson & Leurs, 2020). In response to the affective intensities of control, Chinese international students living in Melbourne, Australia, were found to engage in intimate practices of disconnection, refraining from specific *QQ* or *WeChat* use to escape parental surveillance (Zhao, 2019; see also Lee, 2020).

Furthermore, partner relations in transnational families may also be shaped by intimate forms of surveillance. In the case of non-migrant Senegalese women married to migrant Senegalese men, the digital surveillant gaze of jealous husbands was felt as intensely disciplinary and disproportionate compared to the physical gaze of the partner when he was at home. Women were found to be "tethered to their homes by the telephone cord" as they felt obliged to wait for calls from their husbands, wanting to avoid suspicion by being called when they were not at home (Hannaford, 2014, p. 46). Surveillance and care are two sides of the same coin. For a more balanced understanding of the affective intensities of transnational family life, more attention is needed for parental, familial and intimate surveillance, which to date has received far less consideration by researchers. In particular, little is known about the micro-politics of how those under surveillance may circumvent or affectively experience contestations of control.

Home-making

This final section considers the affective intensities of digital home-making. The home can be defined as the place "on which one's affections centre, or where one finds refuge, rest or satisfaction" (Morley, 2000, p. 16). As a centre for projecting one's affections, home-making reflects the desire for shelter, boundedness, stability, comfort and belonging, shared by all. Home-making is a particularly affectively charged process of place-making for migrants and mobile people, who find themselves making a new home away from their homeland or previous home (e.g. Boccagni et al., 2018, offer a bibliography on home and migration). As such, home-making is a form of migrant longing, which, through digital mediation, may also result in finding belonging (Ponzanesi, 2020). In this section we focus on the affectivity of home-making through the prisms of place-making, nostalgia and aspiration, political struggle and intersectional power relations.

Place-making

From literary and media studies as well as anthropology we learn that digital technologies not only function to connect offline locations, they can also feel like places of home-making and belonging in their own right. People can feel at home in the digital diaspora – also described as the e-diaspora, net-diaspora, web-diasporas or ye-diaspora (young-ediaspora) – which is a process of imagination sustained through "cognitive social media" (Chaubey & Rahaman, 2021). For example, the 'floating population' (*liudong renkou*) of rural to urban migrant workers in China negotiate sensations of homelessness on the platforms *QQ* and *WeChat* as they move from one temporary job to another (Costa & Wang, 2020, pp. 519–520). Digital platforms, networks and groups are not neutral and external places for affective home-making. Rather, they are actively made into spaces of belonging as individuals and user collectives negotiate platform interfaces and templates, but also co-shape social dynamics, norms and expectations. To illustrate, Malagasy migrants living in France appropriate Facebook groups and pages to create the 'safe spaces' needed to express emotions and to maintain solidarity networks between Madagascar and the diaspora (Andrianimanana & Roca-Cuberes, 2021). Indian women living in the diaspora perform affective labour in their use of affordances to form sensory and affective digital communities around diasporic food blogs. Feeling they have to take up active ambassadorial roles as Indian regional cuisine experts living abroad, they form affective bonds through their digital diasporic place-making, criticizing stereotypical denouncements of Indian food as strange and spicy (Hegde, 2016). The digital place-making of migrants cannot be considered in isolation from offline dynamics. For example, the Yanacona indigenous community, which has been internally displaced in Colombia, use social media to find their place in the city of Bogotá. By recording and sharing practices of traditional music, they ensure the symbolic and affective transmission needed for their community's cultural survival (Sarria Sanz & Alencar, 2020). In contrast with previous understandings of the digital realm as a disembodied space, combining affect with a spatial approach can show how mobile subjects actively negotiate the affects of 'de-territorialization' they may feel in the physical space (scrutiny, surveillance and stereotyping) by 're-territorializing' (Appadurai, 1996) themselves online and offline with community members.

Nostalgia and aspiration

The search for a place to call home may be coloured by both nostalgia and future aspirations. The word 'nostalgia' is a combination of the two Greek words, *nostos*, meaning 'returning home' and *algia*, meaning 'longing' or 'pain'. As an affective longing, nostalgia is "a sentiment of loss and displacement, but it is also a romance with one's own fantasy" (Boym, 2007, p. 7). The video-sharing platform *YouTube* is used among Uyghurs, a Muslim minority population in northwest China, living in China and abroad, to establish an affective, imagined sense of togetherness and loyalty (Vergani & Zuev, 2011). Youth with a Moroccan migration background in the Netherlands turn to *YouTube* to watch videos shot in Morocco to shift their affective state and negotiate feelings of homesickness and nostalgia (Leurs, 2015).

Besides nostalgia, the digital migrant archive also gathers important texts and affects of aspiration (Appadurai, 2019; Georgiou & Leurs, 2022). Research among Indigenous Remote Northern Territory communities in Australia documented how aspirations of mobility are projected on mobile phones, platforms like *Skype* and digital resources (Taylor, 2012). Among international students living in Melbourne, Australia, digital media platforms are used to create transnational social fields by sharing and discussing dreams. Mobile aspirations emerge from affective drives to building a better life (taking charge over external conditions) and better selves (attending to internal qualities) (Wong, 2021).

Political struggle

Home-making in the digital diaspora also takes the form of political struggle. Home-making is shaped by ideologies and nationalisms, as is observable in the intensely affective negotiation of communities fighting for rights and recognition and negotiating conflicting national and cultural ties. The digital practices of non-state diasporas, such as Kurdish, Uyghur, Rohingya and Basque communities, provide important insights into the affective workings of ethno-nationalism online. In the case of the Basque diaspora, members living in the Basque country (under the administration of France and Spain) and those living abroad form a geographically borderless community together on the basis of affective glue, as they seek to reconstruct, mourn and mitigate cultural loss through digital practices (Oiarzabal, 2020). Kurdish people who have been forcibly displaced in Turkey, use *Facebook* and *WhatsApp* to construct an imaginary Kurdistan homeland (spanning southeastern Turkey, northwestern Iran, northern Iraq and northern Syria) as a "tool against assimilation" (Costa & Wang, 2020, p. 519). Forcibly displaced Rohingya – a mostly Muslim group who fled from the contested region of Rakhine in Myanmar – living in Bangladesh, Malaysia and Australia seek to digitally insert themselves in the emotionally charged ethno-religious conflict by challenging dominant Myanmar discourses (Aziz, 2022; Nasir, 2021).

Intersectionality

The practice of home-making on the basis of the ritualistic use of devices and technologies is shaped by power relations resulting from the intersection of gender, sexuality, religion, race, nationality, generation, age and ability, among others (Cabalquinto, 2018, 2022). Most notably, the home is commonly imagined as a gendered, domestic space outside politics and separated from the masculine-coded public domain. However, migration and digitization unsettle these gendered binary understandings of the private and public. Mobile subjects, particularly migrant women, engage in the public domain digitally, while their corporeal selves may be in private, bricks-and-mortar homes (Gajjala, 2019). The so-called Indian 'High Tech Housewives', who migrated with their spouses, may find themselves stuck in domesticity. To balance their desire for personal development with ideologies of heteronormativity, Hindu nationalism and expectations surrounding their reproductive roles as mothers and partners, they establish affective connections with fellow South Asian diasporic women (Bhatt, 2018). Similarly, temporary Korean migrants with 'dependent-visa' status – so-called 'trailing spouses' – combine affective hostland and homeland media practices to achieve greater autonomy and to distance themselves from Confucian-oriented patriarchal family culture (Lee, 2020, pp. 104–105).

In short, home-making is an affective media practice conducted across online and offline spaces. These practices display different scales and degrees of privateness and publicness. Place-making largely takes place within migrant communities. Nostalgia and aspiration are articulated across personal and private levels. Home-making as a form of political struggle is public and collective. Across transnational, national and personal domains, intersectional power relations pervade all practices of home-making.

Conclusions

For digital migration studies scholars, affectivity and emotionality are important analytic perspectives to understand the feelings and sensations that mobile subjects may have in encountering digital technologies. In this chapter, we developed affectivity into a framework to research the passage from one embodied emotional state to another that migrants may experience in their bodies when they engage with devices, screens and platforms. Emotions then are taken to refer to the conscious processing of these bodily transitions – for example, by expressing them in words – on the basis of one's biography and broader cultural frame of reference. "Affects are not determined in advance" (Ahmed, 2004, p. 362) and their proclivity for indeterminacy and change make this perspective particularly productive.

Twenty-five years ago, Arjun Appadurai (1996) argued the relations between media and migration could best be understood by addressing them as "ethno-, techno-, finance-, media and ideoscapes". Questions of ethnicity/race, technology, finance, mediation and ideology remain pertinent, but as Sandra Ponzanesi (2020) recently proposed, we should add the "affect scape" to our critical repertoire to address the non-rational dimensions of migration and medation. By approaching digital migration as an affectscape, we can grasp how cultural emotional practices impact local, national and transnational scales; scrutinize the implications of affective care online *vis-à-vis* emotional precarity; and trace how affects are distributed, surveilled and challenged across communities, networks and borders. In this chapter, four key themes that characterize research on the digital migration affectscape were presented: the political economy of affect, intimacy, transnational families and home-making. When drawing on affectivity to study digital migration, we can produce new important knowledge on how top-down forms of migration governance and bottom-up networks and their interrelationships are differently sensed in the bodies of mobile subjects.

Research Dialogue VII: Saskia Witteborn on technologies, migration and affect

Saskia Witteborn (PhD, University of Washington) is Associate Professor in the School of Journalism and Communication at The Chinese University of Hong Kong (CUHK). She specializes in the study of communication, technology and migration. She has worked with various migrant groups in the United States, Europe and East Asia and has written on geopolitics and collective identity formation, technology and political mobilization, technology and affect, the datafication of forced migration management and data privacy. She was a visiting scholar at the Free University of Berlin, at the Berlin Institute for Migration and Integration Research at Humboldt University, at Télécom Paris and the London School of Economics and Political Science. Her research has appeared in edited collections and in leading journals, including the *Journal of Communication, Cultural Studies, Research on Language and Social Interaction*, the *Journal of Refugee Studies*, and *Telematics and Informatics*. She has co-authored *The SAGE handbook of media and migration*, with Kevin Smets, Koen Leurs, Myria Georgiou and Radhika Gajjala (2020) and *Together: Communicating Interpersonally: A social construction approach* (6th edition, 2005), with John Stewart and Karen Zediker, published by Oxford University Press. Her latest book *Unruly Speech: Displacement and the politics of transgression* (2023) is published by Stanford University Press.

1. How did you come to the critical study of mobility and technology?

I grew up in East Germany and was lucky to see the fall of the Berlin Wall, which enabled me to travel more widely and learn English in the UK before moving to former West Germany for my MA degree and to the US for my PhD. As someone who has experienced the impact of heavily restricted transnational mobility in East Germany, I became deeply interested in mobility justice and transnational migration from early on. In East Germany, there were workers from Vietnam, contracted by the East German government to work in the state factories, international students from 'socialist brother countries' (e.g. Angola or Cuba), and soldiers from what was then the Soviet Union who were stationed in the country. Generally, migrants were supposed to leave East Germany once their contract or studies were finished. Contact with the local population was kept to a minimum. Therefore, my intellectual journey is based on experiences of spatial arrest and carefully choreographed interactions between locals and 'outsiders'. These experiences led to my great curiosity about life beyond the electric border fences of East Germany and the limited number of Eastern

Bloc countries we could travel to. I wanted to explore the conditions for and consequences of difference and the question of how strangers shape their identities in the tension between opportunity, socio-cultural isolation and structural pressures. Over time, digital technologies in all their iterations have assumed a key role in shaping mobilities and their management, transnational identities and mediated imaginaries about the other. They play a central role in my research.

2. How do you define and methodologically operationalize affectivity and emotions in your work?

I would like to make a disclaimer and position myself as a transnational (forced) migration and technology researcher, not a researcher of affect and emotions in the narrower sense. I tend to approach my work on emotions and technologies through a co-constitutive practice lens that focuses on the intersections between technologies, emotions and politics. I have found Anna Wierzbicka's work (e.g. Wierzbicka, 1999) helpful for approaching the question of the cultural translatability of emotions from a linguistic and cognitive perspective. I have also built on the well-known work by Sara Ahmed (2004, 2014) on how emotions come into being through the co-constitution and circulation of historically embedded figures and symbols.

Overall, I examine emotions as practices which enact the link between the personal, social and political. For example, when refugees I worked with felt ashamed or fearful, they did not only refer to an inner state of feeling but to larger social and political patterns and structures which amplified particular emotions, from living in shared asylum accommodation in Germany to navigating cultural expectations about gender in this environment. The built environment gestures to the socio-political mechanisms – material and immaterial – which tell us about how a society controls difference in the name of national security, resource management and technocracy (Witteborn, 2014). This built environment becomes part of the emotional practices which structure the daily life of people.

Unsurprisingly, I have found fear and hope to be emotions which are present in displaced populations across space and time (e.g. from Europe to East Asia). Fear of digital surveillance made people seeking asylum proceed very carefully when posting or commenting on Facebook in my research in Germany in 2010–2013. Despite this fear, however, the people engaged with social media to become visible on their own terms beyond the label 'asylum seeker' or 'refugee' and to mobilize politically (Witteborn, 2015). At the same time, video chats, live-streaming and social media comments co-constituted hope, from imagining the future, feeling supported by family and friends, to education and romantic love (Witteborn, 2015, 2021a). The studies highlighted again that emotions are shaped by socio-political, historical and technological processes and what has been called migration infrastructure (Xiang & Lindquist, 2014). This infrastructure increasingly datafies mobilities and migrants' digital practices and quantifies migrants into abstract data markers (Witteborn, 2022b).

3. **In reviewing digital migration studies of affectivity and emotionality, we considered the four themes of political economy, intimacy, transnational families and home-making. How does your work speak to these themes?**

I would situate my work at the moment within the political economy of transnational migration. A political economy approach enables me to explore the role of supranational and (inter)governmental institutions in structuring the movement of people fleeing conflict. This approach highlights the material dimensions of migration. In my recent research, mentioned above, I have examined the role of governmental and intergovernmental organizations in choreograph-ing transnational mobilities through digitalization and datafication practices and a technocratic imaginary of automation (Witteborn, 2022b). I have also explored the actors who keep displaced people in transit infrastructures in the context of Hong Kong SAR (Witteborn, 2021b).

In addition, my work speaks to physical and digital place-making through the connective affordances of digital technologies. People can build homes in a physical and digital place (see Halegoua & Polson, 2021) and migrants contribute to local contexts by emplac-ing themselves. This was one of the conclusions that Paola Monachesi and I (2021) have drawn from our study of skilled creative migrants in Amsterdam. The architects and designers shaped the discourse on technology, sustainability and innovation, and were engaged with the city and its people. They contradicted the notion of the place-less expatriate who works and plays hard and does not engage with the local (Robbins, 1998). At the same time, the migrants did pro-mote the Western model of the smart city and reinforced Western hegemonic imaginaries about place, progress, innovation and green living. I also want to point out that digital place enables people to become mobile on their own terms, specifically women, who can emancipate themselves financially through platform-enabled trade

(Xie & Witteborn, 2020). In a forced migrant context, digital place also becomes a space of memory. Karina Horsti, for example, wrote impressively about digital place and the politics of mediated memory (Horsti, 2017, 2019). You have illustrated how refugees use smartphones as archives and as a place to actualize the right to information and to cultural identity (Leurs, 2017). At the same time, a narrow view of migrant subjectivities and agency only gets us so far, as your book points out so elaborately.

Overall, I have to reflect constantly on the dilemma of representation in my research with displaced people and what it means to be a privileged white scholar and teacher who works with underserved and marginalized populations. Some of my answers are involving participants in research projects, making research insights relevant to the respective communities, volunteering, rigorous theoretical and methodological reflection, teaching these reflections to my students and learning from them.

4. **As a result of Covid-19 lockdown measures beween 2020 and 2022, people across the world became more aware of the vital role of technologies to maintain social relations and intimacy across distance. Where do you see gaps in the existing scholarship on affect?**

One gap I see is the question of how affect/emotions are co-constituted in and through immersive realities. The pandemic seems to have given a push to immersive technologies – immersive virtual reality (VR) in particular. A new generation of VR has emerged (VR film or cinematic virtual reality), in which viewers experience immersive, 360° films through image and sound. Organizations like the United Nations High Commissioner for Refugees (UNHCR) have used those VR films in their work. Humanitarian VR films move the viewer into a strong affective and moral space (see Nash, 2018, on the concept of improper distance). Within this space, emotions are produced (e.g. suffering or hope) which are propositions about how to act as a morally responsible and responsive viewer and citizen of the world. This is what Tim Gruenewald and I discuss in our piece in Cultural Studies *(2022). The discourses on helping, healing and empathy – which were important during the pandemic as well – disguise that VR film is part of a political economy of proselytizing liberal values and of normalizing the neoliberal consumption of suffering. Humanitarian VR films can present a victimized Other and divert attention away from the historical, economic and political conditions causing humanitarian crises. Emotions like suffering and hope can activate empathy through the simulation of intimacy. In other words,*

VR *films create the illusion of interpersonal intimacy and provide
an opportunity to feel with the suffering other. The technology
makes viewers consume emotions which are conveniently cleansed
of geopolitical and historial detail. The consumption of experience
takes centerstage, not the deeper engagement with acting upon unjust
historical and socio-political patterns. Nevertheless, VR will play
an even greater role in our daily lives in the future and shape how
migrants are imagined and how they become mobile.*

*Data privacy and affect is another research angle that deserves
more attention, I think. I have focused on the cultural variants of
data privacy in the contexts of migration (Witteborn, 2021a). By
cultural variant, I do not mean national or ethnic culture. I refer to
a culture of displacement. When engaging with social media, safety
was the main premise for displaced people, growing out of living
with fear and uncertainty. In turn, this need to be and feel safe
on social media did not always translate into appropriate privacy
practices, sometimes for lack of technical and legal knowledge
(Witteborn, 2021a). Examples are posting pictures on social media
to perform particular aspirations, such as financial security, consumption or just having fun. Although those are pretty standard
social media practices, visual, textual and geolocation evidence can
now be used for asylum claim decisions in several countries (Brekke
& Balke Staver, 2019), and images of posing in front of expensive
cars, having a party or enjoying the beach could potentially become
incriminating evidence against persecution claims.*

*I would like to point here to the importance of tracing concepts
through time and cultural space. I see privacy as a cultural concept.
Many migrants know about the importance of protecting their data.
Nevertheless, privacy practices are linked to social roles which in
turn need to be understood in their historical, spatial and cultural
context. For example, young women from the Iraq, Syria and
Palestine regions who sought asylum in Germany had to share
mobile devices with brothers, not only due to a lack of finances,
but due to gendered norms of technology ownership (Witteborn,
2022a). The women had to go to public internet cafés where they
experienced harassment or saw their data leaked to parents in the
name of cultural reproduction. The women found themselves in the
tension between shame, excitement, fear and digital empowerment.
This was a very real experience for the young women and could be
taken as a point of departure to explore even more the constitution of affect in contexts of technology and its social and political
implications.*

5. **What practical advice would you give to those aspiring to contribute to digital migration studies?**

I would encourage new generations of migration and technology researchers to focus on the material and ethical aspects of technologies and movement across space as well as their discursive dimensions. What is the material and algorithmic make-up of the digital practices and processes which select, order, include and exclude people and things from moving across space? As of 2023, communication and migration researchers still sometimes lack coding and computer engineering knowledge, which might help shed light on the more technical aspects of the mechanisms that sort mobilities. At the same time, the ethical aspects of the digitalization and datafication of migration should be highlighted more. I had the opportunity at CUHK to participate in a project on the ethical aspects of AI from a comparative country perspective. I learnt a lot from interdisciplinary discussions with my colleagues from legal studies, security studies, political science and the world of advocacy, including cases from India, China, Australia and Austria (Daly et al., 2019). Interdisciplinary work is key in my view to explore complex topics, such as data, automation and migration or the implications of digital identity for human communication and autonomy. Finally, I am currently interested in the potentials and challenges of immersive realities and blockchain technology for mobility and migration processes, including the future of (migrant) labour and rethinking the concept of co-presence in the context of Web 3.0. Computational methods in combination with solid theoretical training will be essential for making sense of the large amount of data materials available on different platforms. Interdisciplinary and inter-methodological research teams can be a productive solution to ask new questions about communication, migration and mobilities, and to revisit existing theories on affect and technologies.

Research Dialogue VIII: Earvin Charles Cabalquinto on what practices and affects of (im)mobility reveal about power and agency

Earvin Charles B. Cabalquinto is an Australian Research Council DECRA Fellow and Senior Lecturer in the School of Media, Film and Journalism (MFJ) at Monash University, Australia. He is the principal investigator of the 'Exploring the digital divide in the ageing migrant's personal home' project. Cabalquinto's research interests lie in the intersections of digital media, mobilities and migration. In particular, he has contributed important insights on the affective possibilities and limits of digital media use in the conduct of personal, familial and social relations beyond borders. Most recently, he published the monograph *(Im)mobile Homes: Family life at a distance in the age of mobile media* (Oxford University Press, 2022).

1. **How did you come to the study of media, migration and mobility?**

Studying the impacts of modern communication technologies on migration experiences is close to my heart. I, myself, am a Filipino migrant in Australia who relies heavily on digital platforms to sustain ties and relationships with my left-behind family members, relatives and friends across the world. My migration journey began in 2008 when I moved to Brunei Darussalam to work as a professional in an advertising company. For more than four years, I relied on using a 3G phone and a laptop to sustain ties with my loved ones in the Philippines. During those years, through friendships and networks I developed with other migrant Filipinos and communities, I witnessed and embodied how digital technologies facilitated the re-staging of family rituals up to management of multiple crises. This understanding propelled my interest to investigate the role of digital technologies in shaping migration experiences. I developed a PhD proposal in 2012, which I submitted to and discussed with my former PhD supervisor, Professor Brett Hutchins. He introduced me to the mobilities lens developed by the late British Sociologist John Urry (2007). This lens has become an instrumental framework across my research, thinking processes and critical approaches on topics situated within the growing field of digital media and migration study. In the fall of 2012, I moved to Australia and commenced my PhD project, focusing on how temporary Filipino migrants and their left-behind family members use an array of digital communication technologies and online platforms in sustaining a home from afar.

2. How do you define and methodologically study affectivity and emotions in your work, while also attending to the broader context of the digitalization of mobility/immobility?

I approach affective and emotive experiences as (re)produced and constantly negotiated as a result of the influences of asymmetrical social structures and technological infrastructures on transnational and digital practices. To begin with, I was inspired by the work of Mirca Madianou (2012) on how Filipina migrants in the United Kingdom sustained ties with their left-behind family members in the Philippines through polymedia. She particularly exposed the ambivalent experiences of migrant Filipina mothers who perform the role of care providers in a transnational home. Complementing her work, my research has highlighted how affective and emotive digital and transnational practices are shaped by familial and gendered norms, values and expectations, as well as access to digital media access and competencies. For instance, a migrant Filipina mother feels a sense of joy by providing care and love to her left-behind children in the Philippines through constant videoconferencing and phone calls. A migrant Filipino father experiences a sense of fulfilment by transferring money online to his left-behind family members, reinforcing the providing and authoritative role in the family. Moreover, migrant adult children's provision of moral, emotional and practical care to their ageing left-behind parents and siblings through digital media use contributes to the fulfilment of filial piety and generates happiness. However, frustrating and unsettling affective experiences also manifest in digital exchanges. To capture this point, I coined the term 'ambivalent intimacies' to highlight how digital media use among transnational families triggers contradictory affective experiences (Cabalquinto, 2018). As a result of uneven living conditions, structural constraints and uneven digital access, transnational family members experience both pains and gains. An individual stays connected yet may also feel excluded, unsettled and frustrated due to stringent familial expectations and digital asymmetries.

Methodologically, I investigate the affective outcomes of digital media use among dispersed family members through multi-sited ethnography and visual methods. I conducted in-depth interviews among temporary migrants in Melbourne, Australia, and their left-behind family members across selected regions in the Philippines to understand how differential living, socio-cultural, material and infrastructural conditions shape everyday digital practices. Noting the influence of entwined materiality and digitality (Horst & Miller, 2012), the in-depth interviews allowed the research to unravel the benefits and constraints of digital media use in enabling transnational connections. Moreover, considering the importance of kinship (Baldassar, Baldock & Wilding, 2007) in shaping digital media use, I engaged with how familial obligations and norms mould the performance of family life at a distance. More importantly, my work deployed visual methodologies, such as photo elicitation and photo documentation, to capture how affective digital practices are engendered and undermined by the exchange of visual contents, such as photos, videos, stickers, memes, and so forth. These methodological interventions offer new means to study the diverse and often differential affective and emotive digital practices of dispersed family members.

3. In reviewing digital migration studies of affectivity and emotionality, I discerned the four themes of political economy, intimacy, transnational families and home-making. How does your work speak to these themes?

In my recent book, I coined the term '(im)mobile homes' to capture the paradoxical outcomes of digital media use in sustaining family life at a distance among dispersed family members (Cabalquinto, 2022). This body of work encapsulates my critical interrogation of the intersecting four themes of political economy, intimacy, transnational families and home-making. I situate my critical investigation of the impacts of increased digitalization of migration experiences within the context of the migrant's home. For migrants and their dispersed family members, the home is an affective, imagined and highly networked space mediated by the advent of ubiquitous digital technologies. Echoing the work of Pink (2004), the home is characterized through its sensorial and affective dimension, which for dispersed family members are experienced and embodied through the materiality and digitality of media technologies. Here, moving in and through smartphone, tablet, computer, social media and mobile applications enables a sense of intimacy despite physical separation across borders. Additionally, the home, as a symbolic space, is reproduced through kinship, values and negotiations of familial values (Boccagni, 2017). Indeed, a sense of home, intimacy and belonging are performed and experienced through everyday digital practices.

I consider the migrant's home as symptomatic of the existing inequalities in our contemporary society. Noting the politics of performing intimacy in a transnationally networked home, I elucidate everyday digital media use as a key coping strategy for physical separation

*among transnational family members. Importantly, the physical frag-
mentation yet virtual connectedness of transnational families is a by-
product of structural inequalities of our global economy. For instance,
members of Filipino households often bear the burden of the lack of
access to social welfare services and public systems, compelling them
to leave the Philippines in search of a job that would support them
and meet their families' needs. This condition is a colonial legacy,
making the national economy and governance reliant on foreign control and international investors (Aguilar, 2014). Notably, the government also promotes overseas employment as a solution in addressing
underemployment and unemployment in the country (Rodriguez,
2010). In a transnational setting, Filipino migrants and their distant
kins reclaim a sense of home by using digital technologies to perform
familial and gendered roles and fulfil obligations. Paradoxically, the
emotionally-driven digital practices of the transnational Filipino family
in re-constructing a sense of home are leeched on by an economic
and political system that constantly promotes and relies on overseas
labour migration and remittances to keep the national economy afloat
without a strong commitment to create durable jobs and opportunities domestically and foster sustainable family reunification. These
outcomes tend to be overshadowed by a celebratory rhetoric of global
mobility and connectivity.*

4. **As a result of Covid-19 lockdown measures, people across the world
   became more aware of the vital role of technologies to maintain social
   relations and intimacy. Where do you see gaps in our scholarship on
   affect and emotion and what topics do you think we should pursue
   further in the future?**

*During the Covid-19 pandemic, pervasive mobile communication
technologies have allowed individuals to forge and maintain intimate
ties at a local and transnational level. Forced physical immobilities generated through stringent lockdowns, curfews, travel ban, and
cross-border shutdowns have been traversed through virtual mobility.
Building on my current study on investigating how ageing migrants
in Melbourne, Australia, use digital communication technologies in
navigating a forced physical immobility, such as a lockdown, I have
begun examining how affective experiences are shaped by both movements and stasis in and through mobile technologies. Within the growing body of work on the intersections of digital media and migration,
several scholars have begun exploring how forced physical immobility*

is dealt through digital media use (Patterson & Leurs, 2020; Smets, 2019; Twigt, 2022).

Drawing on my work on ageing migrants' digital practices during a lockdown, I contend the need to interrogate how affective experiences are enabled through mobilities in and through digital media. But it is crucial to pay attention to how emotive and intimate practices are informed by mediated immobilities or stasis is created through digital media use. Importantly, thinking about (in)voluntary immobility allows us to rethink the (re)production of agency and exclusion in a digital era. For instance, individuals who know how to navigate the affordances of online technologies are able to voluntarily pause and opt not to share information in order to preserve relationships. This shows how a sense of closeness is enacted through mediated immobility. However, some experience forced mediated immobility, especially when they do not have access to a stable internet connection or lack technological competencies. Some also face difficulties when their networks experience the same disadvantages in digital spaces. By closely examining these outcomes, we see how tech-based immobility has a physical, affective and relational dimension. Noting this, I argue that future work should contribute a more nuanced understanding of what it means to be mobile and still at a time when stringent mobility regimes are erected and there's an increasing reliance on digital technologies to access a diverse range of tools and services to sustain personal, familial and social ties.

5. **What practical advice would you give to those aspiring to contribute to digital migration studies?**

Over the past years, a plethora of work has been produced that examines the role of digital media technologies and online platforms in shaping the migration experiences of mobile bodies, such as migrants, refugees and asylum seekers. During the pandemic, researchers were forced to suspend ethnographic and place-based fieldwork on the digital lifeworlds of migrants, refugees and asylum seekers. However, similar to the experiences of other researchers, I shifted to deploying remote data gathering for my research on ageing migrants' digital practices during a lockdown. Personally, deploying remote interviews – using a phone call and Zoom – allowed me to rethink the meanings and practices of a 'fieldwork'. It has led me to consider the role of digital technologies as a conduit for understanding 'fieldwork' as 'field events' or a series of activities shaped by digital technologies (Ahlin & Li, 2019).

For instance, I embodied a sense of co-presence with my participants when a Zoom interview allowed the participants to move their camera to point at an object in their house. The set-up of a Zoom interview also revealed the relationships participants had with their close networks. Family members often assisted the ageing participants in using Zoom. However, digital media use also illuminated digital inequalities. Some participants opted for a phone call because of a lack of knowledge in using Zoom. Further, some participants were unable to access a video-conferencing session with their peers because of their lack of digital skills to address technical issues. I contend that these field events present new insights on approaching and understanding the digital lifeworlds of migrants. Importantly, I used Lego, as a tool in visualizing narratives (Gauntlett, 2007), to represent the everyday, intimate and (im)mobile experiences of the participants (see Figure 4.1 and 4.2 below). Here, the Lego visuals illustrated the ecology of technologies, objects and symbols constitutive of the digital lifeworlds of the participants.

Building on my ongoing research on the formation and negotiation of everyday (im)mobilities in and through digital media, I recommend future research to interrogate the digital lifeworlds of (im)mobile bodies by thinking beyond online platforms and their affordances. Certainly, technological features shape how intimate, affective ties and belongingness are performed, experienced and negotiated. However, as I highlight in my conception of "(im)mobile homes", there is a need to pay close attention to how digital practices are shaped by unequal social, economic, political and technological forces (Cabalquinto, 2022). In doing so, our scholarship can offer rich insights in exposing intimate practices and networked spaces as crucial sites for revealing and addressing structural inequalities on a global stage.

Furthermore, I encourage scholars who are interested in digital media and migration studies to consider how lifeworlds are shaped by (in)voluntary movements and stillness in and through digital media. To redress this, future interventions can also look into what mediating and representing (im)mobilities reveal about agency, marginalization, and even subversion. One may ask, how does a text, image or video mobilize and immobilize an individual? What does it mean to broadcast or curate a block of (im)mobile people or groups represented through data visualization? How are class, gender, ethnicity, race and dis/ability interlinked with the politics of (in)visible and (im)mobile social actors? These emerging inquiries may provide a starting point to help us understand the complex meanings and practices of moving and pausing in and through digital technologies in volatile times.

Figures 4.1 and 4.2   An ageing participant using a tablet computer to watch *YouTube* videos on gardening (top photo). An ageing participant surrounded by a laptop, a smartphone and money to sustain connections among local and overseas loved ones (bottom photo)

Photos by Earvin Charles Cabalquinto.

5

Histories

The digital migration practices and technologies discussed in previous chapters, such as biometric passports, body scanners or remittance networks, do not come from an a-historical void. Rather, technologies, together with their accompanying use, norms and protocols, reflect both a particular moment in experiencing and governing migration, and a distinctive moment in media history. To date, however, in the words of media scholar Philipp Seuferling, "a fundamental historical exploration of media shaping structures and agencies for forced migrants is lacking" (Seuferling, 2021, p. 28). Here, we can add that a fundamental historical account of the role of media governance and experience is lacking not only for forced migrants but also for migrants and mobile subjects in general. To begin to address this gap in the scholarship, in this chapter we develop a *longue durée* perspective to trace historical relations between migration and media technologies.

The historical *longue durée* (e.g. Braudel & Wallerstein, 2009) is a productive perspective to analyze the historical lineages and evolution – also sometimes called the 'deep time' – of pre-digital migration technologies across extended historical time periods. Observed over the long term, historical patterns, trends, continuities, breaks and failures can serve as a basis from which to draw conclusions about the interrelations between histories, the present and possible desirable or undesirable futures. Such a diachronic perspective considers historical moments and periods as interconnected in contrast to a synchronic perspective, which seeks to isolate and zoom into a particular period in history. With a focus on the mediated management of mobility of people in time and space and experiences of mobility, such a genealogical approach compares epochs of migration, mobility and technologies by tracing continuities, changes, ruptures and critical junctures.

What can we learn from the development, use and experience of pre-digital and early-digital technologies? By taking a *longue durée* perspective on digital migration technologies, we can pursue the following goals:

- Evaluating, nuancing and challenging scholarly 'firstist' claims. In addressing the 'newness' of technological innovations and experiments, scholars commonly take a-historical perspectives. A historical perspective allows us to develop a counterpoint and debunk claims about the exceptionality or uniqueness of technological developments in the context of migration and mobility.

- Develop a greater understanding that seemingly high-tech, advanced technologies of the present are not a logical end-point, a culmination of linear progression, or a causal process of innovation, but are always peculiar, distinctively located and contingent.
- Insights into historical lineages offer a means to question and denaturalize the making of migration and mobility through contemporary categories, procedures and borders as well as how they are mediated by digital technologies.
- We can draw on historical technological developments to question (future) dystopian consequences for some mobile subjects – and we can draw on historical insights to imagine, articulate and pursue utopian alternatives.

This chapter first defines historical approaches to migration and media. Subsequently, following the themes addressed in the previous chapters, historical accounts of migration infrastructures, connectivity, representation and affectivity are discussed.

Historical media dispositions of migration

The premise that "all history has media" (Edwards et al., 2011, p. 1400) will inform our historical scrutiny of the technologies of migration and mobility. A lot of work needs to be done to draw out the nuances of monolithic understandings of migration in relation to technologies. From the perspective of multi-directionality, we can remind ourselves, for example, that even though we know that a potentiality for contestation is materially embedded in any technology (Chun, 2006), few systematic historical studies exist on how migrant and mobile people have experienced, negotiated and/or resisted technologies (e.g. Arnold, 2005; Rohrlich, 2000; Seuferling, 2021).

To frame our *longue durée* approach, we connect discussions from historiography (the study of the concepts and methods in producing historical knowledge), migration and media history.

From historiography, we can inform ourselves about the trap of "presentism": the tendency to conduct historical research to validate contemporary situations. For example, a historical approach is important to trace common claims about the newness of our digital society, such as "surveillance capitalism is young, barely 20 years in the making" (Zuboff, 2020, n.p.). For this purpose, we may de-centre our focus on the present and try to grasp how histories shape the present, how historical eras can be understood in their own right, besides considering how present perspectives retrospectively can inform our understanding of historical eras. Taking a "multi-directional approach" (Rothberg, 2009), we can avoid pursuing universalizing grand narratives about the past. Rather than seeing history as a singular discourse which results from a competitive zero-sum game, histories are contextual, dialogic, processual and multiple (Scott, 1990; Stoler, 2009, 2016).

History scholarship commonly overlooks migrants and refugees. When they are considered, they are commonly framed as victims, not as "agents of change" (Gatrell, 2017, p. 175). Critical scholars of migration history offer an alternative perspective. They address the particular historical constellations – laws, policies, institutions, agencies, practices and discourses – that have constructed particular dominant conceptions of migration in distinct temporal and spatial contexts. An important case in point is the historical production of the refugee regime (Gatrell, 2013, 2017). This paradigm is committed to writing histories from below – beyond the exertion of power by supra-national or national bodies. It advances agency-centric approaches to acknowledge how, where and why migrants themselves have contributed. Finally, historians of migration call for an awareness that migrant journeys are not random but commonly display a particular "path dependency", associated with historical journeys, diasporic formations or previous generations (BenEzer & Zetter, 2015).

Following the research principles of media archaeology (a branch of media history), we can learn to avoid seeing media history as a continuous process of accelerated technological innovation or linear progression. The geological concept of "deep time" invites us to consider earthly timescales that span across human lifetimes (Zielinski, 2006). Media archeological research seeks to excavate – in a literal, material sense as well as a metaphorical sense – the materiality, but also the accompanying procedures, protocols and practices of particular media epochs (Huhtamo & Parikka, 2011). This way, we can move away from considering newly invented technologies as a *tabula rasa* (in the absence of earlier assumptions or preconceived ideas) (e.g. Gitelman, 2006). Rather, with the concept of deep time, we can "find something new in the old" (Zielinski, 2006, p. 3) and conduct archeological investigation of the materialities, practices and imaginaries of technological development (Leurs & Seuferling, 2022). By studying how "media of different epochs are layered palimpsestically" (Mattern, 2015, p. 103), we can dig up the multiple criss-crossing paths of technological experimentation and innovation with mobile subjects. As such, we can trace how the "wake" or afterlives of slavery (Sharpe, 2015) haunt the anti-blackness and white supremacy discernible in media-technological systems and processes of contemporary migration management and governance.

Therefore, the media of different particular periods of time can be scrutinized to reveal how they encapsulated particular dispositions towards particular groups of people. The notion of the "media dispositif" has been proposed as a heuristic tool to consider these dispositions, in particular by teasing out the complex ways in which media technologies and texts of a particular period (can aim to) produce particular subject positions (Kessler, 2006). For example, biometric technologies such as finger-printing date from colonial era South Africa and India. Through time, they have been deployed to facilitate measurement, administration and ranking for the purpose of ensuring particular forms of mobility of particular groups of people (Breckenridge, 2014; Pugliese, 2010).

Media technologies of particular epochs can be seen as interlinked. In parallel to migration history, and also in media history, the conceptual model of "path dependency" can be useful. In our case, it can help us recognize how the channels, protocols and spaces of "preceding technologies" of migration steer the development of "successor technologies" (Mattern, 2015, p. 106). This is not to say that technologies determine certain outcomes. Awareness is also needed about how serendipity and historical social, cultural and political factors impact technological development. Media forms borrow, change, replace and adapt to other media forms, a process called "remediation" (Bolter & Grusin, 2000). Analyzing and comparing the path dependencies of media and migration developments can offer insights into the power-ridden processes of how technologies have served to position particular mobile people similarly or differently through time.

In the following sections, we will encounter exemplary studies that offer practical insight in choosing between and operationalizing historical approaches to media and migration.

Historicizing infrastructures

To date, the histories of migration infrastructures are understudied, as the geographer Francis L. Collins observed: "While much research on migration industries and infrastructure has to date focused on contemporary patterns, many of their functions and effects have substantial historical lineages that have yet to be sufficiently examined" (2021, p. 873). Communication scholar Karim Karim's foundational text *The media of diaspora* (2003a) reminds us that 19th-century infrastructural investments in news agencies, telegraph, telephone and transport, which sustained transnational media forms between the colonies and the colonial metropolis, increased the sphere of control, influence and the cultural dominance of the colonizer. The historical roles and operation of such infrastructures can be teased out by addressing the four perspectives on infrastructures outlined in Chapter 1: social brokering, materiality, relationality and the imaginary.

Histories of the social brokering of migration

What are the historical genealogies of the social brokering of migration? Historical research shows that "migration brokers and the organization of human mobility did not always exist in a black box" (McKeown, 2012, p. 21). Rather, in the three decades preceding the early 20th century, as Adam McKeown argues, lawmakers, officials and journalists were chiefly focused on recruitment, financing, transporting and connecting employers with migrant workers. Only from the late 19th century did infrastructural brokering become black-boxed, as the discourse on the brokers and middlemen of migration shifted from facilitators to smugglers. Brokers became increasingly stereotyped as the source of migration evils. Laws that aimed to regulate brokering pushed migration underground. This happened while, simultaneously, understandings of the migrants as 'free' and self-motivated individuals became dominant, which took place in a wider context where the focus shifted from facilitating and regulating the process of migration to enforcing border control (McKeown, 2012).

A historical focus on migrant brokerage provides insights from the middle, a view that is neither top-down nor bottom-up. For example, in the early modern period (1571–1669), mobile elites, such as traders, which E. Nathalie Rothman (2014) terms "trans-imperial subjects", travelled between Venice and Istanbul, and thereby circulated changing views in the Mediterranean of the Ottoman empire and Venetian institutions. Through the negotiating of cultures and languages of commerce, law, religion and diplomacy, they functioned as "imperial boundary-makers", raising questions about the genealogy of the politics of belonging from the early modern times to our own current days (Rothman, 2014). Besides providing historical insights into how brokering shaped belonging, historical studies also reveal the role of governmental interference and the persistence of unequal power relations along the lines of race and gender, among others.

Illustratively, between 1885 and 1945, generations of Chinese brokers, mostly businessmen who competed for ethnic leadership, served important roles as intermediaries, interacting between Chinese and Anglo communities and politics, in Canada, at a time when most Chinese immigrants were considered illegal (Mar, 2010). In the period between 1949 and 1989, humanitarian brokers, NGOs, churches and Chinese community organizations were largely unsuccessful in countering the Canadian state who would classify Chinese migrants fleeing China as illegals rather than refugees (Madokoro, 2012). In the United States in the 19th century, domestic servitude, which bordered on indentured or coerced labour, was brokered by white upper- and middle-class Americans and the state, at the expense of Black, Chinese and white Irish immigrants, particularly women (Urban, 2017). Between 1910 and 1930, particularly the first generation of pioneering Japanese colonial settlers, including merchants, traders, sex workers, journalists and teachers, actively mediated in the colonial settlement of Korea, and contributed to the imperial expansion project of Japan (Uchida, 2014). While historical research on brokering is emerging, there is a lack of attention paid to the historical roles of pre-digital media technologies in how people such as entrepreneurs, officials, lawmakers and middlemen (and women performing intermediary roles) infrastructurally organized human movement.

Histories of the materialities underpinning migration infrastructures

What can we learn from addressing the historical materialities of migration and media infrastructures? We can scrutinize these interlinkages by literally digging into the earth to uncover geologies of media-technological-migration histories. From a genealogical perspective, we can assume that successor technologies do not supersede old ones, but follow previously established pathways. Following the path dependency principle, we can consider how previous infrastructures have served as the foundation for modern-day systems. For example, telephone lines follow predecessor paths such as the telegraph and railroads. Of particular interest for digital migration studies scholars, as media scholar Nicole Starosielski (2015) has documented, the historical telegraph network and the fibre-optic cables which make up the backbone of the internet today are routed through an 'undersea network', which follows the pathways of former colonial shipping routes, such as the transatlantic triangular slave trade.

Between the 16th and 19th centuries, this pathway of extraction and exploitation involved three continents. White European traders set sail, shipping arms, textiles and wine and buying people from West and West Central Africa, who were forcibly transported. An estimated 12.5 million Black people were transported in dehumanizing conditions during a 6–8-week Middle Passage to the Americas. Those who survived (an estimated 10.7 million people) were sold as chattel and forced to work as enslaved labourers. The Europeans returned with the resources produced by the enslaved labourers, including sugar, coffee, rice, tobacco and cotton, which met the demands of European markets (e.g. Browne, 2015; Smith & Paquette, 2010). Partly following colonial shipping routes, the "All Red Line" copper telegraph cable network, completed in 1902, connected the British colonies, through a similar mix of public and private enterprise (Starosielski, 2015). The routing of prominent undersea fibre-optic cables, which serve as the physical infrastructure of the internet too, partially follows the geographies of the transatlantic triangular trade system (Rezaire, 2020).

Similar to how the telegraph can be understood as a strategic material technology of colonial control, the material infrastructure of the internet today can be understood as being haunted by modes of control and exclusion, as it was not developed to benefit the formerly colonized people. For the digital humanities scholar Dhanashree Thorat, the new fibre-optic oceanic pathways linking South Asia, East Africa and the Middle East through different routes can therefore be understood as "decolonial infrastructural models", as they envision different organizations of ownership, cooperation and governance (2019, p. 252). Further critical analysis is urgently needed to inquire into the genealogies of the material infrastructures of rule (Bhat, 2021), by tracing the infrastructural path dependencies of migration and media technologies, and the implications and possibilities of decolonial disruptions of those paths.

Historical relationalities of infrastructures

Scholars of science and technology studies have advocated a relational view on contemporary infrastructures to acknowledge better the interrelationships between the contemporary moment and the past. This view emphasizes not novelty but continuity and consistency. For this purpose, infrastructures can be addressed from the perspective of the 'long now' (Bowker et al., 2010). The 'long now' stretches over two centuries, a period when "two suites of changes began to occur in the organization of knowledge" (ibid., p. 40). In this time span, states have exponentially increased their information-gathering activities while, simultaneously, the technologies and practices to generate, store and sort information have also grown exponentially. During the colonial era, subordinated people and places were used as a testing ground for infrastructural technological development and information gathering and analysis (Adas, 2015; Harding, 2011), as we can learn from works such as Helen Tilley's *Africa as a living laboratory* (2011) or Rudolf Mrázek's *Engineers of happy land: Technology and nationalism in a colony* (2002). This process continued from the colonial period until the 20th century, as studies of infrastructural entanglements show, for example of refugee management in Germany after World War II (Seuferling, 2021) and the technopolitics of the Cold War (Hecht, 2011).

In the 20th century, biometrics on the basis of statistical documentation and analysis of biological data points were used to differentiate between races and 'objectively' prove white superiority over non-white races. Gradually, with the formalization of finger print technologies, biometrics became understood in light of automated identification. In South Africa, biometric registration supported the apartheid regime and the broader information-based police state (Breckenridge, 2014). From the perspective of the "coloniality of biometric power", the geographer Hidefumi Nishiyama (2022) argues that we can chart pathways of racialized control through biometrics across historical and geographical contexts. In imperial Japan, finger prints and palm prints were interpreted to prove biological inferiority and superiority. The 1926 "finger print index", devised by forensic pathologist Furuhata Tanemoto, was used to classify national subjects and indigenous populations from across the world in a page-long table. In its hierarchy, it was suggested that in comparison to other Asians, Japanese bodies were biologically more closely related to Europeans (Nishiyama, 2022, p. 125). Future research is needed to pursue such historical relationalities of migration infrastructures, to account, for example, for how, to date, "the most powerful biometric surveillance systems are being developed in the poorest countries, the former colonies of European empires" (Breckenridge, 2014, p. 17). To pursue further inquiry into these interrelationships, new dialogues between postcolonial, decolonial, indigenous and STS perspectives are needed.

Historical infrastructural imaginaries

The lens of deep time can be taken up to study – over the course of a longer period of time – the role of the imagination in the formation of particular status quos of technology and migration: how have infrastructure developments that serve/contain particular mobile people been imagined diachronically?

For this purpose, we can explore how 'deep' approaches to history, migration and technology can be aligned. In the humanities and social sciences, the geological metaphor of deep time enables a non-linear imagination of history (Leurs & Seuferling, 2022; Zielinski, 2006). In trying to discover what developments have shaped the "deep fault lines of the world today", such as uneven possibilities for mobility, the historian Ann Stoler invites us to consider how logics and sensibilities of colonial governance and imperialism left durable marks and thereby function as "deep pressure points" (2016, pp. 5–6).

Although often heralded as efficient, neutral and objective, infrastructures imagined as a tool to expedite control have not emerged from a void. Desires of complete knowing in order to rule subjects are reflected in the infrastructural developments of colonial conquest and extraction of resources as well as fascist rule by Nazi Germany. These efficiency-driven, administrative technologies reflect a "concentrationary imaginary" (Pollock, 2015, p. 5). There is great potential in tracing how the anti-Blackness and white supremacy of historical infrastructures reflect the "carceral imaginary" (Benjamin, 2019b) of present-day migration infrastructures. An important case in point are the violent state desires of knowing and controlling its population and state borders by governing and othering particularly racialized bodies (Pugliese, 2010). Policy and the Silicon Valley expectations of artificial intelligence can be traced back to a white male superiority and imperialist worldview reflecting the context of the Cold War military-industrial complex from which it emerged (Katz, 2020).

Throughout history, desires of control and containment are commonly projected on technological advancements. For example, "biometric imaginaries" that display forensic fantasies of identification and classification based on eugenic ideals follow historic pathways (Kang, 2022). For example, at the turn of the 20th century, French authorities developed an "anthropometric nomad passbook" to racially identify "gypsies" and "nomads" on the basis of apparent scientific features such as skin tones (Kang, 2022). Such paper-based classification and ordering tools are pre-digital precursors to contemporary algorithms. Louise Amoore has traced which historical logics haunt contemporary bordering. She argues that discriminatory design and programming in the contemporary digital border demonstrate that they "enact the colonial continuities of racist discrimination and partition" (Amoore, 2021, p. 7). The contemporary "deep border", which results from states incorporating deep learning and neural network algorithms, display states' desires to govern mobility by tapping into computer science imaginations of complex thinking and problem solving (ibid.).

Beyond infrastructural imaginaries projected on technologies, imaginaries of migrants are historically used to legitimate infrastructural solutions. Migrants are commonly perceived to carry contagious diseases, warranting containment as a security measure. Following the announcement of the Covid-19 lockdown measures in India, the health risk posed by millions of migrant wage workers who got stuck in their travels from cities to rural areas caused a public outcry (Shah, forthcoming 2023; Sreedhar Mini & Baishya, 2022). Studies on the contemporary health governance of migrant workers during the Covid-19 pandemic can be expanded by relating them to historical legacies of infrastructural imaginaries. For example, in the early 20th century, following public fears for the spread of tuberculosis, Mexican labourers in the United States were quarantined and subjected to experimental medical treatments (Perreira, 2019). Studying medical archives thus allows us to reconstruct historically how migrants are perceived to carry contagious diseases, warranting infrastructural containment as a security measure.

Historicizing connections

The history of migrant connectivity practices can shed light on how digitalization has resulted in ontological changes in maintaining relations across distance and space-making. In other words, technologies have allowed for a new sense of co-presence to be felt across distance (see Chapter 1 and Chapter 4). However, it is also important to remind ourselves that we should not only chase the newest technological developments. Migrants have always used media practices to stay connected to family, friends and the diaspora. As Karim Karim reminds us, "diasporic media have frequently been at the leading edge of technology adoption" (2003b, p. 12). Before the advent of digital media, the connections that were fostered consisted largely of asynchronous modes of communication. That is, connections were never instant, direct or happening at the same time (Wood & King, 2001). When reflecting on the past from the digital present, one can easily assume that in pre-digital periods migrants experienced a sense of "double absence". Being doubly absent refers to feeling out of sync because of limited abilities to take part in two societies at once as a result of being uprooted from a country of origin and remaining an outsider in the country of arrival (Sayad, 1999; see also Research Dialogue III). However, contextualized historical accounts of experiences of migrant connectivity can yield a more nuanced picture. Below we separate out historical geographies of connectivity and historical information practices, rights and repression.

Historical geographies of connectivity

Comparative historical overviews of migrant connectivity practices and technologies throughout time do not currently exist. However, there is scope to connect distinctive mobile people's media histories and networking across geographies. One could, for example, study letter writing among missionaries in ancient history, the role of newspapers and the telegraph under colonial rule in the 19th century, the circulation of letters, remittances and material goods among diasporic groups in the 20th century, and their subsequent adoption of video cassette recorders and satellite television in the late 20th century.

For example, missionaries of the world religions, including Buddhism, Christianity and Islam, could be a starting point to address how mediated forms of transnational connectivity have developed throughout time. In ancient times, the multi-directional movement of Buddhist traditions across Central and South Asia relied on the establishment of networks, cross-cultural exchanges and trade. These were sustained by the media technology of the time, which included scriptures and rock carving (petroglyphs) and travellers writing graffiti on rocks, among other things (Neelis, 2011). From 1540, over the course of several decades, Jesuits (a religious order of the Catholic Church) established missions in over 100 countries across Europe, the Americas, Africa and Asia. By circulating letters between missions and Europe and manually duplicating and distributing these in large numbers, a sense of networked Jesuit identity was maintained (Nelles, 2019).

Telegraph communication is a colonial technology based on the transmission of information over a wire mediated through series of electrical current pulses (usually in Morse code). In the Netherlands East Indies (present-day Indonesia), the first telegraph line was laid in 1856 between Weltevreden (a mostly Dutch residential suburb of the capital of Batavia) and the summer location of the government in Buitenzorg. Here, the writings of Raden Adjeng Kartini, who was born into the Javanese aristocracy at the time of the Dutch colonial occupation and who paved the way for gender emancipation and Indonesian independence, are illustrative of the feelings of proximity that telegraph communication promised. Kartini was highly enthusiastic about the potential of sending and receiving telegraph messages (also known as "wires", "calls" and "cables") for achieving co-presence. In reflecting on telegraphs, she referred to the "secret telephone-cable" that ran between her and her father's heart (Mrázek, 2002, pp. 161–163).

From the 19th to the late 20th century onwards, migrant networks were sustained through the circulation and importation of newspapers, books and magazines, and gradually cassettes, videotaped films and television programmes in minority languages (Hopkins, 2009). In her work with Punjabi diasporic families living in Southall, London, Marie Gillespie found that many had already acquired video cassette recorders (VCRs) in 1978, "well before most households in Britain" (1995, p. 79), in order to watch Hindi films on videotape, at home. In the 1990s, as the market grew and prices decreased, low-budget international phone calls enabled everyday forms of co-presence, serving as the main "social glue of migrant transnationalism" (Vertovec, 2004a). Indicatively, between 1995 and 2001, calls from Pakistan to Canada increased by 556%, calls from the UK to India grew by 439% and calls between the USA and the Philippines grew by 452%, illustrating how it became more "common for a single family to be stretched across vast distances and between nation-states, yet still retain its sense of collectivity" (Vertovec, 2004a, p. 222). Later in the 2000s, text messaging offered a new means of connectivity. Internal migrants from the Nuba Mountains of Sudan living in the capital Khartoum embraced text messages to exchange poetry and song lyrics. Through this portable medium, they established new means of appropriating Arabic-Islamic traditions, patterns of keeping in touch and maintaining an imagined community of Nuba people (Lamoureux, 2009).

Contemporary mobile people are said to navigate a polymedia landscape, choosing between distinctive platforms and affordances to convey their messages (see Chapter 2: Connections). However, there is scope to change our perspective and reconsider the abundance of pre-digital media as an analogue polymedia landscape. For example, in the late 1990s, Camilla, a mother living in Huancayo, Peru, was documented as maintaining ties with her daughters living overseas in Italy through telephone calls, and by circulating goods such as letters, parcels, cassettes, photographs, taped videos, money and cultural artefacts (Tamagno, 2001, p. 108).

Historicizing information practices, rights and repression

The literature on historical community media and ethnic media offers cues to historicize forms of migrant connectivity from the perspective of information practices and from the perspective of human rights and repression.

We can, for example, consider the role of information practices among French, German, Italian, Polish, Norwegian, Slovak, Hungarian, Slovenian, Ukrainian, Bohemian and Yiddish migrants settling in the United States in the 18th and 19th centuries. These communities set up their own presses to produce ethnic newspapers. Until World War I, ethnic newspapers faced few restrictions. Most were short-lived as a result of financial obstacles, but initiatives rapidly succeeded one another. While German-American and Japanese-American presses faced bans and intense scrutiny during World War I and World War II, the German-Jewish press became an important 'lifeline' for Jewish refugees fleeing from Europe, providing details underreported in the mainstream press. Ethnic media also served as a similar lifeline connecting migrants serving in the armed forces with the diaspora living in the United States. For example, outlets like the *Chinese Times* in San Francisco or the *China Daily News* in New York published soldiers' reports from the frontlines, which included accounts of the discrimination they experienced (Matsaganis, Katz & Ball-Rokeach, 2011, p. 36). Around the same time, between 1880 and 1940, African-owned newspapers in British West Africa (now The Gambia, Sierra Leone, Ghana and Nigeria) printed anonymous letters, fiction and poetry that commented upon, altered and played with discourses of colonial power and African identity (Newell, 2013).

Community media scholars have shown how migrant media initiatives catered to their communities grew into subaltern counter publics by providing a means to contest and challenge the mainstream public sphere (Siapera, 2011, see Chapter 3: Representations). Between the 1960s and 1980s, BBC Radio Leicester produced broadcasts on, for and with post-war Asian migrants in England, while the West German public service radio offered airtime to *Gastarbeiter* (guest workers) and *Spätaussiedler* (German repatriates from Eastern Europe) (Hilgert, Just & Khamkar, 2020). Radio remains a pivotal outlet for migrant communities across the world (see De Koning et al., 2019). For example, the Shan migrant community in Chiang Mai, Thailand, set up Map Radio FM 99 to enable the community to adapt to Thai society, by circulating information and promoting community cohesion (Jeon, 2020).

Historical accounts of queer media representation offer important insights into pre-digital forms of transnational community formation. The internet – through enabling the circulating of non-mainstream information and voices – is considered as the chief medium of globalization. However, before the internet, a variety of media forms connected audiences and communities. For example, taking a historical transnational approach to the study of mediated sexuality, Łukasz Szulc (2018) has documented how, in the 1980s, gay and lesbian presses operated across transnational scales. The cross-border flow of gay and lesbian magazines from and to late communist Poland during the Cold War in Europe networked transnational homosexual readers and identities, but also served to challenge misrepresentation and non-representation. Such analogue, community-oriented information activism had great potential to foster self-awareness and acceptance of non-heteronormative love (see Research Dialogue X by Łukasz Szulc).

As these examples show, it is important to focus not on what predecessor technologies have lacked, or to romanticize them, but to approach distinctive historical usages in their own situated context by considering particular medium-specific characteristics, their affordances and the broader space- and time-specific media culture. In this way, we do not assume a teleological progression towards an ultimate contemporary form of polymedia connectivity, but rather consider situated usage while simultaneously remaining aware of how certain path dependencies have shaped the use of media technologies to sustain connectivity across distance.

Historicizing representations

In Chapter 3, we addressed the politics of representing migration by exploring who can speak about who, why and how. For this purpose, we distinguished between two sides of representation: (1) top-down institutionalized gatekeepers, who were argued to give shape to particular representational regimes (actors – particularly those in power – represent by speaking in the name of and by portraying migrants, in particular, often in reductionist, stereotypical, hierarchical and homogenizing ways); and (2) migrants' bottom-up self-representations that allow for the construction of voice, identity and personal archives that could diversify migration discourse.

Representation regimes

Present-day digital media representational regimes that stereotype, homogenize, exoticize and racialize migrants can be traced to a longer past. Illustratively, in the context of Spain and South America, current racist discourse in telenovelas, novels, literature, school textbooks and television advertising have been traced back to the Reconquista (the battles waged from 801 to 1492 to expel Muslim settlers, known as Moors, from Spanish soil), which was followed from 1492 onwards by the Spanish colonial conquest of South America and the spread of Catholicism among the indigenous populations. Together, these have historically reinforced the racialized marginalization of Arabs, Jews and sub-Saharan Africans in Spain and in South America, both on the level of materiality and on the level of discursive representation (Van Dijk, 2005).

Exhibitions devised to entertain and 'educate' audiences also inform and haunt contemporary regimes of representation. In Denmark, between 1870 and 1920, over 50 exhibitions of real people took place. These were exhibitions of so-called 'exotic people', who were expected to perform their everyday life in 'villages' that were constructed in the middle of the Copenhagen Zoo. Such ethnic human exhibitions, (re)producing European colonial concepts of race, gender and sexuality, linger in contemporary popular cultural representations of 'exoticness' (Andreassen, 2015). Sarah Bartmann, an indigenous Khoi-San woman from South Africa – a community labelled 'hotentot' or 'bushmen' by the Dutch settlers – was exhibited at freak shows and fairs across Europe. Causing particular fascination and exoticization by her bodily appearance (broad hips, prominent buttocks and altered genitals), she was presented in popular media and scientific discourse as the living proof and representation of an essentially different class of human species (Buikema, 2018). The study of whether and how contemporary representations of migrants reflect European 19th-century exhibition practices, which emphasized the excessive sexuality of non-white women and the primitiveness, animality, masculinity and danger of non-white men, is long overdue.

As in the current digital era, mainstream media representation of migration has been predominantly incident-based. It either dominantly reinforced othering or spurred sympathy with migrants. For example, on the one hand, the centre-left newspaper *La Repubblica* discursively constructed consensus in favour of evicting over 1,000 migrants living in the La Pantanella squat, an abandoned factory in Rome, Italy (Walter, 1996). In a comparative study of the representation of migration in the Spanish newspapers *El País* and *ABC* and *The Irish Times* and the *Irish Independent*, from 1990 to 2000, homogenizing collective us-versus-them discourses were apparent (Ramos, 2002). On the other hand, sympathy for the eviction of 'sans-papiers' (undocumented migrants) from the Saint-Bernard church in Paris, France, was constructed through visual narratives on television screens and in printed cartoons (Rosello, 1998).

Beyond the ebb and flow of incident-based news reporting, journalists have sought to represent the structural racialized condition of migrant and minority communities. John Howard Griffen's *Black like me* (1961) describes the experiences of African Americans living under segregation in the south of the United States. In 1969, Grace Halsell published *Soul Sister*, which covered the exploitative and humiliating experiences of Black domestic servants who worked for white employers. In Europe, the 1985 *Ganz unten* by Günter Wallraff recounts the experiences of Turkish guest workers in Germany. All these books became bestsellers, impacting public debate about migrant and minority communities. However, these books were all written by white journalists, who darkened their skins, dressed up and sought to pass for African-American men, women and guest workers, respectively, which raises questions about the ethics of representation, exploitation and cultural appropriation. Moreover, these books promised readers a sense of immersion and close encounter with the workings of racialization and discrimination. For example, Griffen described experiences of dehumanization, such as the 'hate stare' that some white people would give him out of horror and disgust.

A similar promise of immersion accompanies recent virtual reality installations. For example, VR representations can provide audiences with a first-hand experience of daily life in a refugee camp. These VR devices are now seen as machines that may promote empathy (Studt, 2021). In invading the personal and private space of marginalized groups such as refugees, this can become a form "toxic empathy" that only serves the desire for authenticity of white audiences (Nakamura, 2020). Further comparative analysis is needed to see how the hopeful expectations projected on virtual reality might similarly have surrounded the historical non-fiction bestsellers mentioned above. In parallel, historical awareness offers tools to study the representational politics of VR installations in terms of ownership, cultural appropriation and exploitation.

Self-representation repertoires

A variety of migrant-produced self-representational media can be found in the archives. Migration and media histories converge, as migrant self-representational media repertoires reflect the technological affordances of particular historical eras. Preserved archival materials reflect historical societal standings. From the colonial period particularly, for example, media utterances of elite mobile subjects are available.

Colonial travel writing, letters and memoirs are suitable for historicizing, comparing and contextualizing contemporary repertoires of self-representation. Predominantly written by privileged, mobile white Europeans, such records indicate how boundaries between the self and others were drawn, how belongingness was carved out beyond the nation, how subjects navigated languages, cultures and translations, and how intersectional, transnational power relations along the lines of gender, sexuality, race and nationality were inscribed and maintained (Boter, Rensen & Scott-Smith, 2020). However, there has also long been a market for autobiographical narratives of non-elite mobile subjects, such as enslaved people. Works by authors such as Ukawsaw Gronniosaw, John Marrant and Olaudah Equiano circulated widely from the 1770s onwards. Equiano's *The interesting narrative of the life of Olaudah Equiano, or Gustavus Vassa, the African* (2003 [1789]) was reprinted nine times in the author's lifetime, and

Jean-Jacques Rousseau's *The confessions* (1953 [1790]) also circulated widely in Europe. The latter has gained status as the inaugural modern western autobiographical text, indicating how the genre was also implicated in the western imperial project (Moore-Gilbert, 2008, pp. xi–xii). Shipboard periodicals, the newspapers written, edited and printed by mostly white, European elite travellers aboard intercontinental ships in the 19th century, are another example. In reporting general announcements, including births, marriages and accidents, alongside everyday life aboard, such as religious services, concerts and auctions, these offer an insider's view of how people confined in a small space for weeks to months developed mobile communities and othered oriental people and lands after docking in ports such as Colombo, Cape Town or Port Said (De Schmidt, 2016).

In reading institutional colonial archives against the grain, subaltern self-representational efforts can be recovered. For example, local clerks, interpreters and informants – as colonial intermediaries – have been documented as engaging in complex self-representational practices, sometimes furthering and sometimes complicating the knowledge-producing ambitions of the occupying regimes. For example, in British India, the intelligence work of local informants had a profound impact, even resulting in occasional "information panics" among the occupiers (Bayly, 1996, pp. 147–149). The Malian interpreter and clerk Wangrin was celebrated in Amadou Hampâté Bâ's *The fortunes of Wangrin* (2000), as a rogue and heroic manipulator of the French colonial state. Messaoud Djebari, a North African Muslim colonial subject born in Algeria was similarly able to instigate mass media controversies in France, Tunisia and Algeria at the turn of the 20th century (Asseraf, 2022). Attending to the multiplicity of historical self-representational narratives provides a means to unpack how historical views are constructed and to understand how, as a result of evolving power relations, some historical self-representations have become dominant (and preserved) while others were ignored.

One key reference point in the history of 20th-century European and US media and migration is *The Polish peasant in Europe and America: Monograph of an immigrant group* (Thomas & Znaniecki, 1918–1920), a five-volume academic study which drew extensively from migrant self-representations, including, most notably, a collection of letters from Polish migrants and their families. A second key reference is *A seventh man: A book of images and words about the experience of migrant workers in Europe* by John Berger and Jean Mohr (2010 [1975]). At that time in Germany and England, one in seven manual workers was a migrant. Envisioned as a documentary and family photo album, eventually the makers settled on a book due to financial constraints. The book includes several forms of self-representation, including photographs and poetry – which are not unlike the potential use of refugee selfies in the current era – that sought to rehumanize the experience of migration and generate solidarity among all workers (Berger & Mohr, 2010 [1975]).

From the 1990s onwards, migrant self-representational repertoires converged in analogue and digital media forms. This development also parallels the evolution of ethnic media and community media research. These branches of media studies were initially focused on media production and consumption among audiences living in specific geographic locations. Gradually they also brought into focus cross-border flows of media content within transnational migrant communities. Postcolonial media scholar Hamid Naficy's ethnographic study of Iranian television in Los Angeles, USA (1993) depicts how migrant agency emerges from the production and consumption of ethnic media, and provides insight into how these media forms also impact upon the larger political economy of North American mainstream television. Ambiguity and heterogeneity were key analytic registers in Myria Georgiou's study with Greek Cypriots living in London and New York (2006), as she articulated the contextual spatial dimension of diasporic media consumption at the local level of urban spaces, at the transnational level of networks and in global media culture. The Shan community in Myanmar pirated Thai television soap operas to construct a transnational identy beyond the nation (Jirattikorn, 2008). Similarly, through their consumption of audiovisual media, the Chinese, Indian, Vietnamese and Thai diasporic communities in Australia constructed and participated in alternative media environments (Cunningham & Sinclair, 2001). From the 1990s, migrant, postcolonial and third cinema also expanded, complicating further the geo-politics and aesthetics of migration-related representational registers (Bayraktar, 2016; Ponzanesi & Waller, 2012). Overall, these studies rendered visible how the production and consumption of ethnic and community media offered a means to assert hybrid, in-between and third identities and cultures, providing important grounds to question the dominant understandings of mainstream media consumption.

Later in the 1990s and early 2000s, studies appeared on migrants' digital media use, initially focusing mostly on text-based email lists and message boards. Scholarship on digital diaspora, which has proliferated in recent years, originates from these discussions. For example, Radhika Gajjala theorized South Asian women's (SAW) use of the SAWnet email list as a Cyborg-Diaspora (2004). Message boards are web-based spaces for text-based interaction that evolved from the dial-up bulletin board system (BBS), newsgroups and electronic mailing lists of the 1970s. Scholars argued that the self-representational repertoires of the message boards of Chinese migrants in the UK (Parker & Song, 2006), of Asian-Americans, Mexican-Americans and African-Americans (Byrne, 2008) in the US and of Russian LGBTs and queers in Israel (Kuntsman, 2008) provided a way for migrants to voice themselves. For example, South Asian women used boards to contest biases in the "traditional structures of speaking power", illustrating how they sought to take "a place at the table" (Mitra & Watts, 2002, p. 489). These studies commonly highlight the shortcomings of governmental media policies that overlook minority needs. Growing attention was also paid to the technological affordances that allowed the expression of multi-layered and complex self-representations. For example, the ability to create a complex narrative by hyperlinking between various texts presented a new aesthetic for expressing diversity and a metaphor for addressing cultural encounters online (Odin, 2010).

In sum, pre-digital and early-digital diasporic media production and consumption practices have historically mediated multi-layered cultural identities. There is an urgent need to probe further into how such anti-essentialist discourse has historically circulated to add nuance to the dominant claims that equate a democratic potential of self-representation with the emergence of social media platforms.

Historicizing affects and emotions

Migrant digital practices, including selfies, memes and TikTok videos, mediate sensations in particular ways. These practices can be understood in a long lineage of a complex "archive of feelings" (Cvetkovich, 2003) constituted by migrant and mobile people. Digital migration scholars can study how (in the present and) in pre-digital contexts technologies mediated, circulated and archived affects. Following the structure of Chapter 4 on affects and emotions, below we cover histories of the political economy of affect, intimacy, transnational families and home-making.

Political economy

When studying affect, also historically, it is not only the messages exchanged that demand our attention: affects are encoded in the contents of texts, but also in their production and reception practices. As such, migrant archives – digital and paper-based ones – are not simply dry "storehouses of memory" (Appadurai, 2019, p. 564). They contain highly emotional traumatic "stories of suffering" and serve important roles as "aspirational maps" to reflect and project desires, hopes and fantasies of longing (ibid.). Archives are not innocent; they play a pivotal role in institutionalization and state formation. Through gathering and presenting particular artefacts and records, a particular status quo can be maintained, which in the case of migration often relies on bordering, classifying populations and policing, surveillance and governmentality. However, outside the state, as Arjun Appadurai elaborates, the "personal diary, the family photo album, the community museum" present us with vital alternative insights on the lived experiences and feelings of migration (2003, p. 16). For example, discussions about money have long been not only a financial but also a highly emotional concern in transnational migrant families. By way of illustration, a corpus of letters archived from Eastern and Western European families who migrated to the US include common requests, such as "If it is not too expensive then you can send me sugar. Here one cannot get it" (Cancian & Wegge, 2016, p. 10). Financial difficulties and restraints resulting from or despite migration, alongside hopes surrounding remittances, were common, emotionally charged concerns.

Intimacies

In the pre-digital era, migrants could circulate intimacy with loved ones by sending letters, and later on by posting audio-cassettes and making long-distance telephone calls, which became more affordable from the 1970s. Like in the current polymedia landscape, in a pre-digital media landscape migrants too engaged in a complex negotiation of personal preferences and distinctive medium-specific affordances, including the transmission of a personal and affective touch (hand-writing, doodling, sprinkling perfume on a letter or tape-recording one's voice). However, the number of communicative channels was limited, and the frequent time-lag of these channels presented a significant drawback. Historical "letters have been at the center of scholars' preoccupation with mobility" (Borges & Cancian, 2016, p. 282), particularly in the context of North America. Letters offer a means to include migrant perspectives in the study of migration, to trace the impact of technologies and changing family relations, to understand the moti-vations for migration, and to investigate migrants' daily lives.

In recent years, interest in "the history of emotions" (ibid.) in migrant corre-spondence has grown. For example, the historian Sonia Cancian (2012) analyzed the love letters of a couple living apart – one in Italy and one in Canada – in the post-World War II period. The corpus of over 460 love letters offers a close-up view on how intimacy and desire were mediated in the search for solace and comfort, and to overcome feelings of loneliness. Such letters also offer a means to scrutinize how normative gender ideologies where accepted, resisted and challenged (ibid.). Migrant letters reflected how a variety of emotions were communicated and exchanged. Emotions range from "tensions, disappointments, misunderstandings, often combined with hope, nostalgia, and joy" (Cancian & Wegge, 2016, p. 352). Migrant letters, as historical cultural artefacts produced by non-professionals, offer grounds to discern the historical patterns of how people have mediated their everyday relationships at a distance.

Transnational families

Historical sources offer a way to trace how transnational family relations and their means of communication have evolved over time and to understand what has remained stable. The emotionally charged process of keeping in touch has also historically been documented as a careful balancing of networking affec-tion and obligation. The written correspondence between two brothers, one of whom migrated to Canada in the 1820s while the other remained in Scotland, displays how affection, frustration and obligation tied family members together while living at distance (Errington, 2008). The correspondence details everyday life and major events, including births, deaths, marriages, work, leisure, faith, hope and dreams. The letters sustained "familial webs of affection" (ibid., p. 3) in their attempts to replace face-to-face encounters. Not unlike the nagging frustra-tions experienced as part of sustaining digitally mediated togetherness, written correspondence could also not fully replace the affective sensations of physical co-presence: "I almost despair of your wishes of our meeting again with the rest of my family around my fireside", concluded a 1829 letter (ibid., p. 13). For over 150 years, letter writing remained an important way of maintaining a sense of connected presence across distance. Letters offered particular affordances for conveying emotions and affects (including, for example, the personality of hand-writing), as well as a large capacity for storing information and giving the recipient something physical to hold and smell, and they represented the time-investment and devotion of the sender and allowed the receiver the comfort of keeping and re-reading them. Sending letters also came with particular constraints, such as the time-lapse in correspondence.

Between the 1970s and the 1990s letters were increasingly accompanied with audio-cassettes, the new medium of that time. In their oral history research with transnational Filipino parents living in the UK and the Philippines, media scholars Mirca Madianou and Daniel Miller found that while cassette tapes lacked the personalization of handwritten letters, they did offer a stronger sense of co-presence and "emotional immediacy" by being able to share and hear voices of loved ones, including children (2011, p. 269). While letters were experienced as carefully crafted, cassettes offered 60- or 90-minute snippets of spontaneous 'real life', including songs, music and celebrations (ibid., p. 260). With audio-cassettes, concerns of storage and longevity grew, as they could easily become useless if they were broken, cut or became distorted from over-playing. The use of audio-cassettes among transnational migrants sheds light on how concerns about navigating between the different affective affordances and expectations surrounding communicative channels are not new, but pre-date the current digital landscape.

Home-making

Historical migrant home-making practices offer another window on the emotional consequences and affective experiences of migration. The home environment is a material and affective "warehouse" (Lawrence, 1985), indicative of the customs, routines and rituals of previous generations. For this purpose, already in 1985, Roderick J. Lawrence called for researchers to study the "ordering of home environments through the passage of time", by combining personal histories and the social history of architecture, technology and space-making (1985, p. 114). To date, this call for research remains pertinent, as there is a scarcity of historical research on migrant home-making.

Feminist scholars have undertaken some important groundwork. They have documented and conceptualized the profound ambivalence of the home – as a space where stereotypical gender roles are enacted and as a space in which to fight oppression. Historically, the domestic space has been maintained at the expense of women, who in hetero-patriarchic societies have been expected to act as housekeepers. However, women have also enacted the home differently, by asserting their own subjectivities and desires (Young, 2005). As bell hooks (1991) demonstrated, the home could bring Black women a sense of self-esteem and a means of resistance against gendered and racialized oppression. Alongside being mindful of the ambivalent workings of power, future histories of home-making in the context of migration and technology may better tease out how home-making is not a "continuous progression through time", but results from multiple, interacting and conflicting "temporal regimes" of home-making (Nieto, 2021, p. 92).

Conclusions

To historicize digital migration, this chapter proposes that migration history is fundamentally intertwined with media history. As such, the contemporary embrace of technosolutionism in migration governance and control does not come from a void. Rather, technologies and ideas surrounding migration come from somewhere. In our contemporary moment, migrants maintain digital networks across borders and we witness advanced experiments with digital border technologies across the world. These developments are not unidirectional, causal results of a teleological project of technological advancement. Some processes have remained unchanged, while others have only existed for a brief period of time. Seemingly new technologies are haunted by past developments. Taking a *longue durée* perspective on migrant infrastructure, connections, representations and affect alerts scholars of digital migration studies to avoid producing static, a-contextual and singular accounts of migration and media history. Rather, we can account for dynamism, change and multiplicity by considering how a variety of aspirations, actions and the situated experiences of the relevant actors involved shaped particularly situated historical media dispositions. By doing so, we can acknowledge how, throughout media and migration histories, power flowed in multiple directions. Following historical pathways, future research can draw out how media have enabled and contained particular forms of mobilities. In addition, further insights are needed into how migrant media practices have also resulted in changes in institutions, corporations and policies.

Research Dialogue IX: Philipp Seuferling on media, migration and borders, and their histories

Philipp Seuferling is a Fellow at the Department of Media and Communications at London School of Economics and Political Science. He holds a PhD in Media and Communication Studies from Södertörn University, Stockholm, Sweden. His research interests comprise the intersections of media, migration and borders, and their histories. In 2021 he defended his PhD thesis, titled *Media and the refugee camp: The historical making of space, time and politics in the modern refugee regime*. The thesis explored media practices among refugee camp residents and authorities in Germany since 1945. In the spring of 2022, Philipp was a visiting postdoc scholar at New York University's Department of Media, Culture, and Communication. For his current project, he is tracing the deep times of so-called 'smart borders', studying the roles of media technologies in border governance in historical contexts, such as Ellis Island in New York City.

1. **How did you come to study media and migration from a historical perspective?**

   During my undergraduate years in Hamburg, Germany, I worked as a student assistant at the Research Center for Media History at the Leibniz-Institute for Media Research. I shared a desk with Alina Just, who worked on historical film representations of German expellees and refugees after World War Two (Tiews, 2017). With our long discussions on refugee and media history in mind, I moved to Lund, Sweden, for a Master's degree – in the late summer of 2015 – coinciding with what was to be called a European 'refugee crisis'. I quickly found the historical parallels striking. After all, how do we call something a 'crisis', leading to borders being closed, when not even 70 years before millions of Europeans were displaced themselves, several even in my own family? And is the experience different today just because refugees have smartphones?

   I continue to be fascinated by the contingencies and alternatives you can observe across history, and questioning what remains the same, and what changes. The repetitiveness of how migration does (and does not) unfold over again, and how media have always been made complicit in it, is striking to me.

2. **How do you conceptualize and methodologically operationalize your media historical perspective?**

   I think there lies great potential in combining perspectives of media history with research on migration. Media history, and especially approaches along the lines of media archaeology, offer more than a chronological account of things that happened in the past. In fact, they alert us to a broad concept of media as material and symbolic environments, practices and cultural techniques that enable the production and circulation of knowledge, communication and meaning at a very fundamental level. I am here inspired by the work of, for example, Shannon Mattern (2017), Lisa Gitelman (2006), John Durham Peters (2015) and Markus Krajewski (2018).

Looking at migration over time from this perspective brings into focus diverse forms of mediation and communication that have always conditioned and enabled mobility and border-crossing, alerting us to how migration was produced, experienced and governed through mediation. While many studies focus on all the revolutions and radical alterations coming with the digital, a broad media concept and attention for the longue durée *can make 'the digital' take a backseat. In my PhD thesis (Seuferling, 2021), I drew on the concept of 'media practices' to trace how constellations of technologies, and motivations and imaginaries, have shaped media practices that characterize being and being made a refugee. From this lens, we can observe different media practices over time and across distinct technologies: such as connecting across distances, creating diasporic communities, enacting voice and representation, or the governing of mobility and borders. In our co-authored article (Seuferling & Leurs, 2021), we employed the perspective of 'imaginaries' to study solutionist projections on media infrastructures in humanitarianism and migration governance. And in my current project, I am using the term 'cultural techniques' to conceptualize how bordering is realized in co-dependencies of technology and practice, be it in contemporary 'smart border' projects in the EU, or at Ellis Island immigration station in New York City (USA) in the 1890s and 1910s.*

Essentially, these concepts are different ways of addressing continuity and change between media technologies and social and political practices, and how they over time affect the production and experience of migration. By tracing how such practices and techniques materialized at different points in time, we can also question if it is really media that showcase the biggest revolutions, or rather larger political conditions of global refugee regimes, and political fantasies of statehood and citizenship that become embedded and reflected in media practices. In that sense, we can de-centre and re-centre media at the same time. There remains work to be done to assess genealogies of media and of migration and how they intersect. Being open to multiple temporalities of continuities and changes is a helpful starting point.

*Finally, this perspective not only rewrites migration history through
a media lens. Also, media history can ultimately be re-understood by
focusing on seemingly marginal spaces of media practices and technological development, such as migrant communities, refugee camps or
border stations.*

3. **What are the main challenges you face(d) and how do (did) you
negotiate them?**

*Usually, historical methods are not the ones most familiar to media
and communication scholars, nor to migration scholars. So, a challenge
is to find both theoretical and methodological entry points to be able
to study media practices and media technologies in the past and how
they relate to the present. This journey led me to the archives, trying to
excavate previous forms of mediation from archival files and materials.*

*The first challenge, when I was interested in media practices among
historical refugees, was to find archives and sources that would somehow speak to that. There is no media historical refugee archive, and
in general migrants and refugees are marginalized and muted groups
in the archival landscape and its files. To tackle that issue, combining
institutional state archives with other forms of community archives
(such as activist archives) is a good way to diversify and cross-check
voices in the material.*

*Second, postcolonial studies scholars like Ann Stoler have sug-
gested ways of studying colonial archives "along and against the grain"
(Stoler, 2009), meaning that even government documents can reveal
how media practices among migrants could and could not unfold. This
leads to the second challenge: making sure to maintain an agency-
focused analysis. Especially when studying infrastructures and forms
of governance, one can easily overlook forms of resistance, obfusca-
tion and circumvention, when heavily relying on official records.
Again, including a broad range of source material, such as community
archives, but also novels, films or oral history reports, helps to counter-
balance the discourses of institutional archives, which often remain
fantasies, imaginaries and plans.*

*Ultimately, the challenge of any historian is to build a substantiated
narrative out of the collected material, without falling into a positivist
trap of history as 'wie es eigentlich gewesen ist' ('as it actually was').
Instead, I think the value of historicizing approaches in media and
migration can rather lie in radically reflecting on the present-day as the
distinctively situated positionality, out of which one looks at historical files. There are multiple histories that become apparent, depending
on which perspective one takes. Digitalization and large-scale global*

migration are the dominant, situated perspectives of today, that we can
address anew by attending to the longue durée *of mediation and its*
entanglement with cross-border mobility. This (contingent) perspective
ultimately determines how one interprets the archives, and forms the
value of historicization for the present moment.

4. **In reviewing historical approaches to (pre- and early digital) media and migration, we considered the thematic entry points of infrastructure, connectivity, representation and affect. How does your work speak to these themes?**

First, I think it is productive to use concepts like the ones structuring
this book as points of departure for historicization. They can be sen-
sitizers for tracing the meanings and forms of mediation across time,
and across concrete media technologies. Sometimes these concepts are
enveloped with a 'firstist' rhetoric of newness and seen as intrinsically
tied to the affordances of digital media. However, in my work so far,
it has become clear how deeply historically migration is structured by
media practices as infrastructures for communication and mobility,
enablers of connectivity, possibilities of representations, and sources of
affect and emotion.

In my PhD study on historical media practices in refugee camps,
I showed how media technologies had infrastructural meaning on a
very existential level: access to food, beds, benefits and information
has been regulated via media infrastructures, such as paper. Camp
cinemas, radios, newspapers or the mail service were highly controlled
areas, too, leading to struggles over connectivity and (self-)representation
between camp residents and authorities. While studying affect histori-
cally is very tricky and based on many assumptions, the sources gave
impressive insights into the deep, emotional importance that media
and possibilities of communication carried for forced migrants long
before the smartphone.

Ultimately, while digital technologies have partly intensified and
sped up infrastructures, connectivity, representations and affect in con-
texts of migration, these concepts are also highly historical elements of
what migration is, how it is produced by states, and how it is experi-
enced by people on the move.

5. **Where do you see gaps in our (historical) digital migration scholarship and what topics do you think we should pursue further in the future?**

Combinations of studying media and communication, migration
and their histories together are still rare. One path forward in this

*intersection should definitely be to further de-Westernize and decolo-
nize media histories of migration. This includes studying deep times of
media across global, local and vernacular contexts of migration and
bordering, but also tracing how histories of media technologies, and
technologies of bordering and population containment themselves, are
fundamentally shaped and developed within colonial and imperialist
frameworks. The contemporary migration and border regimes, and
the technologies they are enabled by (such as biometrics), are results
of historical projects, such as colonialism, slavery, eugenicism, racism,
fascism or policing vagrancy. How digital borders embody these legacies is little explored, and even more so in contexts beyond the Global
North. The same applies to digging deeper into historical media representations of migration: how changing public spheres have negotiated
meanings of migration and legitimized its governance, as well as how
acts of self-representation have contested borders ever since. Lastly,
there is always a need for more voices and more hidden sources to fill
blind spots of history-writing. Methods of oral history and other forms
of action-research with communities can further diversify insights into
media experiences of migration, and should be documented while wit-
nesses are alive. Uncovering, archiving and making accessible more
voices, experiences and media practices of perhaps forgotten groups of
migrants, and finding new ways of telling such histories, should definitely be explored further.*

6. **What practical advice would you give to those aspiring to contribute
   to digital migration studies?**

*There are many unexplored angles in studying intersections of digital
and non-digital media and migration. Even within the few years that
I have been exploring this field myself, I see fast, and often volatile,
changes in media technologies and how they seep through migration
(e.g. artificial intelligence). I think in going forward, it is important to
both keep track of such new developments, but also make use of the
power of history: taking the wider perspective, zooming out of fast-
paced temporalities of such technologies, and trying to critically understand novelties and changes. For instance, trajectories between eugenics
and artificial intelligence have recently been explored more systematically (Chun, 2021). In that sense, I hope that more scholars engage in
using the perhaps 'slow' historical insights for critiques of the 'fast-
moving' present.*

Research Dialogue X: Łukasz Szulc on pre-digital histories of migration and transnationalism

Łukasz Szulc is a Lecturer in Digital Media and Society in the Department of Sociological Studies at The University of Sheffield, United Kingdom. He specializes in critical and cultural studies of digital media at the intersections of gender, sexuality and transnationalism with a focus on Central and Eastern Europe. He recently published the book *Transnational homosexuals in communist Poland: Cross-border flows in gay and lesbian magazines* (2018) and the report *Queer #PolesinUK: Identity, migration and social media* (2019).

1. **How did you come to study media, nationalism, transnationalism and sexuality, and what where your motivations to add a historical perspective to your research agenda?**

   My research interests reflect my personal trajectory. I became interested in queer digital cultures when I began exploring my sexuality (at that time, mainly through homepages, chatrooms and porn sites) and I added the migration component when I became a migrant myself. Questions about nationalism and transnationalism also reflect my own struggles with national identity – with queerness being excluded from the dominant version of Polishness – and my uncanny feelings of belonging to the global queer culture – dominated by Western ideas, images and sensibilities.

   Never trained as a historian, I was not originally attracted to a historical perspective. That is, until I learned about underground gay and lesbian magazines published in communist Poland. With questions about globalization and geopolitical power relations always on my mind, I hoped that the magazines would help me explore the 'authentic' Polish queerness, the one before the Westernization and commercialization of Polish culture that happened after the fall of communism in the country in 1989. What I found out instead were stories of migration and cross-border flows, both within the Eastern Bloc and between the Eastern and Western Blocs, which I recounted in my book Transnational homosexuals in communist Poland: Cross-border flows in gay and lesbian magazines (Szulc, 2018).

   While I usually work on contemporary digital queer cultures, the project on gay and lesbian magazines published in the 1980s helped put my research into a historical perspective. One example is my current work on ethnic and racial imaginations in dating app cultures. While many researchers investigate the use of ethnic or racial labels in contemporary dating app cultures, it is useful to consider the mediation of the same or similar practices in the 'older' media, for example in personal ads in gay and lesbian magazines (prominent before the popularization of the internet) and in chatrooms (popular among queers in the 1990s and the early 2000s). Such a historical perspective helps make broader observations about media change and cultural change.

2. **How do you conceptualize and methodologically operationalize your media historical perspective?**

One of the key concepts in my scholarship is that of 'context', which helps me stay attentive to both historical and geographical specificities of the things I do research about (Dhoest & Szulc, 2016; Szulc, 2020b). I am interested in the importance of both time and place, history and culture, or indeed historical context and cultural context in queer media cultures.

I think of context as an assemblage of multiple, diverse and volatile historical periods and geographical scales (Deleuze & Guattari, 1988). In my book, I showed how gay and lesbian magazines published in communist Poland were products of a combination and imbrication of different times and places, be it the moment of relaxation of state censorship in the Soviet Union and the People's Republic of Poland in the second half of the 1980s or the location of some authors of the magazines in a city at the Baltic Sea, which gave them access to gay sailors who were bringing queer magazines from abroad. Context understood as an assemblage blurs the clear-cut divisions between historical periods (e.g. before and after 1989) and geopolitical borders (e.g. between Eastern and Western Blocs).

Methodologically, I think about my way of doing research as cruising, in which I am inspired by a queer tradition of wandering around in public spaces to make sexual or romantic connections; wandering around different times and places that assemble a meaningful context for my research (Anderson, 2017; Basiuk & Burszta, 2021; Szulc, 2022). Cruising is driven by desires and involves patience, openness and curiosity. It is about following what attracts us rather than conducting any sort of systematic or structured analysis, as if it was ever possible. Cruising archives or interfaces is about slowing down and hanging around with the hope of running into something or someone we long for and are ready to hook up with.

3. **What are the main challenges you face and how do you negotiate them?**

One consequence of thinking about doing research as cruising is that it makes the research process more fun, since it takes away the positivist pressures of completeness, objectivity or systematization. For me, it was adventurous to track copies of gay and lesbian magazines in queer archives such as Lambda Warszawa, IHLIA LGBTI Heritage in Amsterdam and Schwules Museum in Berlin. It was also exciting trying to locate people who made those magazines and Facebook turned out to be an invaluable help in that. Discovering new issues of the magazines or getting replies from the people who made them evoked feelings comparable to finding out that your crush is into you too.

At the same time, this process is very time-consuming and it also costs a lot of money to travel between cities and countries, sometimes with little result. I was lucky that my work on the book was supported by the Research Foundation Flanders, providing me with necessary resources so I could actually do the cruising the way it should be done: taking time to hang around and follow up clues. Compared to research on contemporary digital cultures, it also takes disproportionately more time to find out basic facts about who was doing what and when. Days, and sometimes weeks, of work resulted in one sentence in my book. And it is much more difficult to study media consumption, reception or use in the past. While I managed to locate nearly all issues of the magazines and I connected with three people who were making them, I still do not know much about who their readers were, what they were thinking about the magazines and how important they were to them.

4. **Where do you see gaps in our scholarship and what topics do you think we should pursue further in the future?**

The magazines I was analyzing were overwhelmingly created by and for gay men. I was not able to locate any periodicals created in Poland in the 1980s by and for lesbians or other groups than gay men from the broad spectrum of gender and/or sexually non-conforming people. I doubt that any such periodicals existed. This, however, does not mean that those groups did not communicate with each other and did not create their own communities. We know, for example, that some lesbian cultures were formed around bookstores or during summer camps (e.g. Adams, 1998). To recognize these cultures and tell more inclusive stories, we need to expand our definition of 'media'. The limits of what we consider as 'media' become the limits of what we imagine as media cultures.

In the same vein, it becomes beneficial to shift the focus from migration to mobility (Szulc, 2020a). The transnational stories of the magazines I analyzed indeed included some stories of migration (one of the magazines was published by a Polish migrant to Vienna), but they also included more casual travels, be it for love, work or holidays. They also included transnational connections that did not involve any travelling – connections maintained by, for example, sending letters and making phone calls. The travelling of people is different from the travelling of texts, images or objects, but the latter should not be disregarded as less important for the studies of transnational cultures.

The travels I tracked in my research were also much messier than simple migration stories from one country to the other. They involved multiple journeys of different lengths within a country and between two, three or more countries. The human geographer Andrew Gorman-Murray (2007, p. 106) makes an interesting provocation to treat the body itself as a scale in queer migration research, suggesting that we follow "the actual movement of the queer body through space". As media scholars, we may think about the actual movement of the body through digital spaces as intertwined with physical space. Following the body may protect us from falling into the trap of both methodological nationalism and media centrism.

5. **What practical advice would you give to those aspiring to contribute to media, nationalism, transnationalism and sexuality and the broader interdisciplinary research area of digital migration studies?**

The first piece of advice that comes to my mind is to follow your passions. Conducting research about the topics that many find controversial and within often very rigid institutional boundaries can be a struggle. Being truly passionate about what you do helps you face the struggles, as does having a support network of like-minded people, both inside and outside academia. Another piece of advice I could offer is to consider different media, different methods and different mobilities. By different I mean strange to the academic canon but familiar to the everyday lives of people you work with. For me, for example, these included cruising as method and body as scale. I also find it important to engage with history even if you do not conduct historical research. This will help you put your work in context (context as assemblage), recognize broader patterns, continuities and ruptures, and question the newness of new media. Finally, avoid fetishizing media and nations. They both matter in many different and important ways but we tend to give them more credit than they deserve. Study everyday life as it is actually lived, with and without media, and appreciate complicated entanglements of times and places.

Conclusions

Digital migration studies scholars seek to unpack the complex relationships between migration and digital technologies. In this book, we use the term 'digital migration studies' to refer to an emerging, interdisciplinary area of research. In the previous chapters we covered theories and empirical work by scholars from fields including media and communication studies, migration studies, geography, sociology, anthropology, psychology and human rights, among others. In presenting an overview of perspectives, this book offers readers a critical toolbox to comprehensively understand digital migrants and the datafication of migration. The toolbox allows researchers to pick and choose from approaches, for example to gain a better understanding of the "techno-hype" (Marino, 2021, p. 125) surrounding contemporary efficiency-driven technological disruption. Technological innovation includes the datafication of biometrics, blockchain, algorithmic modelling and/or machine learning, which are embraced across sectors of migration governance, management, control and humanitarianism. For example, a recent manifesto entitled "If algorithms dream of Customs, do custom officials dream of algorithms? A manifesto for data mobilisation in Customs" called for an international network of customs officials to embrace data in their everyday practices (Mikuriya & Cantens, 2020, p. 1).

Contemporary migration reflects a digitally mediated state of being and a digitized and datafied condition. This state of being a digital migrant and the condition of digitized migration results from bottom-up meaning-making and the emotional digital practices of migrants, and top-down forms of monitoring, governing, surveilling and coercing migrants. This condition has not emerged from a void, and we have discussed the importance of understanding technological dispositions from the historical perspective of deep time (see Chapter 5: Histories). In the previous chapters, we have learned that the relationships between migration and digital technologies are complex and multi-layered:

1. Digital technologies have impacted upon migration processes and experiences. Vice versa, migration processes and contexts have contributed to the development of new technologies. However, no causal, linear or unidirectional relationships between migration and digital technology development exist. We thus have to focus on how migration and digital technologies mutually shape and co-constitute one another across space and time.

2. The relationships between migration and digital technologies are shaped by a variety of actors. The actors involved in digital migration range from migrants themselves to states, corporations, supra-national organizations, non-governmental organizations, social movements, advocacy groups, activists, facilitators as well as non-human actors such as patrol dogs. Therefore, a multi-stakeholder approach will be the most promising viewpoint by which to understand the variety of interests that impact on the digitization and datafication of migration processes and experiences.

3. The relationships are formed on the basis of a variety of technologies, including smartphones, social media platforms, drones, cameras and sensors at borders that enable the datafication of movement, databases of biometrics and traces of migration, algorithms, machine-learning and artificial intelligence (AI) to support decision making, predictive analytics and modelling. We thus should be careful to single out or isolate particular technologies as individual technologies operate in broader situated and contextualized assemblages.

4. A multi-scalar approach is promising to draw attention to how the relationships between migration and digital technologies are shaped between and across local, national, regional, transnational, global and translocal scales.

5. Hierarchical power relations are formed, reproduced and challenged as a result of an intricate interplay of top-down policies, procedures and laws that seek to digitally channel, curtail and control mobility, and migrants' bottom-up digital practices and networks.

In this concluding chapter, we take an overview of perspectives, address the shared concerns that have been covered and propose an agenda for future digital migration studies research.

Infrastructures, connections, representations, affects and emotions, histories

The five thematic chapters of infrastructures, connections, representations, affects and emotions, and histories offer particular entry points to comprehensively understand the multiplicity, multi-layeredness and dynamic relationships between migration and digital technologies. Each chapter is accompanied by two Research Dialogues with colleagues with various sets of expertise. The chapters and Research Dialogues provide us with the analytic apparatus needed to highlight how actors, discourses, ideas, technologies, policies and emotions together construct digital migration in deeply contextualized and situated spaces and times. Beyond the various uses of the term infrastructure a buzzword, by using infrastructures as a critical lens (see Chapter 1), we can open up 'the black-boxed' inner workings of technologies, processes and procedures surrounding and impacting upon migration. Infrastructures enable or disable the circulation of power, people, ideas and goods, which we addressed by zooming in on the role of social brokering, material stuff, relationality and imaginaries. The perspective of connections (see Chapter 2) emphasizes how digitally connected migrants can sustain a presence across distance, maintaining relationships between partners, family, kin and friends in different locations. The intricacies and challenges of maintaining co-presence also became familiar to non-migrant people all over the world during the global Covid-19 health pandemic (2020 onwards), when, as a result of lockdowns, people were forced to keep in touch via their screens and devices. Connectivity is an important focus to reconsider the interrelations between integration and transnationalism as non-mutually exclusive, dynamic processes. Information flows are shaped by a top-down process of information provision from government agencies or humanitarian organizations and the bottom-up practice of information sharing. A focus on digital networks also offers a means to explore both how migrants make human rights claims digitally and how governmental actors and non-governmental groups can digitally repress migrants. The thematic focus of representation (see Chapter 3) provides a means to study the digital politics of representation. With this analytic lens, we can study how, why and when migrants are objectified in digital media representations, such as social media memes or VR installations, and how, why and when digital self-representations, such as selfies or *TikTok* videos, can function as a site of agency and empowerment. The thematic focus of affects and emotions (Chapter 4) can be taken up to produce knowledge about the sensations and feelings migrants may have. This might include migrant bodies encountering administrative or bureaucratic procedures and digital systems of surveillance and control, or using digital devices and social media platforms to maintain intimate relationships at distance. In Chapter 4, we tease out the emotional and affective dynamics of the political economy of digital migration, digital intimacies, transnational families and home-making. Finally, the thematic focus of histories (see Chapter 5) develops a *longue durée* perspective to trace which historical genealogies have shaped relations between migration and media technologies over time. The chapter historicizes infrastructures, connections, representations, and affectivity and emotions, providing a means to question dominant a-historic and 'firstist' accounts of high-tech innovations.

Migration governance, technocracy and dataism

Digital migration studies, on the ontological level, aim to offer a systematic account of how migration and the digital encounter mutually shape one another. Migration does not exist outside digital mediation and technological innovation, while global technological development increasingly relies on migrant populations as ideal test subjects. In their encounter, we can observe how the hegemonic rationalities surrounding migration and technology reinforce each another. Reflecting colonial genealogies, the rationality of migration as something that may and should be governed and channelled for the benefit of some and at the expense of others, dominates global policies of migration governance. The rationality of technocracy, based on efficiency-driven technological and data solutionism, is dominant in technology policies. Migration and technology rationalities mutually strengthen each another. In migration contexts, no one is unaffected by digital practices and data politics.

In the technocratic solutionist rationality of dataism, data is no longer only an analytical abstraction from the real world (Aradau & Blanke, 2022). Rather, dataism accepts that digital datasets shape a "new structural condition" (Halpern et al., 2022, p. 199). The notion of "surplus data" (ibid.) captures how this condition is formed, as data not only abstracts but also is increasingly used as a basis to materialize what it describes. The materialization of migration through databases, artificial intelligence and/or machine learning has particular repercussions for particular groups of migrants: "data determine how we can or cannot move through the world and whether we are considered to be threats, risks, victims or assets" (Leese, Noori & Scheel, 2022, p. 6). The ongoing militarization and securitization of asylum and refugee migration serves as a painful reminder of how data may unequally co-shape the migrant condition.

As a first example, we can consider how, beyond physical sites, datafication changes borders into deterritorial, mobile and privatized entities (Chouliaraki & Georgiou, 2022; Dijstelbloem, 2021). The consequences of these developments vary for different groups of mobile people. For some, this means the border travels with them wherever they move, as they carry it with them on their own smartphones. As anthropologists Carolina Sanchez Boe and media scholar Henry Mainsah (2022) document in the context of the United States, digital facial recognition software is deployed as an alternative to detention by Immigration and Customs Enforcement (ICE). After crossing the border, selected asylum seekers enter the 'Intensive Supervision and Appearance Program' (ISAP) for the purpose of 'digital confinement'. Under this programme, asylum seekers are required to have their smartphones charged at all times, to have Global Positioning Services (GPS) turned on and to use their own smartphones to do weekly 'check-ins' by uploading a selfie to the facial recognition app SmartLINK. Asylum seekers are not informed about how long digital monitoring and broader asylum procedures last (Sanchez Boe & Mainsah, 2022, p. 290). In parallel, in the United Kingdom, experiments with facial recognition smart watches are planned to monitor migrants who were convicted of crimes. The monitoring system will require wearers to take and share up to five photos per day (Kelly, 2022). What are the consequences of using technology to control and govern forms of migration (Ticktin & Youatt, 2022)? Future research should theorize, empirically document and question the consequences of such experiments with mobile borders. For this purpose, we can adopt the critical framework of "carceral migrations" to address racialized, spatialized regulation and punishment of migration and mobility (Kurwa & Gurusami, 2022, p. 353). Carceral migrations result from decisions shaping legal frameworks and procedures. There is scope to chart how these are designed in tandem with the technologies envisioned to support or facilitate punitive trajectories of mobility and immobility (see Benjamin, 2019b).

Second, we can address the possible implications of the material conditions of digitization and datafication by turning to the everyday life of migrant labourers. Migrant workers have contributed to the spectacular recent rise of the so-called gig economy. Migrant gig work and platform work are currently understudied. As media scholars Niels van Doorn and Darsana Vijay argue:

> there is an urgent need to center migrant experiences and the role of migrant labor in gig economy research, in order to generate a better understanding of how gig work offers certain opportunities and challenges to migrants with a variety of backgrounds and skill levels. (2021, p. 1)

Early studies suggest that migrant gig work and platform labour dynamics may create and deepen inequalities. For example, the geographer Dalia Gebrial (2022) argues that cheap migrant labour is monetized at the intersections of racial capitalism and platform capitalism. She conducted research on the basis of interviews and 'ride-alongs' with taxi drivers in London, the UK. She conceptualizes the conditions of vulnerability that migrant Uber drivers face as a form of "racial platform capitalism" (Gebrial, 2022). The embrace of digital and datafied solutions also impacts upon other migrant subjects, such as asylum seekers and refugees. Across geographies, they are expected to become resilient and self-supporting individuals by embracing technology-centred entrepreneurial subjectivities (Georgiou, 2019; Leurs, 2022). Further research from a political economy perspective is needed to question to what extent policies of resilience, for example, result in further abandoning asylum and refugee migrants.

Beyond the ontology of migration governance and technocracy, it is important that digital migration studies scholars remain attentive to alternative ontologies that continue to exist outside official domains. The autonomy of migration perspective, for example, assumes that mobility is an ontological foundation of being human, and that a pursuit of freedom of movement also forms the basis of individual and collective political subjectivity. This perspective shifts attention from borders to centring migrants, in relation to states and capital. From this perspective, researchers have highlighted the "mobile commons" (Papadopolous & Tsianos, 2013) of collectively shared informal knowledge supporting migrant movement. Those who are successful in navigating diasporic and informal mediated flows of information and who have avoided surveillance are empowered, as communication scholar İlke Şanlıer Yüksel documents in her work with asylum migrants in Turkey (2022). Governments and authorities increasingly seek to tap into these informal domains of knowledge production and sharing for the purpose of predicting migrant flows or verifying individual asylum claims. As a result, migrants are increasingly expected to develop sophisticated abilities and literacies (Drolia et al., 2020; Vollmer, 2019) to 'read' stringent policies, uncertainties and often hostile offline and online environments. More attention is needed on those migrants and mobile people who succeed in these increasingly digitalized processes of "social navigation" (Wall, 2019), as well as on those who do not, and why.

Challenges in doing digital migration studies

While there is great urgency to address the fast-paced policy developments and technological innovations, digital migration studies face a number of obstacles, which include: the politics of categorization and naming; limited access to and contextualized understanding of datasets, algorithms and programming decisions; and ethical engagement with migrants, technology and data.

Migration is a technology, as it is an organized system, based on legal frameworks, procedures and agreements, that governs, stratifies and sanctions mobile subjects along the lines of race, gender, sexuality, class, nationality, age and ability, among others. Digital migration studies scholars therefore face major difficulties not only in the practices of defining, categorizing and naming mobile groups and practices (Hamlin, 2021), but also in conceptualizing and methodologically operationalizing studies which avoid reproducing methodological nationalism or colonial legacies (Scheel & Tazzioli, 2022). Migrants and mobile subjects often do not fit into neatly separable categories or boxes. Rather, we can approach mobile subjects alongside a spectrum of power, ranging from privilege to marginalization, to understand the situated lives, practices and procedures that affect global elites, expatriate migrants, global nomads, manual labour migrants, refugees or queer migrants. For this purpose, scholars have sought to develop alternative vocabularies to account for the convoluted histories and political implications of established terminologies (Pallister-Wilkins, 2022). For example, the sociologists Anna Wyss and Janine Dahinden suggest a framework of "entangled mobilities" to move beyond "nationality- and ethnicity-centred epistemologies" and colonial aphasia (2022, p. 1). In parallel, the anthropologist Miriam Ticktin and political scientist Rafi Youatt propose a framework of "intersecting mobilities" (2022). With this framework, Ticktin and Youatt seek to shed light on how at the intersections of mobilities, contact zones are formed, which may offer a basis for alternative political imaginations (2022). These frameworks can serve as important analytic lenses for digital migration studies, as they invite researchers to address how interrelations and interdependencies shape unequal mobility regimes dynamically and in relation to the multiple mobilities that underpin individual and collective biographical trajectories.

Another challenge is getting access to the datasets, algorithms and decision-making processes surrounding technological procedures and experiments with migrant people. The dataism underpinning technocratic migration management and governance demands independent scrutiny. There is a lack of effective regulation and oversight of the artificial intelligence and big data deployed in migration management and governance. These processes are, however, increasingly black-boxed, as a result of security measures or to protect corporate and commercial interests. In consequence, and worryingly, increasingly "neither migrants (as the producers of this data) nor migration scholars (as scientific experts on the topic) are in a position to monitor or control how governments and corporations use such data" (Bircan & Korkmaz, 2021, p. 1). Luděk Stavinoha shows how Freedom of Information (FOI) requests can be appropriated as a research methodology to study digital migration. FOI requests are a legal mechanism, which has been established across various geographical and institutional contexts, that allows one to demand access to previously confidential documents held by public bodies. Stavinoha used this approach to study the governmental outsourcing of migration management to consultancy firms. He argues that FOI requests can be a means to get access to otherwise unavailable "backstage texts", to study the discourse, decision-making and everyday practices of officials, policy makers and bureaucrats, and how they communicate with private actors (Stavinoha, 2023, forthcoming). Thematically, the workings of datafication across global migration contexts demand us to reconsider the analytic potential of existing, often US and Eurocentric, frameworks. There are strong limitations in taking the individual liberal data subject as a mould for data justice, data protection and privacy in situated non-Global North contexts. Rather, we need to develop an eye for contextualized data subjects, on an individual and collective level (Witteborn, 2021a). For example, the notion of the "afrofuturist data subject" can be taken up to foreground the racial dimensions, the radical subjectivity and the collectivity of Black struggle (Kadiri, 2021), which are of great relevance in the contexts of migration and digitization.

Finally, caring, transparent, accountable, engaged and community-centred digital migration studies research demands substantial ethical reflection and commitment (see Sandberg et al., 2022). To what and to whom do we want to contribute with our digital migration studies research? The technologies and datasets surrounding migration are increasingly difficult to access and study. Thus, for many reasons, including their mobile state and often precarious legal, socio-cultural or political position, migrants are often a 'hard to reach' population. Digital techniques, such as smartphone surveys or research apps, do not provide an easy solution to overcome this obstacle (e.g. Keusch et al., 2021). Rather, the research discussed in the thematic chapters indicates that strong commitments and long-term investment are often required for doing digital migration studies research. The research discussed above includes a variety of digital, participatory and co-creative approaches, which have in common a commitment to establish rapport and create a culture of listening and meaningful exchange (see also Lane et al., 2019). While we should be committed to 'doing no harm' to the migrants and mobile subjects participating in our studies, scholars have also issued important calls to pursue normative research and have decided to try 'doing harm' and 'pushing back' against situations, policies and digital procedures that marginalize, invisibilize or dehumanize mobile and migrant subjects and communities (Stierl, 2022).

Future research directions

In reviewing and synthesizing existing scholarship, we have gained a better overview of aspects that have been put on the agenda of digital migration studies. We have also encountered a myriad of concerns which have remained understudied, for a variety of reasons. These include:

- The technological mediation and experiences of environmentally-related migration and climate refugees (see Boas, 2020; Boas, Dahm & Wrathall, 2020).
- The political economy of digital migration. This includes the flow of capital in the military-industrial complex and private-public partnerships that increasingly securitize migration and borders. In addition, it includes the interrelationships between migration and evolving forms of labour, for example in the 'gig work' of taxi drivers and delivery workers (see Alencar & Wang, 2022; Anwar & Graham, 2020; Gebrial, 2022; Martin-Shields, 2022; Ping & Yujie Chen, 2021) or the 'platform work' of migrant influencers (see He, Leurs & Li, 2022; Jaramillo-Dent, Contreras-Pulido & Pérez-Rodríguez, 2022).
- The proliferation and mobility of digital borders (see Sanchez Boe & Mainsah, 2022). For example, this is apparent from the securitization and surveillance of the 'backstage' of private digital communication on smartphones and social media (see Bolhuis & van Wijk, 2021; Lunau & Andreassen, 2022).
- The development and testing of technologies on refugees in camps in relation to the grey areas of existing law and human rights frameworks (see Maxwell & Tomlinson, 2022; Molnar, 2020; Sandvik, 2020).
- The external surveillance of cross-border migrants, by state and non-state actors, particularly pertaining to authoritarian regimes worldwide, in tandem with internal surveillance among transnational migrant communities and diasporas (see Moss, Michaelsen & Kennedy, 2022).
- Policies of selectively sharing and/or withholding information among governments, NGOs and humanitarian organizations about migration policies, administrative procedures and contact points (see Bishop, 2020; Brekke & Thorbjørnsrud, 2020; Ongenaert, Joye & Machin, 2022; Wall, 2019).
- To avoid a 'firstist' focus on the newness of the concerns listed above, we should research migration and digital technologies in relation to the historical genealogies of colonialism, slavery, exploitation and extraction (see Browne, 2015; Chun, 2021; Katz, 2020; Seuferling, 2021).

Overall, we should come to terms with and challenge some of our own tendencies and preoccupations. Most notably, digital migration studies needs to confront its own biases. Largely, 'technocentric' and 'Eurocentric' approaches (Smets, Toffano & Almenara-Niebla, 2022) have been prioritized. To avoid fetishizing technologies in isolation from their situated contexts and geographies of use, technologies and their promises should be decentred, and people as locally situated, embodied, active agents with personal histories, aspirations and dreams should be centred. Our technocentric research focus also reflects a broader turn towards (big) data, algorithms, AI and machine learning across academia, which is affecting funding opportunities, publications and public debate. This move risks marginalizing the relevance of qualitative, holistic small data research (Leurs & Witteborn, 2021). To be able to level the playing field and embrace non-universality, scholars contributing to digital migration studies need to come to terms with their predominantly Euro- and American-centric conceptual, methodological and empirical foci (Stremlau & Tsalapatanis, 2022). As B. Camminga and John Marnell capture in their anthology *Queer and trans African mobilities* (2022), there is great urgency and potential to pursue intersectional and decolonial approaches and attend to how axes of difference, such as race, gender, sexuality, nationality, ability, generation, age and religion, in their encounter with digital technologies, (re)shape identity and the subordination of distinctively situated migrant subjects and groups.

In this way, we can come to understand digital migration beyond the frame of crisis (Frosh & Georgiou, 2022), and from the perspectives of migrant subjects themselves. For this purpose, we should account for the communities of scholarship we choose to locate ourselves in (and reflect on their inherent limitations), commit to moving beyond our disciplinary silos and, most importantly, commit to knowledge co-creation with migrant subjects and collaboratively setting agendas for research and co-designing alternatives (Costanza-Chock, 2020). By considering top-down and bottom-up approaches, exploring various scales and actors, we can develop the needed flexibility to zoom in on the particular, the situated and embodied experiences and zoom out to understand better the overall socio-cultural, economic and political implications of how relationships between migration and technologies remake worlds unevenly.

References

Abidin, C. (2021). From 'networked publics' to 'refracted publics': A companion framework for researching 'below the radar' studies. *Social Media Society, 7*(1), 1–13.

Acedera, K.A., & Yeoh, B.S.A. (2018). Facebook, long-distance marriages, and the mediation of intimacies. *International Journal of Communication, 12,* 4123–4142.

Acedera, K.A., & Yeoh, B.S.A. (2021). When care is near and far: Care triangles and the mediated spaces of mobile phones among Filipino transnational families. *Geoforum, 121,* 181–191.

Adams, K. (1998). Built out of books: Lesbian energy and feminist ideology in alternative publishing. *Journal of Homosexuality, 34*(3–4), 113–141.

Adamson F.B. (2020). Non-state authoritarianism and diaspora politics. *Global Networks, 20*(1), 150–169.

Adas, M. (2015). *Machines as the measure of men* (2nd edition). Ithaca, NY: Cornell University Press.

Ager, A., & Strang, A. (2008). Understanding integration: A conceptual framework. *Journal of Refugee Studies, 21,* 166–191.

Aguilar, F.J. (2014). *Migration revolution: Philippine nationhood and class relations in a globalized age.* Quezon City, Philippines: Ateneo de Manila University Press.

Ahlin, T., & Li, F. (2019). From field sites to field events. *Medicine Anthropology Theory, 6*(2), 1–24.

Ahmed, S. (2004). *The cultural politics of emotion.* New York: Routledge.

Ahmed, S. (2014). *The cultural politics of emotion* (2nd edition). Edinburgh: Edinburgh University Press.

Akhgar, B., Hough, K.L., Abdel Samad, Y., Bayerl, P.S., & Karakostas, A. (Eds.) (2022). *Information and communications technology in support of migration.* Cham, Switzerland: Springer International.

Alencar, A. (2020). Mobile communication and refugees: An analytical review of academic literature. *Sociology Compass, 14*(8), 1–13.

Alencar, A., & Wang, Y. (2022). Precarious migrants in a sharing economy: Collective action, organizational communication, and digital technologies. *International Journal of Communication, 16,* 5467–5479.

Alinejad, D. (2019). Careful co-presence: The transnational mediation of emotional intimacy. *Social Media + Society, 5*(2), 1–11.

Alinejad, D., & Olivieri, D. (2020). Affect, emotions and feelings. In K. Smets, K. Leurs, M. Georgiou, S. Witteborn & R. Gajjala (Eds.), *Handbook of media and migration* (pp. 54–73). London: Sage.

Alinejad, D., & Ponzanesi, S. (2020). Migrancy and digital mediations of emotion. *International Journal of Cultural Studies, 23*(5), 621–638.

Allen, W.L. (2020). Mobility, media and data politics. In K. Smets, K. Leurs, M. Georgiou, S. Witteborn & R. Gajjala (Eds.), *Handbook of media and migration* (pp. 180–191). London: Sage.

Allen, W.L. (2021). The conventions and politics of migration data visualizations. *New Media & Society*. Online first: https://doi.org/10.1177/14614448211019300

Alonso, A., & Arzoz, I. (2010). An activist commons for people without states by Cybergolem. In A. Alonso & P.J. Oiarzabal (Eds.), *Diasporas in the new media age: Identity, politics, and community* (pp. 65–84). Reno, NV: University of Nevada Press.

Amelung, N., Granja, R., & Machado, H. (2021). *Modes of bio-bordering: The hidden (dis)integration of Europe*. Singapore: Palgrave Macmillan.

Amin, A. (2014). Lively infrastructure. *Theory, Culture & Society, 31*(7–8), 137–161.

Amoore, L. (2021). The deep border. *Political Geography*. Online first: https://doi.org/10.1016/j.polgeo.2021.102547

Anderson, F. (2017). Cruising as method and its limits. *Lux*. Retrieved from: https://lux.org.uk/cruising-method-limits-fiona-anderson/.

Anderson, R. (2014). *Illegality, INC: Clandestine migration and the business of bordering Europe*. Oakland, CA: University of California Press.

Andreassen, R. (2015). *Human exhibitions: Race, gender and sexuality in ethnic displays*. Abingdon, UK: Routledge.

Andrews, K. (2021). *The new age of empire: How racism and colonialism still rule the world*. London: Allen Lane.

Andrianimanana, F.M., & Roca-Cuberes, C. (2021). The Facebook groups and pages of Malagasy migrants in France: Hubs of peer-to-peer and spontaneous solidarity. *Social Sciences, 10*(11), 420, 1–14.

Angulo-Pasel, C. (2018). Navigating risks across borders: The lived experiences of Central American women migrants. PhD thesis, Wilfred Laurier University. Retrieved from: https://scholars.wlu.ca/etd/2019

Anthias, F. (2020). *Translocational belongings*. London: Routledge.

Anwar, M.A., & Graham, M. (2020). Hidden transcripts of the gig economy: Labour agency and the new art of resistance among African gig workers. *Environment and Planning A: Economy and Space, 52*(7), 1269–1291.

Appadurai, A. (1988). Introduction: Commodities and the politics of value. In A. Appadurai (Ed.), *The social life of things: Commodities in cultural perspective* (pp. 3–63). Cambridge: Cambridge University Press.

Appadurai, A. (1996). *Modernity at large: Cultural dimensions of globalization*. Minneapolis, MN: University of Minnesota Press.

Appadurai, A. (2003). Archive and aspiration. In J. Brouwer & A. Mulder (Eds.), *Information lives. Art and theory on archiving and retrieving data* (pp. 14–25). Rotterdam: V2_NAi Publishers.

Appadurai, A. (2015). Foreword. In S. Graham & C. McFarlane (Eds.), *Infrastructural lives: Urban infrastructure in context* (pp. xii–xiii). New York: Routledge.

Appadurai, A. (2019). Traumatic exit, identity narratives, and the ethics of hospitality. *Television & New Media, 20*(6), 558–565.

Aradau, C. & Blanke, T. (2022). *Algorithmic reason*. Oxford: Oxford University Press.

Arendt, H. (1951/2004). *The origins of totalitarianism*. New York, NY: Schocken Books.

Arnold, D. (2005). Europe, technology, and colonialism in the 20th century. *History and Technology, 21*(1), 85–106.

Arora, P. (2019). *The next billion users. Digital life beyond the west*. Cambridge, MA: Harvard University Press.

Arthur, T.O. (2020). The performative digital Africa. In K. Smets, K. Leurs, M. Georgiou, S. Witteborn & R. Gajjala (Eds.), *Handbook of media and migration* (pp. 207–219). London: Sage.

Asseraf, A. (2022). Mass media and the colonial informant: Messaoud Djebari and the French Empire, 1880–1901. *Past & Present, 254*(1), 161–192.

Awad, I., & Tossell, J. (2019). Is the smartphone always a smart choice? Against the utilitarian view of the 'connected migrant'. *Information, Communication & Society, 24*(4), 611–626.

Awumbila, M., Deshingkar, P., Kandilige, L., Kofi Teye, J., & Setrana, M. (2019). Please, thank you and sorry – brokering migration and constructing identities for domestic work in Ghana. *Journal of Ethnic and Migration Studies, 45*(14), 2655–2671.

Aziz, A. (2022). Rohingya diaspora online: Mapping the spaces of visibility, resistance and transnational identity on social media. *New Media & Society*. Online first: https://doi.org/10.1177/146144482211322

Bak Jørgensen, M., & Galis, V. (2022). Introduction. In V. Gallis, M. Bak Jørgensen & M. Sandberg (Eds.), *The migration mobile: Border dissidence, sociotechnical resistance and the construction of irregularized migrants* (pp. 3–24). London: Rowman & Littlefield.

Bakewell, O., Kubal, A., & Pereira, S. (2016). Introduction: Feedback in migration processes. In O. Bakewell, G. Engbersen, M.L. Fonseca & C. Horst (Eds.), *Beyond networks* (pp. 1–17). Basingstoke: Palgrave Macmillan.

Baldassar, L., Baldock, C., & Wilding, R. (2007). *Families caring across borders: Migration, ageing and transnational caregiving.* Basingstoke: Palgrave Macmillan.

Baldassar, L., & Merla, L. (2014). Introduction: Transnational family caregiving through the lens of circulation. In L. Baldassar & L. Merla (Eds.), *Transnational families, migration and the circulation of care* (pp. 3–24). London: Routledge.

Balibar, É. (2004). *We, the people of Europe? Reflections on transnational citizenship.* Princeton, NJ: Princeton University Press.

Balkans Act Now! (2019). *BAN Human Trafficking.* Retrieved from: https://banhumantrafficking.com/en/

Barad, K. (2007). *Meeting the universe halfway.* Durham, NC: Duke University Press.

Baser, B., & Ozturk, A.E. (2020). Positive and negative diaspora governance in context. *Middle East Critique, 29*(3), 319–334.

Basiuk, T., & Burszta, J. (Eds.) (2021). *Queers in state socialism: Cruising 1970s Poland.* New York: Routledge.

Bayly, C.A. (1996). *Empire and information: Intelligence gathering and social communication in India, 1780–1870.* Cambridge: Cambridge University Press.

Bayraktar, N. (2016). *Mobility and migration in film and moving image art.* London: Routledge.

Bayramoğlu, Y., & Lünenborg, M. (2018). Queer migration and digital affects: Refugees navigating from the Middle East via Turkey to Germany. *Sexuality & Culture, 22,* 1019–1036.

BBC (2016). Trafficked. 360 video: Inside the horrors of human trafficking in Mexico. *BBC.* Retrieved from: https://www.bbc.com/news/world-38093431

Beck, U., & Beck-Gernsheim, E. (2014). *Distant love. Personal life in the global age.* Cambridge: Polity Press.

Bellanova, R., & Glouftsios, G. (2022). Controlling the Schengen Information System (SIS II): The infrastructural politics of fragility and maintenance. *Geopolitics, 27*(1), 160–84.

BenEzer, G., & Zetter, R. (2015). Searching for directions: Conceptual and methodological challenges in researching refugee journeys. *Journal of Refugee Studies, 28*(3), 297–318.

Benítez, J.L. (2012). Salvadoran transnational families. *Journal of Ethnic and Migration Studies, 38*(9), 1439–1449.

Benjamin, R. (2019a). *Race after technology: Abolitionist tools for the New Jim Code*. Cambridge: Polity Press.

Benjamin, R. (2019b). Introduction: Discriminatory design, liberating imagination. In R. Benjamin (Ed.), *Captivating technology: Race, carceral technoscience and liberatory imagination in everyday life* (pp. 1–24). Durham, NC: Duke University Press.

Bennet, J. (2010). *Vibrant matter: A political ecology of things*. Durham, NC: Duke University Press.

Benton, M., & Glennie, A. (2016). Digital humanitarianism: How tech entrepreneurs are supporting refugee integration. *Migration Policy Institute*, October. Retrieved from: www.migrationpolicy.org/research/digital-humanitarianism-how-tech-entrepreneurs-are-supporting-refugee-integration

Berger, J., & Mohr, J. (2010 [1975]). *A seventh man: A book of images and words about the experience of migrant workers in Europe*. London: Verso.

Bernal, V. (2014). *Nation as network*. Chicago, IL: Chicago University Press.

Berry, J.W. (1997). Immigration, acculturation, and adaptation. *Applied Psychology: An International Review*, 46(1), 5–34.

Berry, J.W. (2005). Acculturation: Living successfully in two cultures. *International Journal of Intercultural Relations*, 29(6), 697–712.

Bhat, R. (2021). From telegraph to fibre optics. *Interventions*. Online first: 10.1080/1369801X.2021.2003230

Bhatt, A. (2018). *High-tech housewives: Indian IT workers, gendered labor and transmigration*. Seattle, WA: University of Washington Press.

Biehl, K. (2015). Governing through uncertainty: Experiences of being a refugee in Turkey as a country for temporary asylum. *Social Analysis*, 59(1), 57–75.

Bircan, T., & Korkmaz, E.E. (2021). Big data for whose sake? Governing migration through artificial intelligence. *Humanities & Social Science Communications*, 8, 241, 1–5. https://doi.org/10.1057/s41599-021-00910-x

Bishop, S. (2019). *Undocumented storytellers: Narrating the immigrant rights movement*. New York: Oxford University Press.

Bishop, S. (2020). An international analysis of governmental media campaigns to deter asylum seekers. *International Journal of Communication*, 14, 1092–1114.

Blindflug studios (2015). *Cloud chasers: Journey of hope*. Retrieved from: http://cloudchasersgame.com

Bloemraad, I. (2012). What the textbooks don't tell you: Moving from a research puzzle to publishing findings. In C. Vargas-Silva (Ed.), *Handbook of research methods in migration* (pp. 502–522). Cheltenham: Edward Elgar.

Boas, I. (2020). Social networking in a digital and mobile world: The case of environmentally related migration in Bangladesh. *Journal of Ethnic and Migration Studies*, 46(7), 1330–1347.

Boas, I., Dahm, R., & Wrathall, D. (2020). Grounding big data on climate-induced human mobility. *Geographical Review*, 110(1–2), 195–209.

Boccagni, P. (2017). *Migration and the search for home: Mapping domestic space in migrants' everyday lives*. Basingstoke: Palgrave.

Boccagni, P., & Baldassar, L. (2015). Emotions on the move: Mapping the emergent field of emotion and migration. *Emotion, Space and Society*, 16, 73–80.

Boccagni, P., Bonfanti, S., Miranda, A., & Massa, A. (2018). Home and migration: A bibliography. *Homing: The Home–Migration Nexus research project*. Retrieved from: https://homing.soc.unitn.it/2018/01/25/homing-working-paper-no-2_2018-home-and-migration-a-bibliography/

Boehm, D.A., & Swank, H. (2011). Introduction: Affecting global movement: The emotional terrain of transnationality. *International Migration, 49*, 1–6.

Boersma, S. (2020). Narrating society: Enacting 'immigrant' characters through negotiating, naturalization, and forgetting. *Global Perspectives, 1*(1), 1–10.

Bolhuis, M.P., & van Wijk, J. (2021). Seeking asylum in the digital era: Social-media and mobile-device vetting in asylum procedures in five European countries. *Journal of Refugee Studies, 34*(2), 1595–1617.

Bolter, J.D., & Grusin, R. (2000). *Remediation: Understanding new media.* Cambridge, MA: MIT Press.

Boochani, B. (2018). *No friend but the mountains: Writings from Manus Prison.* Sydney, NSW: Pan Macmillan Australia.

Boochani, B., & Tazreiter, C. (2019). Notes on exile: Behrouz Boochani in conversation with Claudia Tazreiter. *Australian Journal of Human Rights, 25*(3), 370–375.

Borges, M.J., & Cancian, S. (2016). Reconsidering the migrant letter: From the experience of migrants to the language of migrants. *The History of the Family, 21*(3), 281–290.

Bösel, B., & Wiemer, S. (Eds.) (2020). *Affective transformations: Politics – algorithms – media.* Berlin: Meson Press.

Boter, B., Rensen, M., & G. Scott-Smith (Eds.) (2020). *Unhinging the national framework: Perspectives on transnational life writing.* Leiden: Sidestone Press.

Boullier, D. (2015). The social sciences and the traces of big data: Society, opinion, or vibrations? *Revue Française de Science Politique, 5*(5–6), 805–828.

Boullier, D. (2019). *Sociologie du numérique* (2nd edition). Malakoff: Armand Colin.

Bourdieu, P. (1986). The forms of capital. In J.G. Richardson (Ed.), *Handbook of theory and research for the sociology of education* (pp. 241–258). New York: Greenwood.

Bowker, G., & Leigh Star, S. (1999). *Sorting things out: Classification and its consequences.* Cambridge, MA: MIT Press.

Bowker, G.C., Edwards, P.N., Jackson, S.J., & Knobel, C.P. (2010). The long now of cyberinfrastructure. In W.H. Dutton & P.W. Jeffreys (Eds.), *World wide research: Reshaping the sciences and humanities* (pp. 40–44). Cambridge, MA: MIT Press.

boyd, d. (2010). Social network sites as networked publics: Affordances, dynamics, and implications. In Z. Papacharissi (Ed.), *Networked self: Identity, community, and culture on social network sites* (pp. 39–58). New York, NY: Routledge.

Boyle, E., & Shneiderman, S. (2020). Redundancy, resilience, repair: Infrastructural effects in borderland spaces. *Verge: Studies in Global Asias, 6*(2), 112–138.

Boym, S. (2007). Nostalgia and its discontents. *The Hedgehog Review, 9*(2), 7–18.

Bozdag, C., Hepp, A., & Suna, L. (2012). Diasporic media as the 'focus' of communicative networking among migrants. In I. Rigoni & E. Saitta (Eds.), *Mediating cultural diversity in a globalized public space* (pp. 96–118). Basingstoke: Palgrave Macmillan.

Braudel, F., & Wallerstein, I. (2009). History and the social sciences: The *longue durée*. *Review (Fernand Braudel Center), 32*(2), 171–203.

Breckenridge, K. (2014). *Biometric state: The global politics of identification and surveillance in South Africa, 1850 to the present.* Cambridge: Cambridge University Press.

Brekke, J.P., & Balke Staver, A. (2019). Social media screening: Norway's asylum system. *Forced Migration Review, 61*, 9–11.

Brekke, J.P., & Thorbjørnsrud, K. (2020). Communicating borders. Governments deterring asylum seekers through social media campaigns. *Migration Studies, 8*(1), 43–65.

Brettell, C.B., & Hollifield, J.F. (2023). *Migration theory: Talking across disciplines.* New York: Routledge.

Brickell, K., & Datta, A. (2011). Introduction: Translocal geographies. In K. Brickell & A. Datta (Eds.), *Translocal geographies: Spaces, places, connections* (pp. 3–22). Farnham: Ashgate.

Brinkerhoff, J.M. (2009). *Digital diasporas: Identity and transnational engagement.* Cambridge: Cambridge University Press.

British Dictionary (2021). Representation. *British Dictionary.* Retrieved from: www.dictionary.com/browse/representation

Browne, S. (2015). *Dark matters: On the surveillance of Blackness.* Durham, NC: Duke University Press.

Brudvig, I. (2019). (Im)mobility, digital technologies and transnational spaces of belonging: An ethnographic study of Somali migrants in Cape Town. PhD thesis, University of Cape Town. Retrieved from: https://open.uct.ac.za/handle/11427/30425

Bruns, T. (2023). Thresholds of threat in (historical) security cultures: Overcoming the good-versus-bad mobilities dichotomy. In H. Hein-Kircher & W. Distler (Eds.), *The mobility–security nexus and the making of order: An interdisciplinary and historicizing intervention.* Abingdon, UK: Routledge.

Bryceson, D.F., & Vuorela, U. (2002). Transnational families in the twenty-first century. In D. Bryceson & U. Vuorela (Eds.), *The transnational family* (pp. 3–30). Oxford: Berg.

Bude, H., & Dürrschmidt, J. (2010). What's wrong with globalization? *European Journal of Social Theory, 13*(4), 481–500.

Buikema, R. (2018). The arena of imaginings: Sarah Bartmann and the ethics of representation. In R. Buikema, L. Plate & K. Thiele (Eds.), *Doing gender in media, art and culture* (pp. 81–93). Abingdon, UK: Routledge.

Burns, R. (2019). New frontiers of philanthro-capitalism: Digital technologies and humanitarianism. *Antipode, 51,* 1101–1122.

Burrell, K. (2017). The recalcitrance of distance: Exploring the infrastructures of sending in migrants' lives. *Mobilities, 12*(6), 813–826.

Bustamante Duarte, A.M., Degbelo, A., & Kray, C. (2018). Exploring forced migrants (re)settlement & the role of digital services. In *Proceedings of 16th European Conference on Computer-supported Cooperative Work – Exploratory Papers, Reports of the European Society for Socially Embedded Technologies.* Nancy: EUSSET.

Butler, J. (2001). Giving an account of oneself. *Diacritics, 31*(4), 22–40.

Byrne, D.N. (2008). The future of (the) 'race': Identity, discourse, and the rise of computer-mediated public spheres. In A. Everett (Ed.), *Learning race and ethnicity: Youth and digital media* (pp. 15–38). Cambridge, MA: MIT Press.

Cabalquinto, E.C. (2018). Ambivalent intimacies: Entangled pains and gains through Facebook use in transnational family life. In A.S. Dobson, B. Robards & N. Carah (Eds.), *Digital intimate publics and social media* (pp. 247–263). Basingstoke: Palgrave Macmillan.

Cabalquinto, E.C. (2022). *(Im)mobile homes: Family life at a distance in the age of mobile media.* Oxford: Oxford University Press.

Cabalquinto, E.C., & Wood-Bradley, G. (2020). Migrant platformed subjectivity: Rethinking the mediation of transnational affective economies via digital connectivity services. *International Journal of Cultural Studies, 23*(5), 787–802.

Cabañes, J.V.A. (2019). Information and communication technologies and migrant intimacies: The case of Punjabi youth in Manila. *Journal of Ethnic and Migration Studies, 45*(9), 1650–1666.

Caidi, N., & Allard, D. (2005). Social inclusion of newcomers to Canada: An information problem? *Library & Information Science Research, 27*(3), 302–324.

Caidi, N., Allard, D., & Quirke, L. (2010). Information practices of immigrants. *Annual Review of Information Science and Technology*, 44(1), 491–531.

Cakici, B., Ruppert, E., & Scheel, S. (2020). Peopling Europe through data practices: Introduction to the special issue. *Science, Technology, & Human Values*, 45(2), 199–211.

Camargo, J., Cogo, D. & Alencar, A. (2022). Venezuelan refugees in Brazil: Communication rights and digital inequalities during the Covid-19 pandemic. *Media and Communication*, 10(2), 230–240.

Camminga, B., & Marnell, J. (2022). *Queer and trans African mobilities*. London: Bloomsbury.

Cancian, S. (2012). The language of gender in lovers' correspondence, 1946–1949. *Gender and History*, 24, 755–765.

Cancian, S., & Wegge, S. A. (2016). "If it is not too expensive, then you can send me sugar": Money matters among migrants and their families. *The History of the Family*, 21(3), 350–367.

Candidatu, L. (2021). Diasporic mothering and Somali diaspora formation in the Netherlands. *Journal of Global Diaspora & Media*, 2(1), 39–55.

Carling, J. (2016). Making and breaking a chain: Migrants' decisions about helping others migrate. In O. Bakewell, G. Engbersen, M.L. Fonseca & C. Horst (Eds.), *Beyond networks: Migration, diasporas and citizenship* (pp. 156–182). Basingstoke: Palgrave Macmillan.

Cassidy, E., & Yang Wang, W. (2018). Gay men's digital cultures beyond Gaydar and Grindr: LINE use in the gay Chinese diaspora of Australia. *Information, Communication & Society*, 21(6), 851–865.

Castoriadis, C. (1998). *The imaginary institution of society*. Cambridge, MA: MIT Press.

Çatak, Güven et al. (2017). Game co-design with and for refugees: An intercultural approach. In C. Busch, C. Kassung & J. Sieck (Eds.), *Kultur und Informatik: Reality and virtuality* (pp. 61–73). Frankfurt & Leipzig: Hülsbusch.

Césaire, A. (2000 [1 955]). *Discourse on colonialism*. Transl. by J. Pinkham. New York, NY: Monthly Review Press.

Chadwick, A. (2013). *The hybrid media system*. Oxford: Oxford University Press.

Chandra, G., & Erlingsdóttir, I. (Eds.) (2021). *The Routledge handbook of the politics of the #metoo movement*. Abingdon: Routledge.

Chatman, E.A. (1996). The impoverished life world of outsiders. *Journal of the American Society for Information Science*, 47(3), 193–206.

Chaubey, A.K., & Rahaman, V. (2021). Understanding digital diaspora as cognitive social media. In S. Sharma, V. Rahaman & G.R. Sinha (Eds.), *Big data analytics in cognitive social media and literary texts* (pp. 237–250). Singapore: Springer.

Cheesman, M. (2022). Self-sovereignty for refugees? The contested horizons of digital identity. *Geopolitics*, 27(1), 134–159.

Chen, H. (2020). Left-behind children as agents: Mobile media, transnational communication and the mediated family gaze. In J. Cabañes & C. Uy-Tioco (Eds.), *Mobile media and social intimacies in Asia: Mobile communication in Asia: Local insights, global implications* (pp. 133–153). Dordrecht: Springer.

Chen, X., & Liu, T. (2021). On 'never right-swipe whites' and 'only date whites': Gendered and racialised digital dating experiences of the Australian Chinese diaspora. *Information, Communication & Society*, 24(9), 1247–1264.

Cho, Grace M. (2008). *Haunting the Korean diaspora: Shame, secrecy and the forgotten war*. Minneapolis, MN: University of Minnesota Press.

Chouliaraki, L. (2017). Symbolic bordering: The self-representation of migrants and refugees in digital news. *Popular Communication*, 15(2), 78–94.

Chouliaraki, L., & Georgiou, M. (2022). *The digital border: Migration, technology, power.* New York, NY: New York University Press.

Chouliaraki, L., & Musarò, P. (2017). The mediatized border: Technologies and affects of migrant reception in the Greek and Italian borders. *Feminist Media Studies, 17*(4), 535–549.

Christensen, M., & Jansson, A. (2015). *Cosmopolitanism and the media.* Basingstoke: Palgrave Macmillan.

Chun, W.H.K. (2006). *Control and freedom.* Cambridge, MA: MIT Press.

Chun, W.H.K. (2021). *Discriminating data: Correlation, neighborhoods, and the new politics of recognition.* Cambridge, MA: MIT Press.

Clark, K.E. (2021). Boundary making practices in Virtual Reality. In *Proceedings of DiGRA Australia 2021.* Retrieved from: http://digraa.org/wp-content/uploads/2021/02/DiGRAA2021_paper_27.pdf

Clark-Kazak, C. (2021). Ethics in forced migration research: Taking stock and potential ways forward. *Journal on Migration and Human Security, 9*(3), 125–138.

Clough, P. (2008). The affective turn: Political economy, biomedia and bodies. *Theory, Culture & Society, 25*(1), 1–22.

Cogo, D. (2019). Communication, migrant activism and counter-hegemonic narratives of Haitian diaspora in Brazil. *Journal of Alternative and Community Media, 4*(3), 71–85.

Cole, M. (2021). *Climate change, the fourth industrial revolution and public pedagogies.* Abingdon: Routledge.

Collins, F.L. (2021). Geographies of migration I: Platform migration. *Progress in Human Geography, 45*(4), 866–877.

Collins English Dictionary (2021). Critical infrastructure. *Collins English Dictionary.* Retrieved from: www.collinsdictionary.com/dictionary/english/critical-infrastructure

Collyer, M. (2007). In-between places: Trans-Saharan transit migrants in Morocco and the fragmented journey to Europe. *Antipode, 39*(4), 668–690.

Conradson, D., & Mckay, D. (2007). Translocal subjectivities: Mobility, connection, emotion. *Mobilities, 2*(2), 167–174.

Constable, N. (2020). Afterword: Rethinking ethnographic entanglements of care and control. *Ethnos, 85*(2), 327–334, doi: 10.1080/00141844.2018.1543343

Cook, D. (2020). The freedom trap: Digital nomads and the use of disciplining practices to manage work/leisure boundaries. *Information Technology & Tourism, 22*, 355–390.

Costa, E. (2016). *Social media in South-East Turkey.* London: UCL Press.

Costa, E. (2018). Affordances-in-practice: An ethnographic critique of social media logic and context collapse. *New Media & Society, 20*(10), 3641–3656.

Costa, E., & Menin, L. (2016). Introduction. *Middle East Journal of Culture and Communication, 9*(2), 137–145.

Costa, E., & Wang, X. (2020). Being at home on social media: Online place-making among the Kurds in Turkey and rural migrants in China. In K. Smets, K. Leurs, M. Georgiou, S. Witteborn & R. Gajjala (Eds.), *Handbook of media and migration* (pp. 515–525). London: Sage.

Costanza-Chock, S. (2014). *Out of the shadows, into the streets! Transmedia organizing and the immigrant rights movement.* Cambridge, MA: MIT Press.

Costanza-Chock, S. (2020). *Design justice: Community-led practices to build the worlds we need.* Cambridge, MA: MIT Press.

Couldry, N. (2010). *Why voice matters.* London: Sage.

Cover, R. (2012). Performing and undoing identity online: Social networking, identity theories and the incompatibility of online profiles and friendship regimes. *Convergence, 18*(2), 177–193.

Cranston, S. (2014). Reflections on doing the expat show: Performing the global mobility industry. *Environment and Planning A: Economy and Space, 46*(5), 1124–1138.

Crawley, H., & Skleparis, D. (2018). Refugees, migrants, neither, both: Categorical fetishism and the politics of bounding in Europe's 'migration crisis'. *Journal of Ethnic and Migration Studies, 44*, 48–64.

Cresswell, T. (2006). *On the move.* London: Routledge.

Creswell, T. (2010). Towards a politics of mobility. *Environment and Planning D: Society and Space, 28*, 17–31.

Croucher, S.M., & Rahmani, D. (2015). A longitudinal test of the effects of Facebook on cultural adaptation. *Journal of International and Intercultural Communication, 8*(4), 330–345.

Culpepper, R. (2012). Nationalist competition on the internet: Uyghur diaspora versus the Chinese state media. *Asian Ethnicity, 13*(2), 187–203.

Cunningham, S., & Sinclair, J. (Eds.) (2001). *Floating lives: The media and Asian diasporas.* St Lucia, Queensland: Queensland University Press.

Cvetkovich, A. (2003). *An archive of feelings: Trauma, sexuality, and lesbian public cultures.* Durham, NC: Duke University Press.

D'Ignazio, C., & Klein, L.F. (2020). *Data feminism.* Cambridge, MA: MIT Press.

Dahinden, J. (2016). A plea for the 'de-migranticization' of research on migration and integration. *Ethnic and Racial Studies, 39*(13), 2207–2225.

Dahlberg, L., & Siapera, E. (Eds.) (2007). *Radical democracy and the internet: Interrogating theory and practice.* New York, NY: Palgrave Macmillan.

Daly, A., Hagendorff, T., Li, H., Mann, M., Marda, V., Wagner, B., and Wang, W.W. & Witteborn, S. (2019). Artificial Intelligence, Governance and Ethics: Global Perspectives (July 4, 2019). *The Chinese University of Hong Kong Faculty of Law Research Paper, 033.*

Dasgupta, R.H. (2017). *Digital queer cultures in India.* London: Routledge.

Dasuki, S.I., & Abubakar, N.H. (2019). The contributions of WhatsApp to social inclusion: A case of internally displaced persons in Nigeria. In K. Rannenberg (Ed.), *IFIP Advances in information and communication technology* (pp. 414–424). Cham: Springer International.

Davies, T., Isakjee, A., & Obradovic-Wochnick, J. (2022). Epistemic borderwork: Violent pushbacks, refugees and the politics of knowledge at the EU border. *Annals of the American Association of Geographers.* Online first: https://doi.org/10.1080/2469445 2.2022.2077167

Davis, J.L. (2020). *How artifacts afford: The power and politics of everyday things.* Cambridge, MA: MIT Press.

De Genova, N. (2020). The convulsive European space of mobilities. *Political Anthropological Research on International Social Sciences, 1*(1), 162–188.

De Genova, N. (Ed.) (2017). *The borders of 'Europe': Autonomy of migration, tactics of bordering.* Durham, NC: Duke University Press.

De Genova, N. (2018). The 'migrant crisis' as racial crisis: Do *Black Lives Matter* in Europe? *Ethnic and Racial Studies, 41*(10), 1765–1782.

Dekker, R., & Engbersen, G. (2013). How social media transform migrant networks and facilitate migration. *Global Networks, 14*(4), 401–418.

Dekker, R., Engbersen, G., Klaver, J., & Vonk, H. (2018). Smart refugees: How Syrian asylum migrants use social media information in migration decision-making. *Social Media + Society, 4*(1), 1–11.

De Koning, L., Nolten, E., & Leurs, K. (2019). Community media makers and the mediation of difference. In R. Buikema, A. Boyse & A.C.G.M. Robben (Eds.) *Cultures, citizenship and human rights*, pp. 31–48. London: Routledge.

Deleuze, G. (1988). *Spinoza: Practical philosophy* (R. Hurley, Trans.). San Francisco, CA: City Lights Books.

Deleuze, G., & Guattari, F. (1988). *A thousand plateaus: Capitalism and schizophrenia*. London: Bloomsbury.

De Schmidt, J. (2016). 'This strange little floating world of ours': Shipboard periodicals and community-building in the 'global' nineteenth century. *Journal of Global History*, *11*(2), 229–250.

Deshingkar, P. (2019). The making and unmaking of precarious, ideal subjects – migration brokerage in the Global South. *Journal of Ethnic and Migration Studies*, *45*(14), 2638–2654.

De Tapia, S. (2010). New migratory configurations: Transnationalism/s, diaspora/s, migratory circulation. In C. Audebert & M.K. Doraï (Eds.), *Migration in a globalised world: New research issues and prospects* (pp. 127–142). Amsterdam: Amsterdam University Press.

Dhoest, A., & Szulc, Ł. (2016). Navigating online selves: Social, cultural, and material contexts of social media use by diasporic gay men. *Social Media + Society*, *2*(4), 1–10.

Díaz Andrade, A., & Doolin, B. (2019). Temporal enactment of resettled refugees' ICT-mediated information practices. *Information Systems Journal*, *29*(1), 145–174.

Dijstelbloem, H. (2021). *Borders as infrastructure: The technopolitics of border control*. Cambridge, MA: MIT Press.

Dijstelbloem, H., Meijer, A., & Besters, M. (2011). The migration machine. In H. Dijstelbloem & A. Meijer (Eds.), *Migration and the new technological borders of Europe* (pp. 1–21). Basingstoke: Palgrave Macmillan.

DiMaggio, P., & Garip, F. (2011). How network externalities can exacerbate intergroup inequality. *American Journal of Sociology*, *116*(6), 1887–1933.

Diminescu, D. (2002). La désinstitutionalisation de l'hospitalité et l'intégration par le bas: Le cas des migrants roumains [The deinstitutionalization of hospitality and integration from below: The case of Romanian migrants]. *VEI Enjeux*, *131*, 167–175.

Diminescu, D. (2005). Le migrant connecté: Pour un manifeste épistémologique. *Migrations/Société*, *17*(102), 275–292.

Diminescu, D. (2008). The connected migrant: An epistemological manifesto. *Social Science Information*, *47*(4), 565–579.

Diminescu, D. (2020). Researching the connected migrant. In K. Smets, K. Leurs, M. Georgiou, S. Witteborn & R. Gajjala (Eds.), *Handbook of media and migration* (pp. 74–78). London: Sage.

Dobson, A.S., Robards, B., & Carah, N. (2018). Digital intimate publics and social media: Towards theorising public lives on private platforms. In A.S. Dobson, B. Robards & N. Carah (Eds.), *Digital intimate publics and social media* (pp. 3–27). Basingstoke: Palgrave Macmillan.

Drolia, M., Sifaki, E., Papadakis, S., & Kalogiannakis, M. (2020). An overview of mobile learning for refugee students: Juxtaposing refugee needs with mobile applications' characteristics. *Challenges*, *11*(2), 31. https://doi.org/10.3390/challe11020031

Düvell, F. (2021). Quo vadis, migration studies? The quest for a migratory epistemology. *Zeitschrift für Migrationsforschung*, *1*(1), 215–241.

Easton, A., & Wells, K. (2020). Mobile libraries and information needs in refugee camps. *Pathfinder: A Canadian Journal for Information Science Students and Early Career Professionals, 1*(1), 17–25.

Edwards, A. (2020). Now streaming: Dallas-based AfroLandTV is the new 'Netflix for the global pan African diaspora'. *Dallas Innovates.* Retrieved from: https://dallasinnovates.com/now-streaming-dallas-based-afrolandtv-is-the-new-netflix-for-the-global-pan-african-diaspora/

Edwards, P. (2002). Infrastructure and modernity: Force, time, and social organization in the history of sociotechnical systems. In T.J. Misa, P. Brey & A. Feenberg (Eds.), *Technology and modernity: The empirical turn* (pp. 185–225). Cambridge, MA: MIT Press.

Edwards, P.N., Gitelman, L., Hecht, G., Johns, A., Larkin, B., & Safier, N. (2011). Historical perspectives on the circulation of information. *American Historical Review, 116*(5), 1393–1435.

Edwards, R., & Mauthner, M. (2002). Ethics and feminist research: Theory and practice. In M. Mauthner, M. Birch, J. Jessop & T. Miller (Eds.), *Ethics in qualitative research* (pp. 14–31). London: Sage.

Elias, N., & Lemish, D. (2009). Spinning the web of identity: The roles of the internet in the lives of immigrant adolescents. *New Media & Society, 11*(4), 533–551.

Elliott, A., & Urry, J. (2010). *Mobile lives.* New York, NY: Routledge.

Ellis, D., Tucker, I., & Harper, D. (2013). The affective atmospheres of surveillance. *Theory & Psychology, 23*(6), 716–731.

EMN-OECD (2022). *The use of digitalisation and artificial intelligence in migration management.* European Migration Network – Organisation for Economic Co-operation and Development. Retrieved from: www.oecd.org/migration/mig/EMN-OECD-INFORM-FEB-2022-The-use-of-Digitalisation-and-AI-in-Migration-Management.pdf

Ennaji, M., & Bignami, F. (2019). Logistical tools for refugees and undocumented migrants: Smartphones and social media in the city of Fès. *Work Organisation, Labour & Globalisation, 13*(1), 62–78.

Enright, T. (2022). The infrastructural imagination. *Journal of Urban Technology, 29*(1), 101–107.

Epstein, G.S. (2008). Herd and network effects in migration decision-making. *Journal of Ethnic and Migration Studies, 34*(4), 567–583.

Equiano, O. (2003 [1789]) The *interesting narrative of the life of Olaudah Equiano, or Gustavus Vassa, the African.* London: Penguin.

Erdal, M.B., & Oeppen, C. (2013). Migrant balancing acts: Understanding the interactions between integration and transnationalism. *Journal of Ethnic and Migration Studies, 39*(6), 867–884.

Errington, J. (2008). Webs of affection and obligation: Glimpse into families and nineteenth century transatlantic communities. *Journal of the Canadian Historical Association, 19*, 1–26.

Etem, A.J. (2020). Representations of Syrian refugees in UNICEF's media projects: New vulnerabilities in digital humanitarian communication. *Global Perspectives, 1*(1), 1–17.

EU EPSC (2019). *10 trends shaping migration.* Brussels: European Commission – European Political Strategy Centre. Retrieved from: https://op.europa.eu/en/publication-detail/-/publication/aa25fb8f-10cc-11ea-8c1f-01aa75ed71a1

Fast, K., & Lindell, J. (2016). The elastic mobility of business elites – negotiating the 'home' and 'away' continuum. *European Journal of Cultural Studies, 19*(5), 435–444.

FFunction (2017). (Un)Trafficked. Kailash Satyarthi Children's Foundation and the Children's Investment Fund Foundation. Retrieved from: https://www.idnworld.com/potm/FFunction-Untrafficked

Fischer, F. (1990). *Technocracy and the politics of expertise.* Newbury Park, CA: Sage.

Fotaki, M. (2021). Solidarity in crisis? Community responses to refugees and forced migrants in the Greek islands. *Organization.* Online first: https://doi.org/10.1177/13505084211051048

Foucault, M. (1977). *Discipline and punish: The birth of the prison* (A. Sheridan, Trans.). New York, NY: Vintage Books.

Foucault, M. (2003 [1976]). *Society must be defended. Lectures at the Collège de France,* 1975-76. Transl. by D. Macey. New York, NY: Picador.

Frosh, P., & Georgiou, M. (2022). Covid-19: The cultural constructions of a global crisis. *International Journal of Cultural Studies, 25*(3–4), 233–252.

Gajjala, R. (2004). *Cyber selves: Feminist ethnographies of South Asian women.* Walnut Creek, CA: AltaMira Press.

Gajjala, R. (2019). *Digital diasporas: Labor and affect in gendered Indian digital publics.* London: Rowman & Littlefield.

Galhardi, R. de A. A. (2022). Territories of migrancy and meaning: The emotional politics of borderscapes in the lives of deported Mexican men in Tijuana. *International Journal of Cultural Studies,* Online first: https://doi.org/10.1177/136787792211447

Gao, G., & Sai, L. (2021). Opposing the toxic apartheid: The painted veil of the COVID-19 pandemic, race and racism. *Gender, Work & Organization, 28*(S1), 631–637.

Gatrell, P. (2013). *The making of the modern refugee.* Oxford: Oxford University Press.

Gatrell, P. (2017). Refugees – what's wrong with history? *Journal of Refugee Studies, 30*(2), 170–189.

Gauntlett, D. (2007). *Creative explorations: New approaches to identities and audiences.* New York, NY: Routledge.

Gebrial, D. (2022). Racial platform capitalism: Empire, migration and the making of Uber in London. *Environment and Planning A: Economy and Space.* Online first: https://doi.org/10.1177/0308518X221115439

Georgiou, M. (2006). *Diaspora, identity and the media.* Creskill, NJ: Hampton Press.

Georgiou, M. (2013). Seeking ontological security beyond the nation: The role of transnational television. *Television & New Media, 14*(4), 304–321.

Georgiou, M. (2018). Does the subaltern speak? Migrant voices in digital Europe. *Popular Communication, 16*(1), 45–57.

Georgiou, M. (2019). City of refuge or digital order? Refugee recognition and the digital governmentality of migration in the city. *Television & New Media, 20*(6), 600–616.

Georgiou, M., & Leurs, K. (2022). Smartphones as personal digital archives? Recentering migrant authority as curating and storytelling subjects. *Journalism, 23*(3), 668–689.

Georgiou, M., & Zaborowski, R. (2017). *Media coverage of the 'refugee crisis': A cross-European perspective.* Brussels: Council of Europe. Retrieved from: https://edoc.coe.int/en/refugees/7367-media-coverage-of-the-refugee-crisis-a-cross-european-perspective.html

Gibbs, T. (2014). Becoming a 'big man' in neo-liberal South Africa: Migrant masculinities in the minibus-taxi industry. *African Affairs, 113*(452), 431–448.

Giddens, A. (1990). *The consequences of modernity.* Stanford, CA: Stanford University Press.

Gifford, S.M., & Wilding, R. (2013). Digital escapes? ICTs, settlement and belonging among Karen Youth in Melbourne, Australia. *Journal of Refugee Studies, 26*(4), 558–575.

Gill, J., & Baptista, D. (2022). Digital nomad hotspots grapple with housing squeeze. *Context* Retrieved from: https://www.context.news/socioeconomic-inclusion/digital-nomad-hotspots-grapple-with-housing-squeeze

Gillespie, M. (1995). *Television, ethnicity and cultural change.* London: Routledge.

Gillespie, M., Ampofo, L., Cheesman, M., Faith, B., Illiou, E., Issa, A., & Skleparis, D. (2016). Mapping refugee media journeys: Smartphones and social media networks. *Research report.* Médias Monde, France: The Open University. Retrieved from: http://dx.doi.org/10.13140/RG.2.2.15633.22888

Gillespie, T. (2010). The politics of 'platforms'. *New Media & Society, 12*(3), 347–364.

Gilroy, P. (1993). *The Black Atlantic: Modernity and double consciousness.* Cambridge, MA: Harvard University Press.

Ging, D., & Siapera, E. (Eds.) (2019). *Gender hate online: Understanding the new antifeminism.* Cham, Switzerland: Palgrave Macmillan.

Gitelman, L. (2006). *Always already new: Media, history, and the data of culture.* Cambridge, MA: MIT Press.

Glasius, M. (2018). Extraterritorial authoritarian practices: A framework. *Globalizations, 15*(2), 179–197.

Glaveanu, V.P., & Womersley, G. (2021). Affective mobilities: Migration, emotion and (im)possibility. *Mobilities, 16*(4), 628–642.

Glick Schiller, N., Basch, L., & Blanc-Szanton, C. (Eds.) (1992). *Towards a transnational perspective on migration: Race, class, ethnicity, and nationalism reconsidered.* New York: New York Academy of Sciences.

Goksel, G.U. (2018). *Integration of immigrants and the theory of recognition.* Cham, Switzerland: Palgrave Macmillan.

Gold Extra (2008). *Frontiers: Welcome to fortress Europe.* Retrieved from: https://goldextra.com/en/frontiers.

Golova, T. (2020). Post-Soviet migrants in Germany, transnational public spheres and Russian soft power. *Journal of Information Technology & Politics, 17*(3), 249–267.

Gordano Peile, C. (2014). The migration industry of connectivity services: A critical discourse approach to the Spanish case in a European perspective. *Crossings: Journal of Migration and Culture, 5*(1), 57–71.

Gorman-Murray, A. (2007). Rethinking queer migration through the body, *Social & Cultural Geography, 8*(1), 105–121.

Greene, A. (2020). Mobiles and 'making do': Exploring the affective, digital practices of refugee women waiting in Greece. *European Journal of Cultural Studies, 23*(5), 731–748.

Gregg, M., & Seigworth, G.J. (2009). *The affect theory reader.* Durham, NC: Duke University Press.

Griffen, J.H. (1961). *Black like me.* Boston, MA: Houghton Mifflin.

Griffiths, M. (2020). Affect and displacement. In P. Adey et al. (Eds.), *The handbook of displacement* (pp. 99–107). Cham: Palgrave Macmillan.

Gruenewald, T., & Witteborn, S. (2022). Feeling good: Humanitarian virtual reality film, emotional style and global citizenship. *Cultural Studies, 36*(1), 141–161.

Guardian Staff (2020). Donald Trump calls Covid-19 'kung flu' at Tulsa rally. *The Guardian,* June 20. Retrieved from: www.theguardian.com/us-news/2020/jun/20/trump-covid-19-kung-flu-racist-language

Guevarra, A.R. (2014). Supermaids: The racial branding of global filipino care labour. In B. Anderson & I. Shutes (Eds.), *Migration and care labour: Theory, policy, and politics* (pp. 130–150). Basingstoke: Palgrave Macmillan.

Gunew, S. (2009). Subaltern empathy: Beyond European categories in affect theory. *Concentric: Literary and Cultural Studies*, 35(1), 11–30.

Gutiérrez-Rodríguez, E. (2010). *Migration, domestic work and affect*. London: Routledge.

Haas, H. de (2005). International migration, remittances and development: Myths and facts, *Third World Quarterly*, 26(8), 1269–1284.

Halegoua, G., & Polson, E. (2021). Exploring 'digital placemaking.' *Convergence: The International Journal of Research into New Media Technologies*, 27(3), 573–578.

Hall, S. (2013a). Introduction. In S. Hall, J. Evans & S. Nixon (Eds.), *Representation* (2nd edition, pp. xvii–xxvi). London: Sage/The Open University.

Hall, S. (2013b). The work of representation. In S. Hall, J. Evans & S. Nixon (Eds.), *Representation* (2nd edition, pp. 1–59). London: Sage/The Open University.

Hall, S. (2013c). The spectacle of the 'other'. In S. Hall, J. Evans & S. Nixon (Eds.), *Representation* (2nd edition, pp. 215–269). London: Sage/The Open University.

Hall, S., Evans, J., & Nixon, S. (Eds.) (1997). *Representation*. London: Sage/The Open University.

Halpern, O., Jagoda, P., Kirkwood, J.W., & Weatherby, L. (2022). Surplus data: An introduction. *Critical Inquiry*, 48(2), 197–210.

Halsell, G. (1969). *Soul sister. The journal of a white woman who turned herself black and went to live and work in Harlem and Mississippi*. Cleveland, OH: The World Publishing Company.

Hamlin, R. (2021). *Crossing: How we label and react to people on the move*. Stanford, CA: Stanford University Press.

Hampâté Bâ, A. (2000). *The fortunes of Wangrin* (new edition, Aina Pavolini Taylor, Trans.). Bloomington, IN: Indiana University Press.

Hannaford, D. (2014). Technologies of the spouse: Intimate surveillance in Senegalese transnational marriages. *Global Networks*, 15(1), 43–59.

Haraway, D. (1988). Situated knowledges: The science question in feminism and the privilege of partial perspective. *Feminist Studies*, 14(3), 575–599.

Haraway, D. (1997). M*odest_Witness@Second_Millenium.FemaleMan©_meets_ OncoMouse™: Feminism and technoscience*. New York: Routledge.

Harding, S. (Ed.) (2011). *The postcolonial science and technology studies reader*. Durham, NC: Duke University Press.

Harvey, A. (2020). *Feminist media studies*. Cambridge: Polity Press.

Hasebrink, U., & Domeyer, H. (2012). Media repertoires as patterns of behaviour and as meaningful practices. *Participations: Journal of Audience & Reception Studies*, 9(2), 757–783.

Hasebrink, U., & Hepp, A. (2017). How to research cross-media practices? Investigating media repertoires and media ensembles. *Convergence*, 23(4), 362–377.

Hasić, J., & Karabegović, D. (2020). Diaspora as digital diplomatic agents: 'BOSNET' and wartime foreign affairs. *Migration Letters*, 17(1), 103–113.

Hasisi, B., & Weisburd, D. (2011). Going beyond ascribed identities: The importance of procedural justice in airport security screening in Israel. *Law & Society Review*, 45(4), 867–892.

Hayes, J. (2019). Trajectories of belonging and enduring technology: 2G phones and Syrian refugees in the Kurdistan region of Iraq. *European Journal of Communication*, 34(6), 661–670.

He, G., Leurs, K., & Li, Y. (2022). Researching motherhood in the age of short videos: Stay-at-home mothers in China performing labor on Douyin. *Media and Communication*, 10(3).

He, G., & Zhang, J. (2022). (Im)mobility and performance of emotions: Chinese international students' difficult journeys to home during the COVID-19 pandemic. *Mobile Media & Communication*, 1–23. Online first: https://doi.org/10.1177/205015792211195

Hecht, G. (Ed.) (2011). *Entangled geographies: Empire and technopolitics in the global cold war*. Cambridge, MA: MIT Press.

Hegde, R.S. (Ed.) (2011). *Circuits of visibility: Gender and transnational media cultures*. New York, NY: New York University Press.

Hegde, R.S. (2016). *Mediating migration*. Cambridge: Polity Press.

Hegde, R.S., & Sahoo, A. (Eds.) (2018). *Routledge handbook of the Indian diaspora*. New York, NY: Routledge.

Heidkamp, B., & Kergel, D. (2017). Precarity and social media from the entrepreneurial self to the precariatised mind. In B. Heidkamp & D. Kergel (Eds.), *Precarity within the digital age* (pp. 99–114). Wiesbaden: Springer.

Heller, C., Pezzani, L., & Stierl, M. (2017). Disobedient sensing and border struggles at the maritime frontier of Europe. *Spheres: Journal for Digital Cultures*, 4, 1–15.

Hernández-León, R. (2013). Conceptualizing the migration industry. In T. Gammeltoft-Hansen & N. Nyberg Sorensen (Eds.), *The migration industry and the commercialization of international migration* (pp. 24–44). London: Routledge.

Hilgert, C., Just, A.L., & Khamkar, G. (2020). Airtime for newcomers. *Media History*, 26(1), 62–74.

Hillis, K., Paasonen, S., & Petit, M. (Eds) (2015). *Networked affect*. Cambridge, MA: MIT Press.

Hirata, T., & Leurs, K. (2020). Introduction to the special issue. *Global Perspectives*, 1(1), 1–15.

Hjorth, L., & Lim, S.S. (2012). Mobile intimacy in an age of affective mobile media. *Feminist Media Studies*, 12(4), 477–484.

Hofhuis, J., Hanke, K., & Rutten, T. (2019). Social network sites and acculturation of international sojourners in the Netherlands. *International Journal of Intercultural Relations*, 69, 120–130.

Holt, J., & Vanderau, P. (2015). 'Where the Internet lives': Data centers as cloud infrastructure. In L. Parks & N. Starosielski (Eds.), *Signal traffic: Critical studies of media infrastructures* (pp. 94–112). Urbana-Champaign, IL: University of Illinois Press.

hooks, b. (1991). *Yearning: Race, gender and cultural politics*. London: Turnaround.

Hopkins, L. (2009). Media and migration: A review of the field. *Australian Journal of Communication*, 36, 35–54.

Horst, H., & Miller, D. (2012). Normativity and materiality: A view from digital anthropology. *Media International Australia*, 145, 103–111.

Horsti, K. (2017). Communicative memory of irregular migration: The re-circulation of news images on YouTube. *Memory Studies*, 10(2), 112–129.

Horsti, K. (2019). *The politics of public memories of forced migration and bordering in Europe*. Cham, Switzerland: Palgrave Macmillan.

Hu, Y., Xu, C.L., & Tu, M. (2022). Family-mediated migration infrastructure: Chinese international students and parents navigating (im)mobilities during the COVID-19 pandemic. *Chinese Sociological Review*, 54(1), 62–87.

Huang, Y. (2020). 'Re-feminization' of dependent women migrants: Negotiating gender roles in the Chinese digital diaspora. *Asian Journal of Women's Studies*, 26(2), 159–183.

Huhtamo, E., & Parikka, J. (Eds.) (2011). *Media archaeology: Approaches, applications, and implications.* Berkeley, CA: University of California Press.

Hynnä, K., Lehto, M., & Paasonen, S. (2019). Affective body politics of social media. *Social Media + Society, 5*(4), 1–5.

ID2020 (2021). Why the alliance. *ID2020 Systems.* Retrieved from: https://id2020.org/alliance

Iliadis, A., & Russo, F. (2016). Critical data studies: An introduction. *Big Data & Society, 3*(2), 1–7.

ILO (2019). *Mobile women and mobile phones: Women migrant workers' use of information and communication technologies in ASEAN.* International Labour Organization. Retrieved from: www.ilo.org/asia/publications/WCMS_732253/lang–en/index.htm

ILO (2021). *Use of digital technology in the recruitment of migrant workers.* International Labour Organization. Retrieved from: www.ilo.org/global/topics/fair-recruitment/publications/WCMS_831814/lang–en/index.htm

Impey, A. (2013). Keeping in touch via cassette: Tracing Dinka songs from cattle camp to transnational audio-letter. *Journal of African Cultural Studies, 25*(2), 197–210.

Iñárritu, A.G. (2017). *Carne y Arena.* Retrieved from: https://phi.ca/en/carne-y-arena/

Isin, E., & Ruppert, E. (2020). *Being digital citizens* (2nd edition). London: Rowman & Littlefield.

Jack, V. (2016). Communication of information on the Thai–Burma border. *Forced Migration Review, 52,* 96–98.

Jack, V. (2020). Informing refugee communities in Greece. In J. Matthews & E. Thorsen (Eds.), *Media, journalism and disaster communities* (pp. 201–213). Cham, Switzerland: Springer International.

Jackson, J. (2017). Sojourner communication. In Y.Y. Kim & K.L. McKay-Semmler (Eds.), *The international encyclopedia of intercultural communication* (pp. 1–5). Hoboken, NJ: John Wiley & Sons.

Jamieson, L. (2011). Intimacy as a concept: Explaining social change in the context of globalisation or another form of ethnocentricism? *Sociological Research Online, 16*(4), 1–13.

Jansson, A. (2018). *Mediatization and mobile lives: A critical approach.* New York: Routledge.

Jaramillo-Dent, D., Alencar, A., & Asadchy, Y. (2022) #Migrantes on TikTok: Exploring platformed belongings. *International Journal of Communication, 16,* 5578–5602.

Jaramillo-Dent, D., Contreras-Pulido, P., & Pérez-Rodríguez, A. (2022). Immigrant influencers on TikTok: Diverse microcelebrity profiles and algorithmic (in)visibility. *Media and Communication, 10*(1), 208–221.

Jeon, H. (2020). Articulating the Shan migrant community in Thai society through community radio: A case study of the map radio FM 99 in the city of Chiang Mai, Thailand. *Asia in Focus, 8,* 26–35.

Jiménez Durán, R., Müller, K. & Schwarz, C. (2022). The effect of content moderation on online and offline hate: Evidence from Germany's Netzdg. *CEPR Press Discussion Paper* No. 17554, retrieved from: https://cepr.org/publications/dp17554

Jirattikorn, A. (2008). 'Pirated' transnational broadcasting: The consumption of Thai soap operas among Shan communities in Burma. *SOJOURN: Journal of Social Issues in Southeast Asia, 23*(1), 30–62.

Johnson, M., Lee, M., McCahill, M., & Mesina, M.R. (2020). Beyond the 'All seeing eye': Filipino migrant domestic workers' contestation of care and control in Hong Kong. *Ethnos, 85*(2), 276–292.

Johnson, M., & Lindquist, J. (2020). Care and control in Asian migrations. *Ethnos, 85*(2), 195–207.

Jones, R. (Ed.) (2019). *Open borders: In defence of free movement.* Athens, GA: University of Georgia Press.

JR (2017). Migrants, Picnic across the border. Retrieved from: https://www.jr-art.net/projects/migrants-picnic-across-the-border

Kadiri, A.P.L. (2021). Data and Afrofuturism: An emancipated subject? *Internet Policy Review, 10*(4), 1–26.

Kahn, R., & Kellner, D. (2007). Globalization, technopolitics and radical democracy. In L. Dahlberg & E. Siapera (Eds.), *Radical democracy and the internet: Interrogating theory and practice* (pp. 17–36). New York, NY: Palgrave Macmillan.

Kang, E.B. (2022). Biometric imaginaries: Formatting voice, body, identity to data. *Social Studies of Science, 52*(4), 581–602.

Karim, K. (2003a). *The media of diaspora.* London: Routledge.

Karim, K. (2003b). Mapping diasporic mediascapes. In K. Karim (Ed.), *The media of diaspora* (pp. 1–18). London: Routledge.

Karppi, T., Kähkönen, L., Mannevuo, M., Pajala, M., & Sihvonen, T. (2016). Affective capitalism: Investments and investigations. *Ephemera, 16*(4), 1–13.

Kathiravelu, L. (2012). Social networks in Dubai: Informal solidarities in an uncaring state. *Journal of Intercultural Studies, 33*(1), 103–119.

Katz, Y. (2020). *Artificial whiteness: Politics and ideology in artificial intelligence.* New York, NY: Columbia University Press.

Kaufmann, K. (2018). The smartphone as a snapshot of its use: Mobile media elicitation in qualitative interviews. *Mobile Media & Communication, 6*(2), 233–246.

Kelly, N. (2022). Facial recognition smartwatches to be used to monitor foreign offenders in UK. *The Guardian*, August 5. Retrieved from: www.theguardian.com/politics/2022/aug/05/facial-recognition-smartwatches-to-be-used-to-monitor-foreign-offenders-in-uk

Kessler, F. (2006). Notes on dispositif. *Utrecht University, 15.* Retrieved from: www.frankkessler.nl/wp-content/uploads/2010/05/Dispositif-Notes.pdf

Keusch, F., Leonard, M.M., Sajons, C., & Steiner, S. (2021). Using smartphone technology for research on refugees: Evidence from Germany. *Sociological Methods & Research, 50*(4), 1863–1894.

Khorana, S. (2023). *Mediated emotions of migration. Reclaiming affect for agency.* Bristol: Bristol University Press.

Kim, Y. (2011). *Transnational migration, media and identity of Asian women.* New York: Routledge.

Kim, Y.Y. (2001). *Becoming intercultural: An integrative theory of communication and cross-cultural adaptation.* London: Sage.

Kivikuru, U. (2013). Upstairs downstairs: Communication contradictions around two African refugee camps. *Journal of African Media Studies, 5*(1), 35–51.

Kleinman, J. (2019). *Adventure capital: Migration and the making of an African hub in Paris.* Berkeley, CA: University of California Press.

Kleist, N., & Bjarnesen, J. (2019). Migration infrastructures in West Africa and beyond. *Merian Institute for Advanced Studies in Africa. Working Papers 3.* Retrieved from: www.ug.edu.gh/mias-africa/sites/miasafrica/files/images/191127%20MIASA%20WP_2019%283%29%20Kleist_Bjarnesen.pdf

Koch, R., & Miles, S. (2021). Inviting the stranger in: Intimacy, digital technology and new geographies of encounter. *Progress in Human Geography, 45*(6), 1379–1401.

Komito, L. (2011). Social media and migration: Virtual community 2.0. *Journal of the American Society for Information Science and Technology, 62*, 1075–1086.

Kosciejew, M. (2019). Information's importance for refugees: Information technologies, public libraries, and the current refugee crisis. *The Library Quarterly*, 89(2), 79–98.

Kperogi, F.A. (2020). *Nigeria's digital diaspora: Citizen media, democracy, and participation*. Rochester, NY: University of Rochester Press.

Krajewski, M. (2018). *The server: A media history from the present to the Baroque*. New Haven, CT: Yale University Press.

Krifors, K. (2021). Logistics of migrant labour: Rethinking how workers 'fit' transnational economies. *Journal of Ethnic and Migration Studies*, 47(1), 148–165.

Kumar, P. (2018). Rerouting the narrative: Mapping the online identity politics of the Tamil and Palestinian diaspora. *Social Media + Society*, 4(1).

Kuntsman, A. (2008). Contested borders and the politics of passing in Israel/Palestine and in cyberspace. *Feminist Media Studies*, 8(3), 267–283.

Kurwa, R., & Gurusami, S. (2022). Carceral migrations: Reframing race, space and punishment. *Social Science Review*, 96(2), 353–388.

Labayen, M.F., & Gutierrez, I. (2021). Digital placemaking as survival tactics: Sub-Saharan migrants' videos at the Moroccan–Spanish border. *Convergence*, 27(3), 664–678.

Lamoureux, S. (2009). Imagined connectivity, poetic text-messaging and appropriation in Sudan. In M. Fernández-Ardèvol & A. Ros (Eds.), *Communication technologies in Latin America and Africa: A multidisciplinary perspective* (pp. 221–244). Barcelona: IN3.

Lane, G., Georgiou, M., Dajani, D.S., Kolbe, K., & Theodoropoulou, V. (2019). City of refuge toolkit. *Proboscis*. Retrieved from: http://proboscis.org.uk/6151/city-of-refuge-toolkit/

Langenohl, A., & Van Riet, G. (2020). Security Infrastructures, *Politikon*, 47(1), 1–3.

Larkin, B. (2013). The politics and poetics of infrastructure. *Annual Review of Anthropology*, 42, 327–343.

Latonero, M., Hiatt, L., Napolitano, A., Clericetti, G., & Penagos, M. (2019). Digital identity in the migration and refugee context. *Data & Society*. Retrieved from: https://datasociety.net/library/digital-identity-in-the-migration-refugee-context/

Latour, B. (1996). *Aramis or the love of technology*. Cambridge, MA: Harvard University Press.

Latour, B. (2005). *Reassembling the social: An introduction to actor-network theory*. Oxford: Oxford University Press.

Law, J. (2010). The material of STS. In D. Hicks & M.C. Beaudry (Eds.), *The Oxford handbook of material culture studies* (pp. 174–188). Oxford: Oxford University Press.

Lawrence, R.J. (1985). A more humane history of homes: Research method and application. In I. Altman & C.M. Werner (Eds.), *Home environments* (pp. 113–132). New York: Springer.

Lee, C.S. (2020). *Mediatized transient migrants*. Lanham, MD: Lexington Books.

Leese, M., Noori, S., & Scheel, S. (2022). Data matters: The politics and practices of digital border and migration management. *Geopolitics*, 27(1), 5–25.

Leigh Star, S., & Bowker, G. (2002). How to infrastructure. In L. Lievrouw & S. Livingstone (Eds.), *Handbook of new media* (pp. 151–162). London: Sage.

Leigh Star, S., & Ruhleder, K. (1996). Steps toward an ecology of infrastructure: Design and access for large information spaces. *Information Systems Research*, 7(1), 111–134.

Leppik, M. (2020). The segmented integration and mediated transnationalism of Estonian Russian-speaking populations. PhD thesis, Institute of Social Studies, University of Tartu. Retrieved from https://dspace.ut.ee/handle/10062/70189

Leung, L. (2020). Digital divides. In K. Smets, K. Leurs, M. Georgiou, S. Witteborn & R. Gajjala (Eds.), *Handbook of media and migration* (pp. 79–84). London: Sage.

Leurs, K. (2014). The politics of transnational affective capital: Digital connectivity among young Somalis stranded in Ethiopia. *Crossings: Journal of Migration and Culture, 5*(1), 87–104.

Leurs, K. (2015). *Digital passages: Migrant youth 2.0. Diaspora, gender and youth cultural intersections.* Amsterdam: Amsterdam University Press.

Leurs, K. (2016). Young, connected migrants and non-normative European family life: Exploring affective human right claims of young e-diasporas. *International Journal of E-Politics, 7*(3), 15–34.

Leurs, K. (2017). Communication rights from the margins: Politicising young refugees' smartphone pocket archives. *The International Communication Gazette, 79*(6–7), 674–698.

Leurs, K. (2019). Transnational connectivity and the affective paradoxes of digital care labour. *European Journal of Communication, 34*(6), 641–649.

Leurs, K. (2022). Resilience and digital inclusion: The digital re-making of vulnerability? In P. Tsatsou (Ed.), *Vulnerable people and digital inclusion* (pp. 27–46). Cham, Switzerland: Palgrave Macmillan.

Leurs, K., & Seuferling, P. (2022). Migration and the deep time of media infrastructures. *Communication, Culture & Critique, 15*(2), 290–297.

Leurs, K., & Witteborn, S. (2021). Digital migration studies. In M. McAuliffe (Ed.), *Research handbook on migration and technology* (pp. 15–28). Cheltenham: Edward Elgar.

Lewis, D. (2015). 'Illiberal spaces': Uzbekistan's extraterritorial security practices and the spatial politics of contemporary authoritarianism. *Nationalities Papers, 43*(1), 140–159.

Li, H. (2020). Transnational togetherness through Rela: Chinese queer women's practices for maintaining ties with the homeland. *International Journal of Cultural Studies, 23*(5), 692–708.

Lim, S.S., & Pham, B. (2016). 'If you are a foreigner in a foreign country, you stick together': Technologically mediated communication and acculturation of migrant students. *New Media & Society, 18*(10), 2171–2188.

Lin, W., Lindquist, J., Xiang, B., & Yeoh, B.S.A. (2017). Migration infrastructures and the production of migrant mobilities. *Mobilities, 12*(2), 167–174.

Lindley, A. (2009). The early-morning phonecall: Remittances from a refugee diaspora perspective. *Journal of Ethnic and Migration Studies, 35*(8), 1315–1334.

Lindquist, J. (2015). Anthropology of brokers and brokerage. In J. Wright (Ed.), *International Encyclopedia of Social and Behavioral Science* (pp. 870–874). Amsterdam: Elsevier.

Lindquist, J., Xiang, B., & Yeoh, B.S.A. (2012). Introduction: Opening the black box of migration: Brokers, the organization of transnational mobility and the changing political economy in Asia. *Pacific Affairs, 85*(1), 7–19.

Lloyd, A. (2014). Building information resilience: How do resettling refugees connect with health information in regional landscapes – implications for health literacy. *Australian Academic & Research Libraries, 45*(1), 48–66.

Lloyd, A. (2017). Researching fractured (information) landscapes. *Journal of Documentation, 73*(1), 35–47.

Lo Presti, L. (2020). The migrancies of maps: Complicating the critical cartography and migration nexus in 'migro-mobility' thinking. *Mobilities, 15*(6), 911–929.

Löfflmann, G., & Vaughan-Williams, N. (2018). Vernacular imaginaries of European border security among citizens: From walls to information management. *European Journal of International Security*, 3(3), 382–400.

Lunau, M., & Andreassen, R. (2022). Surveillance practices among migration officers: Online media and LGBTQ+ refugees. *International Journal of Cultural Studies*. Online first: https://doi.org/10.1177/13678779221140129

Lupton, D. (2014). *Digital sociology*. New York: Routledge.

Lupton, D. (2019). Introduction/infrastructure. In J. Vertesi & D. Ribes (Eds.), *digitalSTS: A field guide for science & technology studies* (pp. 263–266). Princeton, NJ: Princeton University Press.

M'charek, A. (2020). *Harraga*: Burning borders, navigating colonialism. *The Sociological Review*, 68(2), 418–434.

Madianou, M. (2012). Migration and the accentuated ambivalence of motherhood: The role of ICTs in Filipino transnational families. *Global Networks*, 12(3), 277–295.

Madianou, M. (2016). Ambient co-presence: Transnational family practices in polymedia environments. *Global Networks*, 16(2), 183–201.

Madianou, M. (2019a). Technocolonialism: Digital innovation and data practices in the humanitarian response to refugee crises. *Social Media + Society*, 5(3), 1–13.

Madianou, M. (2019b). The biometric assemblage: Surveillance, experimentation, profit, and the measuring of refugee bodies. *Television & New Media*, 20(6), 581–599.

Madianou, M., & Miller, D. (2011). Crafting love: Letters and cassette tapes in transnational Filipino family communication. *South East Asia Research*, 19(2), 249–272.

Madianou, M., & Miller, D. (2012). *Migration and new media: Transnational families and polymedia*. London: Routledge.

Madokoro, L. (2012). Unwanted refugees: Chinese migration and the making of a global humanitarian agenda, 1949–1989. PhD thesis, University of British Columbia. Retrieved from: https://open.library.ubc.ca/media/stream/pdf/24/1.0058346/1

Madörin, A. (2022). Postcolonial surveillance: Europe's border technologies between colony and crisis. London: Rowman & Littlefield.

Mahmud, Y. (2020). Organizing refugees. PhD thesis, Stockholm Business School, Stockholm University, Sweden. Retrieved from: www.diva-portal.org/smash/get/diva2:1446161/FULLTEXT01.pdf

Mai, N., & King, R. (2009). Introduction: Love, sexuality and migration: Mapping the issue(s). *Mobilities*, 4(3), 295–307.

Mainsah, H. (2011). 'I could well have said I was Norwegian but nobody would believe me': Ethnic minority youths' self-representation on social network sites. *European Journal of Cultural Studies*, 14(2), 179–193.

Maitland, C. (2018). Information policies and displacement. In C. Maitland (Ed.), *Digital lifeline? ICTs for refugees and displaced persons* (pp. 209–238). Cambridge, MA: MIT Press.

Mallapragada, M. (2006). Home, homeland, homepage: Belonging and the Indian-American web. *New Media & Society*, 8(2), 207–227.

Mancini, T., Sibilla, F., Argiropoulos, D., Rossi, M., & Everri, M. (2019). The opportunities and risks of mobile phones for refugees' experience: A scoping review. *PLoS ONE*, 14(12), e0225684. https://doi.org/10.1371/journal.pone.0225684

Mansour, E. (2018). Profiling information needs and behaviour of Syrian refugees displaced to Egypt: An exploratory study. *Information and Learning Science*, 119(3/4), 161–182.

Mar, L.R. (2010). *Brokering belonging: Chinese in Canada's Exclusion Era, 1885–1945.* Oxford: Oxford University Press.

Marino, S. (2019). Cook it, eat it, Skype it: Mobile media use in re-staging intimate culinary practices among transnational families. *International Journal of Cultural Studies*, 22(6), 788–803.

Marino, S. (2021). *Mediating the refugee crisis.* Cham, Switzerland: Palgrave Macmillan.

Marlowe, J. (2020). Refugee resettlement, social media and the social organization of difference. *Global Networks*, 20(2), 274–291.

Marmaras, I. (2013). Banopticon. *Mig@Net.* Retrieved from: https://banoptikon. personalcinema.org/

Martin, A., & Taylor, L. (2021). Exclusion and inclusion in identification: Regulation, displacement and data justice. *Information Technology for Development*, 27(1), 50–66.

Martín-Barbero, J. (2006). A Latin American perspective on communication/cultural mediation. *Global Media and Communication*, 2(3), 279–297.

Martin-Shields, C. (2022). Ride-sharing apps for urban refugees: Easing or exacerbating a digital transport disadvantage? *Trialog*, 140/141, 58–62.

Martzoukou, K., & Burnett, S. (2018). Exploring the everyday life information needs and the socio-cultural adaptation barriers of Syrian refugees in Scotland. *Journal of Documentation*, 74(5), 1104–1132.

Marx, K. (1852). The Eighteenth Brumaire of Louis Bonaparte. *Die Revolution.* New York. Retrieved from: www.marxists.org/archive/marx/works/1852/18th-brumaire/ch01.htm

Masiero, S., & Bailur, S. (2021). Digital identity for development: The quest for justice and a research agenda. *Information Technology for Development*, 27(1), 1–12.

Massumi, B. (2002). *Parables for the virtual.* Durham, NC: Duke University Press.

Massumi, B. (2015). *The politics of affect.* London: Polity Press.

Matsaganis, M.D., Katz, V.S., & Ball-Rokeach, S. (2011). *Understanding ethnic media.* London: Sage.

Mattern, S. (2015). Deep time of media infrastructure. In L. Parks & N. Starosielski (Eds.), *Signal traffic: Critical studies of media infrastructures* (pp. 94–112). Urbana-Champaign, IL: University of Illinois Press.

Mattern, S. (2017). *Code and clay, data and dirt: Five thousand years of urban media.* Minneapolis, MN: University of Minnesota Press.

Matthes, G. (2022). Bali lures digital nomads despite controversy. *Deutsche Welle.* Retrieved from: https://www.dw.com/en/bali-lures-digital-nomads-despite-controversy /a-63669834.

Maxwell, J., & Tomlinson, J. (2022). *Experimenting in automating immigration systems.* Bristol: Bristol University Press.

Mayblin, L., & Turner, J. (2021). *Migration studies and colonialism.* London: Polity Press.

Mazzucato, V. (2008). The double engagement: Transnationalism and integration. Ghanaian migrants' lives between Ghana and the Netherlands. *Journal of Ethnic and Migration Studies*, 34(2), 199–216.

Mazzucato, V., & Dito, B.B. (2018). Transnational families: Cross-country comparative perspectives. *Population, Space and Place*, 24(7), 1–7.

Mbembé, J., & Meintjes, L. (2003). Necropolitics. *Public Culture*, 15(1), 11–40.

McAuliffe, M. (Ed.) (2021). *Research handbook on migration and technology.* Cheltenham: Edward Elgar.

McAuliffe, M., Blower, J., & Beduschi, A. (2021). Digitalization and artificial intelligence in migration and mobility: Transnational implications of the Covid-19 pandemic. *Societies*, 11(4), 135, 1–13. https://doi.org/10.3390/soc11040135

McIlwain, C. (2020). *Black software: The internet & racial justice, from the AfroNet to Black Lives Matter*. Oxford: Oxford University Press.

McKeown, A. (2012). How the box became black: Brokers and the creation of the free migrant. *Pacific Affairs*, *85*(1), 21–45.

Meeus, B., van Heur, B., & Arnaut, K. (2019). Migration and the infrastructural politics of urban arrival. In B. Meeus, K. Arnaut & B. van Heur (Eds.), *Arrival infrastructures*. Cham: Palgrave Macmillan.

Meraz, S., & Papacharissi, Z. (2016). Networked framing and gatekeeping. In T. Witschge, W. Anderson, D. Domingo & A. Hermida (Eds.), *Handbook of digital journalism* (pp. 95–112). London: Sage.

Metcalfe, P. (2022). Autonomy of migration and the radical imagination: Exploring alternative imaginaries within a biometric border. *Geopolitics*, *27*(1), 47–69.

Mevsimler, M. (2021). Translocal modes of belonging: Diasporic identity and digital media amongst migrant women in London. PhD thesis, Utrecht University, the Netherlands. Retrieved from: https://dspace.library.uu.nl/handle/1874/402150

Mezzadra, S., & Neilson, B. (Eds.) (2013). *Border as method, or, the multiplication of labor*. Durham, NC: Duke University Press.

Mikuriya, K., & Cantens, T. (2020). If algorithms dream of Customs, do custom officials dream of algorithms? A manifesto for data mobilisation in Customs. *World Customs Journal*, *14*(2), 3–22.

Milan, S., & Treré, E. (2019). Big data from the South(s): Beyond data universalism. *Television & New Media*, *20*(4), 319–335.

Milk, C., & Arora, G. (2015). Clouds over Sidra. *UNICEF*. Retrieved from: https://www.unicefusa.org/stories/clouds-over-sidra-award-winning-virtual-reality-experience/29675

Miller, D. (Ed.) (2005). *Materiality*. Durham, NC: Duke University Press.

Missing Link Trust (2016). *Missing: Game for a Cause*. Retrieved from: https://missinggirls.itch.io/missing-game-for-a-cause

Mitra, A. (2001). Marginal voices in cyberspace. *New Media & Society*, *3*(1), 29–48.

Mitra, A., & Evansluong, Q. (2019). Narratives of integration: Liminality in migrant acculturation through social media. *Technological Forecasting and Social Change*, *145*, 474–480.

Mitra, A., & Watts, E. (2002). Theorizing cyberspace: The idea of voice applied to the internet discourse. *New Media & Society*, *4*(4), 479–498.

Mlotshwa, K. (2019). Emotions of belonging and playing families across borders in sub-Saharan Africa. In B. Fox (Ed.), *Emotions and loneliness in a networked society* (pp. 223–238). Cham: Palgrave Macmillan.

Mol, A. (2003). *The body multiple: Ontology in medical practice*. Durham, NC: Duke University Press.

Mollerup, N. (2020). Perilous navigation. *Social Analysis*, *64*(3), 95–112.

Molnar, P. (2020). *Technological testing grounds: Migration management experiments and reflections from the ground up*. EDRi and the Refugee Law Lab. Retrieved from: https://edri.org/our-work/technological-testing-grounds-border-tech-is-experimenting-with-peoples-lives/

Molnar, P. (2022). Territorial and digital borders and migrant vulnerability under a pandemic crisis. In A. Triandafyllidou (Ed.), *Migration and pandemics*. IMISCOE Research Series (pp. 45–64). Cham: Springer International.

Monachesi, P., & Witteborn, S. (2021). Building the sustainable city through Twitter: Creative skilled migrants and innovative technology use. *Telematics and Informatics*, *58*(2), 1–10.

Moore-Gilbert, B. (2008). *Postcolonial life-writing: Culture, politics and self-representation*. London: Routledge.

Moran, C. (2022). The 'connected migrant': A scoping review. *Convergence: The International Journal of Research into New Media Technologies*, 1–20. Online first: https://doi.org/10.1177/13548565221090480

Morley, D. (2000). *Home territories: Media, mobility and identity*. London: Routledge.

Morley, D. (2009). For a materialist, non-media-centric media studies. *Television & New Media*, 10(1), 114–116.

Morley, D. (2017). *Communications and mobility: The migrant, the mobile phone, and the container box*. Chichester: Wiley-Blackwell.

Morozov, E. (2012). The naked and the TED. *The New Republic*. Retrieved from: https://newrepublic.com/article/105703/the-naked-and-the-ted-khanna

Morrissette, J. (2017). Glory to Arstotzka: Morality, rationality, and the iron cage of bureaucracy in *Papers, Please*. *Game Studies*, 17(1), n.p.

Mosco, V. (1996). *The political economy of communication*. London: Sage.

Moscovici, S., & Duveen, G. (Eds.) (2001). *Social representations: Essays in social psychology*. New York, NY: New York University Press.

Moss, D.M. (2018). The ties that bind: Internet communication technologies, networked authoritarianism, and 'voice' in the Syrian diaspora. *Globalizations*, 15(2), 265–282.

Moss, D.M., Michaelsen, M., & Kennedy, G. (2022). Going after the family: Transnational repression and the proxy punishment of Middle Eastern diasporas. *Global Networks*, 1–17. Online first, May 10: https://doi.org/10.1111/glob.12372.

Moulin Aguiar, C., & Magalhães, B. (2020). Operation shelter as humanitarian infrastructure: Material and normative renderings of Venezuelan migration in Brazil. *Citizenship Studies*, 24(5), 642–662.

Mrázek, R. (2002). *Engineers of happy land: Technology and nationalism in a colony*. Princeton, NJ: Princeton University Press.

Musarò, P. (2019). Aware migrants: The role of information campaigns in the management of migration. *European Journal of Communication*, 34(6), 629–640.

Naficy, H. (1993). *The making of exile cultures: Iranian television in Los Angeles*. Minneapolis, MN: University of Minnesota Press.

Naficy, H. (2011). A social history of Iranian cinema, volume 2: *The industrializing years, 1941–1978*. Durham, NC: Duke University Press.

Nakamura, L. (2020). Feeling good about feeling bad: Virtuous virtual reality and the automation of racial empathy. *Journal of Visual Culture* 19(1), 47–64.

Nakamura, L., & Chow-White, P. (2012). Introduction: Race and digital technology: Code, the color line, and the information society. In L. Nakamura & P. Chow-White (Eds.), *Race after the internet* (pp. 1–18). New York NY: Routledge.

Nash, K. (2018). Virtual reality witness: Exploring the ethics of mediated presence. *Studies in Documentary Film*, 12(2), 119–131.

Nasir, K.M. (2021). Virtual Rohingya: Ethno-religious populism in the Asia Pacific. In C. Gomes, L. Kong & O. Woods (Eds.), *Religion, hypermobility and digital media in Global Asia* (pp. 223–245). Amsterdam: Amsterdam University Press.

Nedelcu, M. (2012). Migrants' new transnational habitus: Rethinking migration through a cosmopolitan lens in the digital age. *Journal of Ethnic and Migration Studies*, 38(9), 1339–1356.

Nedelcu, M., & Soysüren, I. (2022). Precarious migrants, migration regimes and digital technologies: The empowerment–control nexus. *Journal of Ethnic and Migration Studies*, 48(8), 1821–1837.

Neelis, J. (2011). *Early Buddhist transmission and trade networks*. Leiden: Brill.

Nelles, P. (2019). Jesuit letters. In I.G. Županov (Ed.), *The Oxford handbook of Jesuits*. Oxford: Oxford University Press.

Nessi, L., & Bailey, O.G. (2014). Privileged Mexican migrants in Europe: Distinctions and cosmopolitanism on social networking sites. *Crossings: Journal of Migration & Culture*, 5(1), 121–137.

Newell, S. (2013). *The power to name: A history of anonymity in Colonial West Africa*. Athens, OH: Ohio University Press.

Ngai, S. (2005). *Ugly feelings*. Cambridge, MA: Harvard University Press.

Nguyen, D., & Nguyen, S. (2022). Data literacy as an emerging challenge in the migration/refugee context: A critical exploration of communication efforts around "refugee apps". *International Journal of Communication*, 16, 5553–5577.

Nieto, A.J. (2021). Temporalities. In A.M. Nieto, A. Massa & S. Bonfanti (Eds.), *Ethnographies of home and mobility* (pp. 91–114). London: Routledge.

Nikunen, K. (2019). *Media solidarities*. London: Sage.

Nishiyama, H. (2022). Bodies and borders in post-imperial Japan: A study of the coloniality of biometric power. *Cultural Studies*, 36(1), 120–140.

Norman, D.A. (2002). *The design of everyday things*. New York: Basic Books.

Nova Refugee Clinic (2022). Digital Migration Podcast. NOVA School of Law/CEDIS Legal Clinic. Retrieved from: https://novarefugeelegalclinic.novalaw.unl.pt/?page_id=3585

NurMuhammad, R., Horst, H., Papoutsaki, E., & Dodson, G. (2016). Uyghur transnational identity on Facebook: On the development of a young diaspora. *Identities*, 23(4), 485–499.

Nyers, P., & Rygiel, K. (Eds.) (2012). *Citizenship, migrant activism and the politics of movement*. London: Routledge.

O'Brien, E., & Berents, H. (2019). Virtual saviours: Digital games and anti-trafficking awareness-raising. *Anti-Trafficking Review*, 13, 82–99.

Odin, J. (2010). *Hypertext and the female imaginary*. Minneapolis, MN: University of Minnesota Press.

Oduntan, O., & Ruthven, I. (2019). The information needs matrix: A navigational guide for refugee integration. *Information Processing and Management*, 56, 791–808.

Oelgemöller, C. (2017). *The evolution of migration management in the global north*. New York, NY: Routledge.

Ofren, K. (2021). The new wave of anti-Indian racism. *Craccum: The University of Auckland Student Magazine*. Retrieved from: http://craccum.co.nz/news/opinion/the-new-wave-of-anti-indian-racism/

Ogunyemi, O. (2017). Introduction: Communicating conflict from the diaspora. In O. Ogunyemi (Ed.), *Media, diaspora and conflict* (pp. 1–18). New York: Palgrave.

Oiarzabal, P.J. (2020). (Re)Loading identity and affective capital online: The case of diaspora Basques on Facebook. In K. Smets, K. Leurs, M. Georgiou, S. Witteborn & R. Gajjala (Eds.), *Handbook of media and migration* (pp. 246–257). London: Sage.

Olivius, E. (2019). Claiming rights in exile: Women's insurgent citizenship practices in the Thai–Myanmar borderlands. *Citizenship Studies*, 23(8), 761–779.

Ongenaert, D., Joye, S., & Machin, D. (2022). Beyond the humanitarian savior logics? UNHCR's public communication strategies for the Syrian and Central African crises. *International Communication Gazette*. Online first, May 6: https://doi.org/10.1177/17480485221097966

Onuoha, M., & Galvin, A. (2021). Becoming data episode 1: Data & Humanity Podcast. *Data & Society*. Retrieved from: https://listen.datasociety.net/episodes/becoming-data-data-social-life/transcript

Osman, I. (2017). *Media, diaspora and the Somali conflict*. Cham, Switzerland: Palgrave.

Otu, K.E. (2021). Queer slacktivism as silent activism? The contested politics of queer subjectivities on GhanaWeb. *Sexualities, 23*(1–2), 46–66.

Oxford English Dictionary (2021a). Affectivity. *Oxford English Dictionary*. Retrieved from: www.oed.com.

Oxford English Dictionary (2021b). Infrastructure. *Oxford English Dictionary*. Retrieved from: www.oed.com.

Oyeleye, A. (2017). Diaspora journalism and conflicts in transnational media circuits. In O. Ogunyemi (Ed.), *Media, diaspora and conflict* (pp. 19–36). New York, NY: Palgrave.

Paige, T.P. (2021). Zombies as an allegory for terrorism. *Law & Literature, 33*(1), 119–140.

Pallister-Wilkins, P. (2022). *Humanitarian borders: Unequal mobility and saving lives.* London: Verso.

Papadopoulos, D., & Tsianos, V.S. (2013). After citizenship: Autonomy of migration, organisational ontology and mobile commons. *Citizenship Studies, 17*(2), 178–196.

Parker, D., & Song, M. (2006). New ethnicities online: Reflexive racialisation and the internet. *The Sociological Review, 54*(3), 575–594.

Parks, L. (2015). Stuff you can kick. In P. Svensson & D.T. Goldberg (Eds.), *Between humanities and the digital* (pp. 355–373). Cambridge, MA: MIT Press.

Parreñas, R. (2005). Long distance intimacy: Class, gender and intergenerational relations between mothers and children in Filipino transnational families. *Global Networks, 5,* 317–336.

Patterson, J., & Leurs, K. (2020). Transnational digital intimacy practices: Paradoxes of transnational connectivity and home-making among young adult expatriates in Amsterdam, the Netherlands. *Global Perspectives, 1*(1), 1–17.

Pelizza, A. (2016). Developing the vectorial glance: Infrastructural inversion for the new agenda on government information systems. *Science, Technology, & Human Values, 41*(2), 298–321.

Pelizza, A. (2020). Processing alterity, enacting Europe: Migrant registration and identification as co-construction of individuals and polities. *Science, Technology, & Human Values, 45*(2), 262–288.

Peng, Y., & Wong, O.M.H. (2013). Diversified transnational mothering via telecommunication: Intensive, collaborative, and passive. *Gender & Society, 27*(4), 491–513.

Peraldi, M. (Ed.) (2001). *Cabas et containers: Activités marchandes informelles et réseaux transfrontaliers* [Shopping bags and containers: Informal market activities and cross-border networks]. Paris: Maisonneuve et Larose.

Perreira, C. (2019). Consumed by disease: Medical archives, Latino fictions and carceral health imaginaries. In R. Benjamin (Ed.), *Captivating technology* (pp. 50–67). Durham, NC: Duke University Press.

Peters, J.D. (2015). *The marvelous clouds: Toward a philosophy of elemental media.* Chicago, IL: The University of Chicago Press.

Pieke, F.N., Van Hear, N., & Lindley, A. (2007). Beyond control? The mechanics and dynamics of 'informal' remittances between Europe and Africa. *Global Networks, 7*(3), 348–366.

Ping, S., & Yujie Chen, J. (2021). Platform labour and contingent agency in China. *China Perspectives, 1,* 19–27.

Pink, S. (2004). *Home truths: Gender, domestic objects and everyday Life.* London: Bloomsbury.

Pink, S., Horst, H., Postill, J., Hjorth, L., Lewis, T., & Tacchi, J. (2016). *Digital ethnography: Principles and practice.* London: Sage.

Piocos III, C.M. (2021). *Affect, narratives and politics of southeast Asian Migration.* Abingdon: Routledge.

Pollock, G. (2015). A concentrationary imaginary. In G. Pollock & M. Silverman (Eds.), *Concentrationary imaginaries: Tracing totalitarian violence in popular culture* (pp. 1–46). London: IB Tauris.

Pollozek, S., & Passoth, J.H. (2019). Infrastructuring European migration and border control: The logistics of registration and identification at Moria hotspot. *Environment and Planning D: Society and Space, 37*(4), 606–624.

Ponzanesi, S. (2004). *Paradoxes of post-colonial culture: Contemporary women writers of the Indian and Afro-Italian diaspora*. Albany, NY: State University of New York Press.

Ponzanesi, S. (2019). Migration and mobility in a digital age: (Re)mapping connectivity and belonging. *Television & New Media, 20*(6), 547–557.

Ponzanesi, S. (2020). Digital diasporas: Postcoloniality, media and affect. *Interventions, 22*(8), 977–993.

Ponzanesi, S., & Waller, M. (Eds.) (2012). *Postcolonial cinema studies*. London: Routledge.

Pope, L. (2013). Papers, please. Retrieved from: https://papersplea.se/

Potter, J., & Wetherell, M. (1987). *Discourse and social psychology: Beyond attitudes and behaviour*. London: Sage.

Pötzschke, S., & Rinken, S. (Eds.) (2022). *Migration research in a digitized world: Using innovative technology to tackle methodological challenges*. Cham, Switzerland: Springer International.

Presti, L. (2020). The migrancies of maps: Complicating the critical cartography and migration nexus in 'migro-mobility' thinking. *Mobilities, 15*(6), 911–929.

Privacy International (2011). *Why we work on refugee privacy*. Retrieved from: https://privacyinternational.org/news-analysis/1322/why-we-work-refugee-privacy

Pugliese, J. (2010). *Biometrics: Bodies, technologies, biopolitics*. Abingdon: Routledge.

Radio Darfur (2010). *On the ground reporter: Darfur*. Retrieved from: http://directiondesign.nl/sites/darfur/

Rae, M., Holman, R., & Nethery, A. (2018). Self-represented witnessing: The use of social media by asylum seekers in Australia's offshore immigration detention centres. *Media, Culture & Society, 40*(4), 479–495.

Rae, M., Russell, E.K., & Nethery, A. (2019). Earwitnessing detention: Carceral secrecy, affecting voices, and political listening in the messenger podcast. *International Journal of Communication, 13*, 1036–1055.

Raessens, J. (2019). Virtually present, physically invisible: Alejandro G. Iñárritu's mixed reality installation Carne y Arena. *Television & New Media, 20*(6), 634–648.

Raiño-Alcalá, P. (2008). Journeys and landscapes of forced migration: Memorializing fear among refugees and internally displaced Columbians. *Social Anthropology, 16*(1), 1–18.

Ramazanoğlu, C., & Holland, J. (2002). *Feminist methodology: Challenges and choices*. London: Sage.

Ramos, F.P. (2002). *Ethnic Alterity in the News: Discourse on Immigration in the Spanish and the Irish Press, 1990–2000* (Doctoral dissertation, Dublin City University. School of Applied Language and Intercultural Studies).

Retis, J. (2019). Homogenizing heterogeneity in transnational contexts. In J. Retis & R. Tsagarousianou (Eds.), *The handbook of diasporas, media and culture* (pp. 115–136). Hoboken, NJ: John Wiley & Sons.

Retis, J., & Tsagarousianou, R. (Eds.) (2019). *The handbook of diasporas, media, and culture*. Hoboken, NJ: John Wiley & Sons.

Reyhan, D. (2012). Uyghur diaspora and the internet. *E-Diasporas Working Papers*. Fondation Maison des sciences de l'homme. Retrieved from: www.e-diasporas.fr/working-papers/Reyhan-Uyghurs-EN.pdf

Reynolds, T., & Zontini, E. (2013). 'Non-normative' family lives? Mapping migrant youth's family and intimate relationships across national divides and spatial distance. In T. Sanger & Y. Taylor (Eds.), *Mapping intimacies: Relations, exchanges, affects* (pp. 228–247). London: Palgrave Macmillan.

Rezaire, T. (2020). Prologue – decolonial healing: In defense of spiritual technologies. In K. Smets, K. Leurs, M. Georgiou, S. Witteborn & R. Gajjala (Eds.), *Handbook of media and migration* (pp. xxix–xliv). London: Sage.

Riklis, E. (2013). *Zaytoun: The game*. Retrieved from: https://zaytounbordertoborder. wordpress.com

Risam, R. (2019). Beyond the migrant 'problem': Visualizing global migration. *Television & New Media*, 20(6), 566–580.

Robbins, B. (1998). *Cosmopolitics: Thinking and feeling beyond the nation*. Minneapolis, MN: University of Minnesota Press.

Robertson, Z., Wilding, R., & Gifford, S. (2016). Mediating the family imaginary: Young people negotiating absence in transnational refugee families. *Global Networks*, 16, 219–236.

Rodriguez, R.M. (2010). *Migrants for export: How the Philippine state brokers to the world*. Minneapolis, MN: University of Minnesota Press.

Rohrlich, R. (Ed.) (2000). *Resisting the Holocaust*. Oxford: Berg.

Rose Mar, L. (2010). *Brokering belonging: Chinese in Canada's exclusion era, 1885–1945*. Oxford: Oxford University Press.

Rosello, M. (1998). Representing illegal immigrants in France: From *clandestins to l'affaire des sans-papiers de Saint-Bernard*. *Journal of European Studies*, 28, 137–151.

Rothberg, M. (2009). *Multidirectional memory*. Stanford, CA: Stanford University Press.

Rothman, E.N. (2014). *Brokering empire: Trans-imperial subjects between Venice and Istanbul*. Ithaca, NY: Cornell University Press.

Rousseau, J.-J. (1953 [1790]). *The confessions*. London: Penguin.

Ruiz, S. (2006). *Darfur is dying*. Retrieved from: https://web.archive.org/web/20060803161433/http://www.darfurisdying.com/

Ruppert, E., & Scheel, S. (2021). *Data practices: Making up a European people*. London: Goldsmiths Press.

Rygiel, K. (2011). Bordering solidarities: Migrant activism and the politics of movement and camps at Calais. *Citizenship Studies*, 15(1), 1–19.

Sadowski, H. (2016). Digital intimacies: Doing digital media differently. PhD thesis, Department of Thematic Studies, Linköping University. Retrieved from: www.diva-portal.org/smash/get/diva2:1047582/FULLTEXT01.pdf

Saha, A. (2021). *Race, culture and media*. London: Sage.

Sai, S. (2021). Benevolent technocracy: The Chinese Protectorate, migration control and racialised governmentality in colonised Malaya. *Journal of Southeast Asian Studies*, 52(3), 441–463.

Said, E. (1979). *Orientalism*. New York: Vintage Books.

Said, E.W. (1997). *Covering Islam*. New York: Vintage Books.

Salah, A.A. (2022). Can big data deliver its promises in migration research? *International Migration*, 60(2), 252–255.

Salah, A.A., Korkmaz, E.E., & Bircan, T. (Eds.) (2022). *Data science for migration and mobility*. Oxford: Oxford University Press.

Salah, A.A., Pentland, A., Lepri, B. et al. (2019). Introduction to the data for refugees' challenge on mobility of Syrian refugees in Turkey. In A.A. Salah, A. Pentland, B. Lepri, & E. Letouzeé (Eds.), *Guide to mobile data analytics in refugee scenarios* (pp. 3–28). Cham, Switzerland: Springer International.

Sampson, T.D. (2012). *Virality: Contagion theory in the age of networks*. Minneapolis, MN: University of Minnesota Press.

Sampson, T.D., Maddison, S., & Ellis, D. (Eds.) (2018). *Affect and social media*. London: Rowman & Littlefield.

Sanchez Boe, C., & Mainsah, H. (2022). Detained through a smartphone: Deploying experimental collaborative visual methods to study the socio-technical landscape of digital confinement. *Digital Culture & Society*, 7(2), 287–310.

Sánchez-Querubín, N., & Rogers, R. (2018). Connected routes: Migration studies with digital devices and platforms. *Social Media + Society*, 4(1), 1–13.

Sandal, H. (2020). Radical queer epistemic network: Kurdish diaspora, futurity, and sexual politics. *Migration Letters*, 17(1), 81–90.

Sandberg, M., Rossi, L., Galis, V., & Bak Jørgensen, M. (Eds.) (2022). *Research methodologies and ethical challenges in digital migration studies*. Cham, Switzerland: Palgrave Macmillan.

Sandoval-García, C. (2013). To whom and to what is research on migration a contribution. *Ethnic and Racial Studies*, 36, 1429–1445.

Sandvik, K.B. (2020). Humanitarian wearables: Digital bodies, experimentation and ethics. In D. Messelken & D. Winkler (Eds.), *Ethics of medical innovation, experimentation, and enhancement in military and humanitarian contexts* (pp. 87–104). Cham, Switzerland: Springer International.

Şanlıer Yüksel, İ. (2022). Empowering experiences of digitally mediated flows of information for connected migrants on the move. *Journal of Ethnic and Migration Studies*, 48(8), 1838–1855.

Sarria Sanz, C., & Alencar, A. (2020). Rebuilding the Yanacona home in the city: The role of digital technologies for place-making practices of displaced indigenous communities in Bogotá, Colombia. *Global Perspectives*, 1(1), 1–14.

Savolainen, R. (2008). *Everyday information practices: A social phenomenological Perspective*. Toronto: Scarecrow Press.

Sayad, A. (1981). Le phénomène migratoire, une relation de domination [The migratory phenomenon, a relationship of domination]. *Annuaire de l'Afrique du Nord*, 20, 365–406.

Sayad, A. (1999). *La double absence: Des illusions de l'émigré aux souffrances de l'immigré [The double absence: The illusions of the emigrant to the suffering of the immigrant]*. Paris: Seuil.

Sayyad Abdi, E., Partridge, H., Bruce, C., & Watson, J. (2019). Skilled immigrants: A resettlement information literacy framework. *Journal of Documentation*, 75(4), 892–908.

Schapendonk, J. (2018). Navigating the migration industry: Migrants moving through an African–European web of facilitation/control. *Journal of Ethnic and Migration Studies*, 44(4), 663–679.

Scheel, S. (2019). *Autonomy of migration? Appropriating mobility within biometric border regimes*. Abingdon: Routledge.

Scheel, S., & Tazzioli, M. (2022). Who is a migrant? Abandoning the nation-state point of view in the study of migration. *Migration Politics*, 1(002), 1–23.

Scheer, M. (2012). Are emotions a kind of practice (and is that what makes them have a history?). *History and Theory*, *51*, 193–220.

Schmidle, N. (2015). Ten borders: A Syrian refugee's epic escape from Syria. *The New Yorker*, October 26. Retrieved from: www.newyorker.com/magazine/2015/10/26/ten-borders

Schoemaker, E., Baslan, D., Pon, B., & Dell, N. (2021). Identity at the margins: Data justice and refugee experiences with digital identity systems in Lebanon, Jordan, and Uganda. *Information Technology for Development*, *27*(1), 13–36.

Scholten, P., Collett, E., & Petrovic, M. (2017). Mainstreaming migrant integration? A critical analysis of a new trend in integration governance. *International Review of Administrative Sciences*, *83*(2), 283–302.

Scott, J.C. (1990). *Domination and the arts of resistance*. New Haven, CT: Yale University Press.

Seuferling, P. (2021). Media and the refugee camp: The historical making of space, time and politics in the modern refugee regime. PhD thesis, Södertörn University. Retrieved from: https://sh.diva-portal.org/smash/get/diva2:1593543/FULLTEXT02.pdf

Seuferling, P., & Leurs, K. (2021). Histories of humanitarian technophilia: How imaginaries of media technologies have shaped migration infrastructures. *Mobilities*, *16*(5), 670–687.

Shah, N. (forthcoming 2023). When immovable bodies meet unstoppable media circulation: The Aporetic body in digital migration studies. In K. Leurs & S. Ponzanesi (Eds.), *Doing digital migration studies* (np). Amsterdam: Amsterdam University Press.

Shah, N. (2020). The cog that imagines the system: Data migration and migrant bodies in the face of Aadhaar. In K. Smets, K. Leurs, M. Georgiou, S. Witteborn & R. Gajjala (Eds.), *Handbook of media and migration* (pp. 464–476). London: Sage.

Shanneik, Y., & Sobieczky, E. (2023). Artistic Methodologies in Forced Migration: Using Body Mapping and Augmented Reality in Syrian Refugees' Narratives. *Arts, 12*(2), 46. MDPI AG. Retrieved from http://dx.doi.org/10.3390/arts12020046

Sharma, S. (2013). Black Twitter? Racial hashtags, networks and contagion. *New Formations: A Journal of Culture/Theory/Politics*, *78*, 46–64.

Sharpe, C. (2015). *In the wake: On blackness and being*. Durham, NC: Duke University Press.

Sheller, M. (2018). *Mobility justice: The politics of movement in an age of extremes*. London: Verso.

Sheller, M., & Urry, J. (2006). The new mobilities paradigm. *Environment and Planning A: Economy and Space*, *38*(2), 207–226.

Shield, A. (2017). New in town: Gay immigrants and geosocial dating apps. In A. Dhoest, Ł. Szulc & B. Eeckhout (Eds.), *LGBTQs, media, and culture in Europe* (pp. 244–261). London: Routledge.

Shield, A. (2019). *Immigrants on Grindr: Race, sexuality and belonging online*. Cham, Switzerland: Springer International.

Shield, A.D.J. (2018). Grindr culture: Intersectional and socio-sexual. *Ephemera*, *18*(1), 149–161.

Shim, D. (1998). From yellow peril through model minority to renewed yellow peril. *Journal of Communication Inquiry*, *22*(4), 385–409.

Shrestha, T., & Yeoh, B.S.A. (2018). Introduction: Practices of brokerage and the making of migration infrastructures in Asia. *Pacific Affairs*, *91*(4), 663–672.

Siapera, E. (2010). *Cultural diversity and global media*. Chichester: Wiley-Blackwell.

Siapera, E. (2011). *Cultural diversity and global media. The mediation of difference*. Oxford: John Wiley & Sons.

Siapera, E. (2018). *Understanding new media* (2nd edition). London: Sage.

Siapera, E., Boudourides, M., Lenis, S., & Suiter, J. (2018). Refugees and network publics on Twitter: Networked framing, affect, and capture. *Social Media + Society*, 4(1), 1–21.

Silverstone, R. (1999). *Why study the media?* London: Sage.

Sim, K., & Cheesman, M. (2020). What's the harm in categorisation? Reflections on the categorisation work of Tech 4 Good. *Big Data & Society* [blog]. Retrieved from: https://bigdatasoc.blogspot.com/2020/03/whats-harm-in-categorisation.html

Simone, A.M.M. (2004). People as infrastructure: Intersecting fragments in Johannesburg. *Public Culture*, 16(3), 407–429.

Sims, S. (2014). From differentiated use to differentiating practices: Negotiating legitimate participation and the production of privileged identities. *Information, Communication & Society*, 17(6), 670–682.

Sinanan, J., & Hjorth, L. (2018). Careful families and care as 'kinwork'. In B. Neves & C. Casimiro (Eds.), *Connecting families?* (pp. 181–200). Bristol: Policy Press.

Sinanan, J., & Horst, H. (2022). Communications technologies and transnational networks. In B.S.A. Yeoh & F.L. Collins (Eds.), *Handbook on transnationalism* (pp. 371–387). Cheltenham: Edward Elgar.

Skrbiš, Z. (2008). Transnational families: Theorising migration, emotions and belonging. *Journal of Intercultural Studies*, 29(3), 231–246.

Smets, K. (2019). Media and immobility: The affective and symbolic immobility of forced migrants. *European Journal of Communication*, 34(6), 650–660.

Smets, K., Leurs, K., Georgiou, M., Witteborn, S., & Gajjala, R. (Eds.) (2020). *Handbook of media and migration*. London: Sage.

Smets, K., Toffano, G., & Almenara-Niebla, S. (2022). Refugee and mediated lives. *Oxford Research Encyclopedia of Communication*. Oxford: Oxford University Press.

Smith, M.M., & Paquette, R.L. (2010). *The Oxford handbook of slavery in the Americas*. Oxford: Oxford University Press.

Sneath, D., Holbraad, M., & Axel, P.M. (2009). Technologies of the imagination. *Ethnos: Journal of Anthropology*, 74(1), 5–40.

Sou, G. (2018). Trivial pursuits? Serious (video) games and the media representation of refugees. *Third World Quarterly*, 39(3), 510–526.

Spivak, G. (1988). Can the subaltern speak? In C. Nelson & L. Grossberg (Eds.), *Marxism and the interpretation of culture* (pp. 271–317). Urbana, IL: University of Illinois Press.

Spivak, G., with Gunew, S. (1990a). Questions of multi-culturalism. In S. Harasym (Ed.), *The post-colonial critic* (pp. 59–66). London: Routledge.

Spivak, G., with Harasym, S. (1990b). Practical politics of the open end. In S. Harasym (Ed.), *The post-colonial critic* (pp. 95–112). London: Routledge.

Sreedhar Mini, D., & Baishya, A. (2022). Reimagining the migrant in the time of the pandemic. In N. Banerjea, P. Boyce & R.K. Dasgupta (Eds.), *Covid-19 assemblages* (pp. 34–44). London: Routledge.

Srinivasan, R., & Pyati, A. (2007). Diasporic information environments: Reframing immigrant-focused information research. *Journal of the American Society for Information Science and Technology*, 58(12), 1734–1744.

Sseviiri, H., Alencar, A., & Kisira, Y. (2022). Urban refugees' digital experiences and social connections during Covid-19 response in Kampala, Uganda. *Media and Communication*, 10(2), 276–286.

Stark, L. (2019). Affect and emotion in digitalSTS. In J. Vertesi (Ed.), *digitalSTS: A field guide for science & technology studies* (pp. 117–135). Princeton, NJ: Princeton University Press.

Starosielski, N. (2015). *The undersea network*. Durham, NC: Duke University Press.

Stavinoha, L. (2019). Communicative acts of citizenship: Contesting Europe's border in and through the media. *International Journal of Communication, 13*, 1212–1230.

Stavinoha, L. (2023, forthcoming). McKinsey consultants and technocratic fantasies: Crafting the illusion of orderly migration management in Greece. In K. Leurs & S. Ponzanesi (Eds.), *Doing digital migration studies*. Amsterdam: Amsterdam University Press.

Stewart, K. (2007). *Ordinary affects.*Durham, NC: Duke University Press.

Stiegler, B. (2013). *What makes life worth living: On pharmacology*. Cambridge: Polity Press.

Stierl, M. (2020). *Migrant resistance in contemporary Europe*. London: Routledge.

Stierl, M. (2022). Do no harm? The impact of policy on migration scholarship. *Environment and Planning C: Politics and Space, 40*(5), 1083–1102.

Stoetzler, M., & Yuval-Davis, N. (2002). Standpoint theory, situated knowledge and the situated imagination. *Feminist Theory, 3*(3), 315–334.

Stoler, A.L. (2009). *Along the archival grain*. Princeton, NJ: Princeton University Press.

Stoler, A.L. (2016). *Duress: Imperial durabilities in our times*. Durham, NC: Duke University Press.

Strauss, C. (2006). The imaginary. *Anthropological Theory, 6*(3), 322–344.

Stremlau, N., & Tsalapatanis, A. (2022). Social media, mobile phones and migration in Africa: A review of the evidence. *Progress in Development Studies, 22*(1), 56–71.

Studt SJ, E. (2021). Virtual reality documentaries and the illusion of presence. *Studies in Documentary Film, 15*(2), 175–185.

Sun, P., & Chen, J.Y. (2021). Platform labour and contingent agency in China. *China Perspectives, 1*, 19–27.

Sun, P., & Zhao, Y. (2022). Platformed distinction work: Rethinking the migration and integration of food delivery workers in China. *Environment and Planning A: Economy and Space*. Online first: https://doi.org/10.1177/0308518X221090245

Sun, W. (2021). Chinese diaspora and social media: Negotiating transnational space. *Oxford research encyclopedia of communication*. Oxford: Oxford University Press.

Sun, W., & Yu, H. (Eds.) (2022). *WeChat diaspora*. London: Routledge.

Sundén, J. (2003). *Material virtualities: Approaching online textual embodiment*. New York: Peter Lang.

Sundén, J. (2018). Queer disconnections: Affect, break, and delay in digital connectivity. *Transformations, 31*, 63–78.

Szulc, Ł. (2018). *Transnational homosexuals in communist Poland*. Basingstoke: Palgrave Macmillan.

Szulc, Ł. (2019). *Queer #PolesinUK: Identity, migration and social media*. London: London School of Economics and Political Science. Retrieved from: http://eprints.lse.ac.uk/101767/

Szulc, Ł. (2020a). Queer migrants and digital culture. In K. Smets, K. Leurs, M. Georgiou, S. Witteborn & R. Gajjala (Eds.), *Handbook of media and migration* (pp. 220–232). London: Sage.

Szulc, Ł. (2020b). Digital gender disidentifications: Beyond the subversion versus hegemony dichotomy and toward everyday gender practices. *International Journal of Communication, 14*, 5436–5454.

Szulc, Ł. (2022). Zza żelaznej firanki. *Dwutygodnik*. Retrieved from: www.dwutygodnik.com/artykul/10045-zza-zelaznej-firanki.html

Taipale, S. (2019). *Intergenerational connections in digital families*. Cham: Springer International.

Talani, L.S. (2015). International migration: IPE perspectives and the impact of globalisation. In L.S. Talani & S. McMahon (Eds.), *Handbook of the international political economy of migration* (pp. 17–36). Cheltenham: Edward Elgar.

Tamagno, C. (2001). 'You must win their affection...': Migrants' social and cultural practices between Peru and Italy. In N. Nyberg Sørensen & K. Fog Olwig (Eds.), *Work and migration: Life and livelihoods in a globalizing world* (pp. 106–125). London: Routledge.

Tarrius, A. (1995). Territoires circulatoires des entrepreneurs commerciaux maghrebins de Marseille: Du commerce communautaire aux réseaux de l'économie souterraine mondiale [Circulatory territories of the Maghreb commercial entrepreneurs of Marseille: From community commerce to the networks of the global underground economy]. *Journal des Anthropologues, 59*, 15–35.

Taylor, A. (2012). Information communication technologies and new indigenous mobilities? Insights from remote Northern Territory Communities. *Journal of Rural and Community Development, 7*(1), 59–73.

Taylor, L. (2017). What is data justice? The case for connecting digital rights and freedoms globally. *Big Data & Society, 4*(2), 1–14.

Taylor, L., & Meissner, F. (2020). A crisis of opportunity: Market-making, big data, and the consolidation of migration as risk. *Antipode, 52*, 270–290.

Tazzioli, M. (2022). Afterword: Counter-mapping the technology hype in migration studies. In V. Gallis, M. Bak Jørgensen & M. Sandberg (Eds.), *The migration mobile: Border dissidence, sociotechnical resistance and the construction of irregularized migrants* (pp. 237–244). London: Rowman & Littlefield.

Tedeschi, M., Vorobeva, E., & Jauhiainen, J.S. (2022). Transnationalism: Current debates and new perspectives. *GeoJournal, 87*, 603–619.

Thomas, W.I., & Znaniecki, F. (1918–1920). *The Polish peasant in Europe and America: Monograph of an immigrant group*. Boston, MA: Richard G. Badger.

Thorat, D. (2019). Colonial topographies of internet infrastructure: The sedimented and linked networks of the telegraph and submarine fiber optic internet. *South Asian Review, 40*(3), 252–267.

Thorpe, H., & Wheaton, B. (2021). Young Gazan refugees, sport and social media: Understanding migration as a process of becoming. *International Migration Review, 55*(3), 902–928.

Thumim, N. (2012). *Self-representation and digital culture*. Basingstoke: Palgrave Macmillan.

Ticktin, M., & Youatt, R. (2022). Intersecting mobilities: Beyond the autonomy of movement and power of place. *Borderlands Journal, 21*(1), 1–17.

Tiews, A.L. (2017). *Fluchtpunkt Film: Integrationen von Flüchtlingen und Vertriebenen durch den deutschen Nachkriegsfilm 1945–1990*. Berlin: Bebra Verlag.

Tiidenberg, K. (2018). Ethics in digital research. In U. Flick (Ed.), *Handbook of qualitative data collection* (pp. 466–481). London: Sage.

Tilley, H. (2011). *Africa as a living laboratory*. Chicago, IL: University of Chicago.

Toivanen, M., & Baser, B. (2020). Diaspora's multiple roles in peace and conflict. *Migration Letters, 17*(1), 47–57.

Trandafoiu, R. (2013). *Diaspora online: Identity politics and Romanian migrants*. Oxford: Berghahn.

Trauttmansdorff, P., & Felt, U. (2021). Between infrastructural experimentation and collective imagination: The digital transformation of the EU Border Regime. *Science, Technology, & Human Values*. Online first: https://doi.org/10.1177/01622439211057523

Trauttmansdorff, P. (2022). Borders, migration, and technology in the age of security: Intervening with STS. *Tecnoscienza. Italian Journal of Science & Technology Studies*, *13*(2), 133–154.

Triandafyllidou, A. (Ed.) (2022). *Migration and pandemics: Spaces of solidarity and spaces of exception*. Cham, Switzerland: Springer International.

Trillò, T. (2018). Can the subaltern tweet? Reflections on Twitter as a space of appearance and inequality in accessing visibility. *Studies on Home and Community Science*, *11*(2), 116–124.

Trimikliniotis, N., Parsanoglou, D., & Tsianos, V. (2015). *Mobile commons, migrant digitalities and the right to the city*. Basingstoke: Palgrave Macmillan.

Tsourapas, G. (2020). The long arm of the Arab state. *Ethnic and Racial Studies*, *43*(2), 351– 370.

Turkle, S. (2012). *Alone together: Why we expect more from technology and less from each other*. New York, NY: Basic Books.

Turner, J. (2020). *Bordering intimacy*. Manchester: Manchester University Press.

Twigt, M. (2022). *Mediated lives: Waiting and hope among Iraqi refugees in Jordan*. New York & Oxford: Berghahn.

Twigt, M.A. (2018). The mediation of hope: Digital technologies and affective affordances within Iraqi refugee households in Jordan. *Social Media + Society*, *4*(1), 1–14.

Twigt, M.A. (2021). The datafication of refugee protection in and beyond the Middle East: A case for digital refugee lawyering. *Maja Janmyr* [blog], May 6. Retrieved from: www.janmyr.org/blog/digital-refugee-lawyering

Uchida, J. (2014). *Brokers of empire: Japanese settler colonialim in Korea, 1876–1945*. Harvard, MA: Harvard University Press.

Umel, A. (2022). Filipino migrants in Germany and their diasporic (irony) chronotopes in Facebook. *International Journal of Cultural Studies*, online first: https://doi.org/10.1177/13678779221126538

Udwan, G., Leurs, K., & Alencar, A. (2020). Digital resilience tactics of Syrian refugees in the Netherlands: Social media for social support, health, and identity. *Social Media + Society*, *6*(2). Online first: https://doi.org/10.1177/2056305120915587

UNHCR (2003). *Handbook for registration: Procedures and standards for registration, population data management and documentation*. Geneva: United Nations High Commissioner for Refugees. Retrieved from: www.refworld.org/pdfid/3f967dc14.pdf

UNHCR (2007). *Against all odds*. UNHCR The Refugee Agency. Retrieved from: https://www.unhcr.org/news/latest/2007/11/4731b5064/refugee-game-offers-fear-flight-safety-click-time.html

UNHCR (2022a). *Digital Inclusion Programme*. Geneva: United Nations High Commissioner for Refugees. Retrieved from: www.unhcr.org/innovation/digital-inclusion/

UNHCR (2022b). *Data Innovation Programme*. Geneva: United Nations High Commissioner for Refugees. Retrieved from: www.unhcr.org/innovation/data-innovation/

UNRIC (2012). *My life as a refugee. United Nations Regional Information Centre for Western Europe*. Retrieved from: https://unric.org/en/my-life-as-a-refugee/

Urban, A. (2017). *Brokering servitude: Migration and the politics of domestic labour during the long nineteenth century*. New York, NY: New York University Press.

Urry, J. (2007). *Mobilities*. Cambridge: Polity Press.

Ustek-Spilda, F. (2020). Statisticians as back-office policy-makers: Counting asylum-seekers and refugees in Europe. *Science, Technology, & Human Values*, *45*(2), 289–316.

Valaskivi, K., & Sumiala, J. (2014). Circulating social imaginaries: Theoretical and methodological reflections. *European Journal of Cultural Studies*, *17*(3), 229–243.

Van den Boomen, M.V.T., Lammes, S., Lehmann, A.S., Raessens, J.F.F., & Schaeffer, M.T. (Eds.) (2009). *Digital material*. Amsterdam: Amsterdam University Press.

Van Dijck, J. (2004). Memory matters in the digital age. *Configurations*, *12*(3), 349–373.

Van Dijck, J. (2014). Datafication, dataism and dataveillance: Big data between scientific paradigm and ideology. *Surveillance & Society*, *12*(2), 197–208.

Van Dijk, T.A. (2005). *Racism and discourse in Spain and Latin America*. Amsterdam: John Benjamins.

Van Doorn, N., & Vijay, D. (2021). Gig work as migrant work: The platformization of migration infrastructure. *Environment and Planning A: Economy and Space*. Online first: https://doi.org/10.1177/0308518X211065049

Van Hear, N., & Cohen, R. (2017). Diasporas and conflict: Distance, contiguity and spheres of engagement. *Oxford Development Studies*, *45*(2), 171–184.

Van Heelsum, A. (2017). Aspirations and frustrations: Experiences of recent refugees in the Netherlands. *Ethnic and Racial Studies*, *40*(13), 2137–2150.

Van Houtum, H., & Bueno Lacy, R. (2020). The migration map trap: On the invasion arrows in the cartography of migration. *Mobilities*, *15*(2), 196–219.

Vergani, M., & Zuev, D. (2011). Analysis of YouTube videos used by activists in the Uyghur nationalist movement. *Journal of Contemporary China*, *20*(69), 205–229.

Vertovec, S. (2004a). Cheap calls: The social glue of migrant transnationalism. *Global Networks*, *4*(2), 219–224.

Vertovec, S. (2004b). Migrant transnationalism and modes of transformation. *The International Migration Review*, *38*(3), 970–1001.

Vertovec, S. (2009). *Transnationalism*. London: Routledge.

Viera Magalhães, J., & Couldry, N. (2021). Giving by taking away: Big tech, data colonialism and the reconfiguration of social good. *International Journal of Communication*, *15*, 343–362.

Viola, L., & Musolff, A. (2019). *Migration and media: Discourses about identities in crisis*. Amsterdam: John Benjamins.

Vis, F., & Goriunova, O. (Eds.) (2015). The iconic image on social media: A rapid research response to the death of Aylan Kurdi*. *Visual Social Media Lab*. Retrieved from: https://pure.royalholloway.ac.uk/ws/portalfiles/portal/41164696/iconic_image_on_social_media.pdf

Vollmer, S. (2019). Digital citizenship for newly arrived Syrian refugees through mobile technologies. In M. Cooke & R. Peutrell (Eds.), *Brokering Britain, educating citizens* (pp. 157–172). Bristol: Blue Ridge Summit.

Volpe, C.R. (2021). 'What kind of girl is she?': Good and bad diasporic daughters on social media. *Journal of Cultural Geography*, *38*(2), 177–205.

Voronova, O., Voronova, L., & Yagodin, D. (2020). Russophone diasporic journalism. In K. Smets, K. Leurs, M. Georgiou, S. Witteborn & R. Gajjala (Eds.), *Handbook of media and migration* (pp. 258–271). London: Sage.

Waldinger, R. (2013). Immigrant transnationalism. *Current Sociology*, *61*(5–6), 756–777.

Wall, M. (2019). Social navigation and the refugee crisis: Traversing 'archipelagos' of uncertainty. *Media and Communication*, *7*(2), 300–302.

Wall, M. (2020). Information precarity. In K. Smets, K. Leurs, M. Georgiou, S. Witteborn & R. Gajjala (Eds.), *Handbook of media and migration* (pp. 85–90). London: Sage.

Wall, M., Campbell, M.O., & Janbek, D. (2017). Syrian refugees and information precarity. *New Media & Society*, 19(2), 240–254.

Wall, M., Campbell, M.O., & Janbek, D. (2019). Refugees, information precarity, and social inclusion. In J. Retis & R. Tsagarousianou (Eds.), *The handbook of diasporas, media & culture* (pp. 503–514). Hoboken, NJ: John Wiley & Sons.

Wallraff, G. (1985). *Ganz unten*. Cologne: Kiepenheuer & Witsch

Walsh, K. (2018). *Transnational geographies of the heart*. Oxford: Wiley Blackwell.

Walter, J. (1996). The social representation of immigrants: The Pantanella issue in the pages of *La Repubblica*. *New Community*, 22(1), 39–66.

Walters, W. (2015). Migration, vehicles, and politics: Three theses on viapolitics. *European Journal of Social Theory*, 18(4), 469–488.

Walters, W. (2018). Aviation as deportation infrastructure: Airports, planes, and expulsion. *Journal of Ethnic and Migration Studies*, 44(16), 2796–2817.

Wang, S., Chen, X., Li, Y., Luu, C., Yan, R., & Madrisotti, F. (2021). 'I'm more afraid of racism than of the virus!': Racism awareness and resistance among Chinese migrants and their descendants in France during the Covid-19 pandemic. *European Societies*, 23(sup 1), S721–S742.

Wang, Y., & Lim, S.S. (2021). ICTs and transnational householding: The double burden of polymedia connectivity for international 'study mothers'. In M. McAuliffe (Ed.), *Handbook of migration and technology* (pp. 207–219). Cheltenham: Edward Elgar.

Watson, A., Lupton, D., & Michael, M. (2021). Enacting intimacy and sociality at a distance in the COVID-19 crisis: The sociomaterialities of home-based communication technologies. *Media International Australia*, 178(1), 136–150.

WCOOMD (2022). International Customs Day 2022. *World Customs Organization/ Organisation mondiale des douanes*. Retrieved from: www.wcoomd.org/en/about-us/ international-customs-day/icd-2022.aspx

Weber, W. (2020). Exploring narrativity in data visualization in journalism. In M. Engebretsen & H. Kennedy (Eds.), *Data visualization in society* (pp. 295–313). Amsterdam: Amsterdam University Press.

Wee, K., Goh, C., & Yeoh, B.S.A. (2019). Chutes-and-ladders: The migration industry, conditionality, and the production of precarity among migrant domestic workers in Singapore. *Journal of Ethnic and Migration Studies*, 45(14), 2672–2688.

Wee, K., Goh, C., & Yeoh, B.S.A. (2020a). Choreographing the rhythms of encounter in Singapore's maid agencies. *Transactions of the Institute of British Geographers*, 45(1), 109–122.

Wee, K., Goh, C., & Yeoh, B.S.A. (2020b). Translating people and policy: The role of maid agents in brokering between employers and migrant domestic workers in Singapore's migration industry. *International Migration Review*, 54(4), 992–1015.

WFP (2005). *Food force*. Retrieved from: https://archive.org/details/Food_Force

Wierzbicka, A. (1999). *Emotions across language and cultures: Diversity and universals*. Cambridge: Cambridge University Press.

Wilding, R., & Baldassar, L. (2018). Ageing, migration and new media: The significance of transnational care. *Journal of Sociology*, 54(2), 226–235.

Wilding, R., Baldassar, L., Gamage, S., Worrell, S., & Mohamud, S. (2020). Digital media and the affective economies of transnational families. *International Journal of Cultural Studies*, 23(5), 639–655.

Williams, M. (2013). *The migrant trail*. Retrieved from: http://theundocumented.com/

Williams, R. (1974). *Television, technology and cultural form*. London: Fontana.

Wimmer, A., & Glick-Schiller, N. (2002). Methodological nationalism and beyond: Nation-state building, migration and the social sciences. *Global Networks*, 2(4), 301–334.

Winner, L. (1980). Do artifacts have politics? *Daedalus*, *109*(1), 121–136.

Winner, L. (1993). Upon opening the black box and finding it empty: Social constructivism and the philosophy of technology. *Science, Technology, & Human Values*, *18*(3), 362–378.

Wise, A. (2013). Pyramid subcontracting and moral detachment: Down-sourcing risk and responsibility in the management of transnational labour in Asia. *The Economic and Labour Relations Review*, *24*(3), 433–455.

Wise, A., & Velayutham, S. (2006). Towards a typology of transnational affect. *Centre for Research on Social Inclusion, Macquarie University*. Retrieved from: www.researchgate.net/publication/242323387_Towards_a_Theory_of_Transnational_Affect_Emotion.

Witteborn, S. (2014). Forced migrants, emotive practice and digital heterotopia. *Crossings: Journal of Migration & Culture*, *5*(1), 73–85.

Witteborn, S. (2015). Becoming (im)perceptible: Forced migrants and virtual practice. *Journal of Refugee Studies*, *28*(3), 350–367.

Witteborn, S. (2018). The digital force in forced migration: Imagined affordances and gendered practices. *Popular Communication*, *16*(1), 21–31.

Witteborn, S. (2019). The digital gift and aspirational mobility. *International Journal of Cultural Studies*, *22*(6), 754–769. https://doi.org/10.1177/1367877919831020

Witteborn, S. (2021a). Data privacy and displacement: A cultural approach. *Journal of Refugee Studies*, *34*(2), 2291–2230.

Witteborn, S. (2021b). Migration and technologies in contexts of uncertainty. *Media and uncertainty* [E-book]. Retrieved from: www.com.cuhk.edu.hk/images/content_people/publication/saskia-book-2021-migration.pdf

Witteborn, S. (2022a). Privacy in collapsed contexts of displacement. *Feminist Media Studies*, *22*(4), 883–897. Online first, November 10, 2020. https://doi.org/10.1080/14680777.2020.1841814

Witteborn, S. (2022b). Digitalization, digitization and datafication: The 'three D' transformation of forced migration management. *Communication, Culture & Critique*, *15*(2), 157–175.

Witteborn, S. (2023). *Unruly speech: Displacement and the politics of transgression*. Redwood City, CA: Stanford University Press.

Wong, J. (2021). Digital environments and the aspirations of international students. In S. Chang & C. Gomes (Eds.), *Digital experiences of international students* (pp. 25–45). Abingdon, UK: Routledge.

Wood, N., & King, R. (2001). Media and migration: An overview. In R. King & N. Wood (Eds.), *Media and migration: Constructions of mobility and difference* (pp. 1–22). London: Routledge.

Worrell, S. (2021). From language brokering to digital brokering: Refugee settlement in a smartphone age. *Social Media + Society*, *7*(2), 1–11.

Wu, S., & Trottier, D. (2021). Constructing sexual fields: Chinese gay men's dating practices among pluralized dating apps. *Social Media + Society*, *7*(2), 1–14.

Wyss, A., & Dahinden, J. (2022). Disentangling entangled mobilities: Reflections on forms of knowledge production within migration studies. *Comparative Migration Studies*, *10*(33), 1–17.

Xiang, B., & Lindquist, J. (2014). Migration infrastructure. *International Migration Review*, *48*(1), 122–148.

Xiang, B., & Lindquist, J. (2018). Postscript: Infrastructuralization: Evolving sociopolitical dynamics in labour migration from Asia. *Pacific Affairs*, *91*(4), 759–773.

Xie, Z., & Witteborn, S. (2020). The mobility–migration nexus: The politics of interface, labor and gender. In K. Smets, K. Leurs, M. Georgiou, S. Witteborn & R. Gajjala (Eds.), *Handbook of media and migration* (pp. 453–463). London: Sage.

Xinghui, K. (2021). 'Small minority' of Singapore residents sowing racism against local, expat Indians. *South China Morning Post*. Retrieved from: www.scmp.com/week-asia/lifestyle-culture/article/3133086/small-minority-singapore-residents-sowing-racism

Yang, F. (2022). From ethnic media to ethno-transnational media: News-focused WeChat official accounts in Australia. In W. Sun & H. Yu (Eds.), *WeChat diaspora* (pp. 57–76). London: Routledge.

Yeoh, B.S.A., Chee H.L., & Baey, G. (2017). Managing risk, making a match: Brokers and the management of mobility in international marriage. *Mobilities*, *12*(2), 227–242.

Yeoh, B.S.A., Somaiah, B.C., Lam, T., & Acedera, K.F. (2020). Doing family in 'times of migration': Care temporalities and gender politics in Southeast Asia. *Annals of the American Association of Geographers*, *110*(6), 1709–1725.

Young, I.M. (2005). House and home: Feminist variations on a theme. In S. Hardy & C. Wiedmer (Eds.), *Motherhood and space* (pp. 115–147). New York: Palgrave Macmillan.

Yu, N., Pan, S., Yang, C., & Tsai, J. (2020). Exploring the role of media sources on Covid-19-related discrimination experiences and concerns among Asian people in the United States: Cross-sectional survey study. *Journal of Medical Internet Research*, *22*(11), e21684

Yuen Thompson, B. (2019). 'I get my lovin' on the run': Digital nomads, constant travel, and nurturing romantic relationships. In C.J. Nash & A. Gorman-Murray (Eds.), *The geographies of digital sexuality* (pp. 69–90). Singapore: Palgrave Macmillan.

Zaborowski, R., & Georgiou, M. (2019). Gamers versus zombies? Visual mediation of the citizen/non-citizen encounter in Europe's 'refugee crisis'. *Popular Communication*, *17*(2), 92–108.

Zanforlin, S.C. & Grohmann, R. (2022). On-demand migrants: Entrepreneurialism, platformization, and migration in Brazil. *International Journal of Communication*, *16*, 5520–5537.

Zapata-Barrero, R., & Yalaz, E. (2020). Qualitative migration research ethics: A roadmap for migration scholars. *Qualitative Research Journal*, *20*(3), 269–279.

Zhao, X. (2019). Disconnective intimacies through social media: Practices of transnational family among overseas Chinese students in Australia. *Media International Australia*, *173*(1), 36–52.

Zielinski, S. (2006). *Deep time of the media: Toward an archaeology of hearing and seeing by technical means*. Cambridge, MA: MIT Press.

Ziems, C., He, B., Soni, S., & Kumar, S. (2020). Racism is a virus: Anti-Asian hate and counterhate in social media during the COVID-19 Crisis. arXiv preprint. Retrieved from: https://arxiv.org/abs/2005.12423

Zijlstra, J., & van Liempt, I. (2017). Smart(phone) travelling: Understanding the use and impact of mobile technology on irregular migration journeys. *International Journal of Migration and Border Studies*, *3*(2/3): 174–191.

Zuboff, S. (2020). The known unknown. *New York Times*, January 24. Retrieved from: www.nytimes.com/2020/01/24/opinion/sunday/surveillance-capitalism.html

Index

www.ingramcontent.com/pod-product-compliance
Lightning Source LLC
Chambersburg PA
CBHW080540030426

42337CB00024B/4807